Pop-Up Books

A Guide for Teachers and Librarians

Nancy Larson Bluemel and Rhonda Harris Taylor

LIBRARIES UNLIMITED

AN IMPRINT OF ABC-CLIO, LLC
Santa Barbara, California • Denver, Colorado • Oxford, England

Library of Congress Cataloging-in-Publication Data

Bluemel, Nancy.
    Pop-up books : a guide for teachers and librarians / Nancy Larson Bluemel and Rhonda Harris Taylor.
        p. cm.
    Includes index.
    ISBN 978-1-59158-398-1 (pbk. : acid-free paper) — ISBN 978-1-61069-154-3 (ebook)
1. Pop-up books—Bibliography.   2. Pop-up books.   3. Pop-up books in education.
4. Education, Elementary—Activity programs—United States.   5. Education, Secondary—Activity programs—United States.   6. Libraries—Special collections—Pop-up books.
I. Taylor, Rhonda Lynette Harris, 1951–   II. Title.
    Z1033.T68B58   2012
    070.5'73—dc23   2011039794

ISBN: 978-1-59158-398-1
EISBN: 978-1-61069-154-3

16   15   14   13   12   1   2   3   4   5

This book is also available on the World Wide Web as an eBook.
Visit www.abc-clio.com for details.

Libraries Unlimited
An Imprint of ABC-CLIO, LLC

ABC-CLIO, LLC
130 Cremona Drive, P.O. Box 1911
Santa Barbara, California 93116-1911

This book is printed on acid-free paper ∞

Manufactured in the United States of America

Contents

Preface

Welcome to the wonderful world of the pop-up book! We hope that this resource will be used in the instructional setting (whether school or home) and in the library, but it is also our goal to simply share with teachers and librarians the wonder and delight of this most clever of books.

PURPOSE

Our intent is to introduce the pop-up (interactive or movable) book to teachers and librarians as a viable and exciting tool that inherently has great appeal not only to students but to many audiences and that can be very easily used for teaching across the curriculum, for enriching programs, and for individual reading and enjoyment.

SCOPE

The audiences for this book are those teachers and school librarians who are not already familiar with the pop-up (interactive or movable) book, but we also believe that those who have experience with pop-up books will find new ideas. We have shaped this book to be both a pathfinder and an instructional guide, using a variety of the best of the pop-up books as exemplars. Because pop-up books can be effectively used at many grades, ages, and interest and ability levels, this resource is appropriate for grades pre-K–12 and even for adult audiences.

Acknowledgments

No book is brought to life without the assistance and encouragement of many individuals, and we are very grateful to the many people who played such important roles in our work for this book.

To Sharon Coatney, senior acquisitions editor, School Library Media, Libraries Unlimited, without whose support of our ideas this book would not have come to fruition.

To Libraries Unlimited, and the many staff members, for making this book possible.

To the wonderful individuals profiled in this book, who welcomed us into their lives to ask too many questions and to listen to what they shared with us.

To our colleagues who were always there with their interest, their questions, and their sharing of pop-up books and resources.

To the many individuals who attended our workshops, conference presentations, and lectures, and who delighted us with *their* delight with the pop-up books that we shared with them—they are the reason for what we do with pop-ups, including this book.

And, most of all, to our families, whose members are our favorite fans, best audiences, and most faithful boosters.

Nancy Bluemel
Rhonda Taylor

1

Introduction

WHAT *IS* A POP-UP?

So, what *is* a pop-up book? **Our definition of a pop-up book is a book that offers the potential for motion and interaction through the use of paper mechanisms such as folds, scrolls, slides, tabs, or wheels** (see this book's Glossary for more explanation of the variations of pop-up books). These books don't necessarily "pop-up," but they have motion.

There are purists who prefer to reserve the term "pop-up" for those books with motion created by illustrations or figures springing from the page. Sometimes these types of books are also called "movable books" or "interactive books." However, while we consider these two phrases to be more accurate than the term "pop-up," they do not seem to be **popularly** used. Our approach is more inclusive. **In this book, we have included books that demonstrate a wide range of mechanisms that lend them motion, and when discussing them, we term all of them "pop-up books." However, for resources listed in activities, we do alert the teacher/librarian to those books that "pop" versus those with non-pop "interactivity."**

We have also seen the term "toy book" used to refer to these wonderful books, particularly in discussions of children's literature. For many people, the term "toy" refers to those things that are representative of the innocence of childhood and are viewed as being spontaneous and fun and bringing you joy. However, too often in contemporary American culture, the word toy, other than when referring to actual play objects of children, is used disparagingly. **So, we always avoid referring to pop-up books as toy books. For the same reason, we always avoid deeming them "novelty books."**

WHO CREATES POP-UP BOOKS?

Who creates these remarkable books? In 1999, David A. Carter and James Diaz, acclaimed paper engineers, produced a fabulous how-to book called *The Elements of Pop-Up: A Pop-Up Book for Aspiring Paper Engineers*. Since we don't think that you can get much more authoritative than the people who create the motion in these fantastic pop-ups, we like to rely on the Carter and Diaz (1999) explanation of what they do: **"A paper engineer is an artist who creates pop-ups using paper as his or her main medium"** (Introduction).

However, a pop-up book, as with regular books, requires a large team to assist in bringing it to life. A pop-up book may utilize the skills of many talents: writers, artists, illustrators, photographers, paper engineers, designers, consultants, researchers, editors, and so on. And, sometimes one of these creators serves multiple roles, such as in the case of a paper engineer who is also responsible for the illustrations. **In our citations for this book, for your information, we have included the names of the various team members, including the paper engineers, given credit in the pop-up books.** We believe that these are useful additions for you, the reader, in decision-making about which books to acquire, in tracking the work of favorite talents and producers, and in revealing the potential careers available to individuals (especially students) interested in the field. However, we do need to point out that, especially in older pop-up books, the names of paper engineers and other individuals who helped to create these works might have been omitted in the books' credits.

WHY POP-UPS IN THE CLASSROOM AND LIBRARY COLLECTION?

For teachers/librarians working with today's young people for whom the printed word suggests text messaging, it may be difficult to garner an enthusiastic response from the audience when the printed word being used is found on a seemingly prosaic medium: paper. However, there is one print format that has an inherent appeal for readers of all ages, from toddlers to adults. It can be used very effectively to promote a love of story, to motivate reading, and to stimulate interest in the subject at hand. That format? Pop-up books!

THE APPEAL OF POP-UPS IN THE CLASSROOM

If your students' attitudes are ho-hum when you announce that the next topic to be studied will be the Beowulf saga or perhaps a compilation of ancient stories from around the world, grab their attention by introducing the first lesson with *Dragons,* paper engineered by Keith Moseley (McQuinn 2006). From the cover replete with textured dragon scales to the double-page pop-up spreads of the awesome creatures, to the background illustrations depicting the time and setting of each story, this book does bring the context and relevant information to life, bristling and vibrant.

OKAY, BUT ARE THEY REALLY LITERATURE?

Though few people can resist the appeal of pop-up books, some still question if they are playthings or literature. Experts of past years called them toy books and had a tendency to dismiss them as quality literature with remarks such as, "Most of the toy books published today have little substance, little beauty, and a minimal amount of ingenuity" (Sutherland and Arbuthnot 1986). With the coming of the contemporary second golden age of pop-ups and as paper engineers' names have become as recognizable as their author/illustrator peers, many authors of contemporary, widely used texts on children's literature now include them in their chapters on categories of literature appropriate for use with children (Lynch-Brown and Tomlinson 1993; Jacobs and

Tunnell 2004). While the term toy books is still used by some critics, currently a more popular phrase used when discussing movable books (pop-up books) is "engineered books," which implies a credibility that we believe is certainly justified. For instance, in this book's Activities chapter, we have included Award Alerts to remind readers of the recognition that has been achieved by some pop-up book titles.

EVALUATING THE POP-UP BOOK AS LITERATURE

Teachers and librarians adhere to professional standards for selecting books to use with students. Many guidelines are available to aid in that selection process. Keeping in mind that art and movement and not storyline are often considered the major attributes of pop-up books, let us examine them using commonly suggested criteria for evaluating picture books and informational books. We have also added criteria for some features specific to the pop-up format.

1. Do the visual elements (line, shape, color, composition, and texture) of the pop-up book serve the same function as they do in quality picture books? Movable art should do more than amaze us by its movement. It should add to the story or information given in the book in one or more ways. Thus, the art in pop-up books should:

   Reinforce the text by making the characters and/or setting come to life.
   Establish the mood of the story through the use of color such as warm or cool, bright, soft, or dark.
   Extend the story by the addition of visual details not described in the text.

2. If the book is informational, it must be evaluated by the same criteria as all other nonfiction books, and then you should ask:

   Is the information accurate?
   Unless the book is of a historical nature, is the information current?
   Does the manner in which the information is presented aid in understanding and stimulate interest in further exploration of the topic?

3. Pop-up books must also be judged on their effectiveness as movable art. Criteria that should be considered include:

   Quality of the paper engineering; how well do the movable parts work?
   Complexity of the engineering; is there intricacy, delicacy, ingenuity?
   Relevance of the engineering; does it extend the text rather than just embellish it?

If the teacher/librarian believes that the main purposes of literature are to create readers by making reading a fun activity and to inform and to inspire a curiosity to learn more, then pop-up books certainly deserve the designation of literature. They are worthy to be included in that larger canon of children's and young adult literature and to be considered a distinctive contribution to the field.

WHY USE POP-UPS IN AN EDUCATIONAL SETTING?

Movable books are full of surprises. Place one in the hands of students of any age and observe their reactions as they turn the pages. There is no doubt that even with those pop-ups where the plot and characterization may be minimal and the factual information may be basic, the reader of these books exhibits an enthusiasm that is not often seen in the perusal of an ordinary book. Interest generates motivation, and no literature instantly captures the interest of children of all ages (adults included) like pop-ups. They appeal to a cross-section of students, from eager learners to those who have a history of being turned off by reading, to those for whom learning is difficult, to those who are grappling with a language other than their first one. That enthusiasm can be channeled into positive experiences for students at every level. Try using pop-up books with:

> young children to develop a love of books and reading;
>
> early childhood learners to bridge the gap between real-life situations and symbolic representation;
>
> older students and/or gifted and talented students to develop critical thinking skills and develop creativity;
>
> reluctant readers, children with learning disabilities, and English as a Second Language (ESL) students to aid in grasping meaning through exciting visual representation and to promote the desire and drive to read independently even if currently struggling with the skills to do so.

HOW TO USE POP-UP BOOKS WITH STUDENTS

Reading aloud has long been recognized as an important activity to share with your students and with your own children—no matter what age they may be. Jim Trelease (2006), author of the acclaimed *Read Aloud* handbooks, has written, "The experts were saying reading aloud was more important than worksheets, homework, assessments, book reports, and flashcards. One of the cheapest, simplest, and oldest tools of teaching was being promoted as a better teaching tool than anything else in the home or classroom."

Even middle- and high-school-age students will sit, quiet and entranced, while being read to from a rousing adventure or a heartbreaking memoir. Adults, even those who are good, capable readers, still enjoy the experience of listening to audio books while driving or sitting in traffic. Reluctant and struggling readers benefit from being able to have a shared literary experience with their classmates, and they gain from hearing a vocabulary that too often they cannot read for themselves. Now add to the richness of the read-aloud experience the magic of motion. That feature initiates an interaction between student and book that involves listening, observing, and a different kind of critical thinking. So, how does that work?

Reading aloud to an entire class can often segue between large group and small group discussion opportunities, creating and managing creative projects, individual and team endeavors, independent research, and further reading and analysis. Pop-up books tend to be short, quick reads. They work nicely within the time constraints of a typical class period, which allows reasonable follow-up time for student activities. If taking instruction time to read aloud is not feasible, pop-ups work equally well as the starting point for assignments in which everyone is responsible for her or his own reading.

Pop-up books are great motivators! Don't limit their use to the obvious language arts curriculum and art class projects. They cover a wide range of other topics from math to science to social studies. They are useful in introducing fine arts and physical fitness. They are excellent tools to inspire careers in illustration, book production, and paper engineering. Use one as a hook to capture your students' attention before moving on to the core of your presentation. For instance, the tabs, wheels, flaps, and pop-ups in *Universe* (Couper and Pelham 1985) will add pizzazz to your earth science unit. Each pop-up is part of a backdrop that rises from a double-page spread. Hold the book in front of a light source for the maximum effect. In its presentation of the history of the universe, this book is sure to spark a lively discussion of the new theories and facts discovered since its publication.

This book's Activities chapters provide many more activities, ideas, and resources.

POP-UP BOOKS IN PUBLIC LIBRARIES

If planning story times or summer reading programs for a public library, consider making use of pop-up books. Using a pop-up book featuring a familiar character or retelling of a favorite story is one way to enliven a revisit to a beloved adventure. A book such as *Clifford, I Love You Pop-Up* (Bridwell 2002) offers bright colors and large pop-ups of Clifford the Big Red Dog springing off the pages, making it easy for an audience of young children to see the motion. Also, *Clifford, I Love You Pop-Up* is one of many potential titles that offer an easy transition to a hands-on activity. For instance, a reading aloud of the book could be followed with children making their own short pop-up book or a card to send to someone dear. This book (which features hearts) and a "make-your own pop-up" activity would be especially appropriate in February, close to Valentine's Day. It is easy for children to make use of pre-cut pictures or cut-out hearts provided by the librarian, their own drawings, or rubber stamps to create the illustrations to be glued to a base that makes them pop up. For more guidance on making pop-ups, from simple to advanced, see the Activities chapter of this book.

Programs with pop-up books should not be restricted to children. Library staff or a community member can do a show-and-tell of pop-up books borrowed from either the library collection or a personal collection or a local special collection and attract an adult audience. The topic can be broad, such as the range of pop-ups available, or thematic, such as those with holiday motifs, those about nature, those that are the products of a particular paper engineer, those designed for adult audiences, those that are reprints of historical pop-ups, those published this year, the best selections for gifts for the child in your life, an introduction to books about how to make pop-ups, and so on. Consider collaborating with the local school district to provide a program, perhaps using the expertise of an art teacher. Also, if the budget allows, consider featuring a paper engineer, perhaps as part of a larger festival or event. For ideas and facts useful for program planning about pop-ups, check out chapter 4, "Taking Journeys through the History of Pop-Up Books," in this book, where we provide descriptions of websites that offer history and online exhibits of outstanding and historical pop-up books, and also chapter 3, "The Enduring Popularity of the Pop-Up Book," where we provide an overview of the range of pop-ups that have popular appeal. Also, visit the activities chapters 6–8, which provide sample activities and programs, and chapter 5, "The Pop-Up Book Creators," which provides a selection of contemporary paper engineers and pioneers in the field.

EMBRACING THE FORMAT!

Concerns about fragility, cost, and availability often deter teachers and librarians from purchasing and using pop-up books with their students and their clientele. These books have been proven by those already using them to be not as fragile as feared. When Robert Sabuda and Matthew Reinhart's pop-up *Encyclopedia Prehistorica: Dinosaurs* (2005) was placed on the Texas Bluebonnet reading list for students grades 3 through 6, Martha Edmundson, who was then youth services manager for the Denton Public Library system, noted in a March 9, 2006, interview with Nancy L. Bluemel that she felt strongly that the books should be made available to their patrons. She purchased several copies and placed them into circulation despite the misgivings of her colleagues. In tracking the number of times each book was checked out, she discovered that they held up very well to frequent use.

The format itself provides a perfect opportunity for teaching younger children how to appropriately handle any book. It is common practice for teachers and parents and other caregivers to help young children master such skills as carefully turning pages of the books to which they are introduced in the classroom or are checking out from the library. Our collective experience has been that even very young readers are so entranced by the format that they are eager to take care of the pop-up books that they encounter. Cost is comparable to traditional books when considering that every pop-up must be assembled by hand, and the "oomph" that you get for that dollar is well worth it. Availability, if you know where to look, is easier than you think, and we give you tips about that adventure in the Finding, Buying, Housing chapter of this book.

So, overcome your apprehension! If you are a teacher, acquire just one awesome pop-up book and use it to introduce a lesson, or to read aloud, or to inspire independent study, or to motivate a reluctant or challenged learner. When you do, you will quickly see the tremendous value of including pop-ups in your bag of sure-thing instructional resources, and you will be out searching for more. (Hint, hint!) If you are a classroom teacher, ask your librarian to start acquiring pop-ups for your school's professional collection. If you are a homeschooling parent, invest in a few pop-up book titles that can be easily used across several subjects and for a range of ages. If you are a school library media specialist, purchase a couple of high-quality, curriculum-related pop-ups, and then encourage your teachers to use them by giving a short hands-on staff development presentation. If you are a children's or young adult librarian, add some outstanding pop-ups to the collection, publicize them, and watch them circulate—and not just to young people. We promise that you won't need encouragement to buy your next pop-up book!

REFERENCES

Bridwell, Norman. 2002. *Clifford, I Love You Pop-Up.* Rev. ed. New York: Scholastic.

Carter, David A., and James Diaz. 1999. *The Elements of Pop-Up: A Pop-Up Book for Aspiring Paper Engineers.* Design assistance and illustration by Leisa Bentley; photography by Keith Sutter; digital production art by Rick Morrison, White Heat; production by Intervisual Books; developed by White Heat. New York: Little Simon.

Couper, Heather, and David Pelham. 1985. *Universe: A Three-Dimensional Study.* New York: Random House.

Jacobs, James S., and Michael O. Tunnell. 2004. *Children's Literature, Briefly.* 3rd ed. Upper Saddle River, NJ: Prentice Hall.

Lynch-Brown, Carol, and Carl M. Tomlinson. 1993. *Essentials of Children's Literature.* Boston: Allyn & Bacon, 1993.

McQuinn, Anna. 2006. *Dragons: A Pop-Up Book of Fantastic Adventures.* Paper engineering by Keith Moseley; illustration by M. P. Robertson. New York: Abrams Books for Young Readers.

Sabuda, Robert, and Matthew Reinhart. 2005. *Encyclopedia Prehistorica: Dinosaurs: The Definitive Pop-Up.* Cambridge, MA: Candlewick.

Sutherland, Zena, and May Hill Arbuthnot. 1986. *Children and Books.* 7th ed. Glenview, IL: Scott, Foresman.

Trelease, Jim. 2006. *The Read-Aloud Handbook.* 6th ed. New York: Penguin Books.

2

Popping Off about Pop-Up Books: Conversing about Collecting with Rhonda Harris Taylor and Nancy Larson Bluemel

INTRODUCING US

Rhonda Harris Taylor is an associate professor in the School of Library and Information Studies, University of Oklahoma, Norman, Oklahoma. Nancy Larson Bluemel is a retired school library media specialist and former school district library coordinator who resides in Texas and is now an adjunct instructor in graduate library education and an independent consultant. Taylor and Bluemel collect pop-up books (and, more casually, pop-up cards and advertising) and have made numerous presentations about them to teachers and to graduate and undergraduate students and to lay audiences. Bluemel and Taylor have been friends and colleagues for two decades, since they met in the graduate library science program at Texas Woman's University and studied for doctoral comprehensive exams and completed dissertations at the same time.

IN OUR OWN WORDS

Rhonda

Beginning the Collecting Journey

I'm not sure that I actually remember when I became a collector of pop-up books. I do remember the first pop-up book that I owned; it was one that I shared with my two nephews and a niece more than 20 years ago. They would come to visit us in the summer and looking at this book became something of a tradition. They were quite entranced by it and remembered it from visit to visit. I read it to them, and we were all fascinated by its action. Because my nieces and nephews range in age from 30-plus years to preschoolers, I have had the opportunity to share pop-ups with kids in my family for a very long time.

However, I would not say that that first pop-up book was actually the beginning of my interest in the three-dimensional potential of paper. I have thought that my interest dates back to early childhood, when I was fascinated by Barnum's Animal Cracker boxes, Cracker Jack toys, and Morton Salt boxes, with the illustration of the girl and the umbrella. What these products all shared in common was a certain amount of illusion and dimensionality. The animal-cracker box, for instance, was actually a circus train, and when I was a child, the wheels could be trimmed out from the bottom to further the illusion. The top of the box was also a cut-out, which became a circus animal; there were different ones on different boxes. The Cracker Jack toys had a variety of iterations, including, at one point, plastic pieces that could be snapped together to create such items as a mannequin whose legs and arms moved. With the Morton Salt box, I was fascinated by the illusion of the girl holding the salt box with a girl holding the salt box with a girl holding the salt box, and so on.

When I was a middle school student, I had a Yogi Bear book that had a zillion pieces that could be snapped out, folded, and put together to create a Jellystone Park scene that literally covered the whole top of the card table. I also had a rather incredible number of paper dolls, and I have always been fascinated by dollhouses and miniatures.

The Boundaries of My Collecting

First I should say that I did not set out to collect pop-up books. It would be more accurate to say that one day I realized that I had begun to collect them. But, my intent of what to collect began to take a utilitarian focus. Somewhat serendipitously, my collection has begun to center on pop-ups reflecting popular culture such as movies, and, more calculatedly, on mathematics and science topics, especially those geared to children and young adults. The first orientation is simply because I have always been fascinated by popular culture in general, and the latter is because that's also an interest that I have as a library professional and educator. Pop-up books are great resources for the presentations about math and science pedagogy that Nancy and I give to teachers and to graduate and undergraduate students and lay people.

While we're talking about what we collect, I have to say that several years ago, Nancy and I realized that our individual collections of pop-up books were going certain directions, and since we often did joint presentations for educators and students that utilized pop-up books, we consciously made a decision to continue in those somewhat separate directions.

Reaping the Benefits of Collecting

Besides the benefits of sharing a common interest with a friend and colleague, one of the best things about collecting anything is that, as a matter of course, one learns about the history and other relevant details about whatever is being collected. With pop-up books, there is a long and respectable history that is relevant to the book arts, to the publishing and printing industries, to marketing, and so on.

A really important benefit is the fun aspect. I remember that one evening I entertained my mother for at least three hours by simply showing her my favorite pop-ups and talking about what I liked about them. But then, moms are obligated to be receptive audiences!

Nancy

Beginning the Collecting Journey

In looking over my collection, I noticed that I do have several books that I bought for my now-adult children when they were small. So, I guess that pop-up books have always attracted my attention. But, I think that I first became passionate about them when I heard children's book illustrator Paul O. Zelinsky speak at a public library. At that time he was discussing the artwork that he had done for *Rumpelstiltskin* (1986). At the conclusion of his talk, he told the audience about his forthcoming book, *Wheels on the Bus* (1990). I was so intrigued that I remember thinking, "I have to have this book when it is published." I watched for it, purchased it, and have been hooked ever since! What appealed to me then, and what still appeals to me now, about this book is the correlation of illustrations with the motions suggested by the text, such as up and down, in and out, and bumpety-bump. Obviously I'm not the only person who was a fan of this book. It was published in 1990 and then, because of its popularity, the book was reissued in 2000 (Zelinsky 1990, 2000) as a 10th anniversary edition.

The Boundaries of My Collecting

In my case, the focus of my collection is on books of classic children's literature, art, and music. My love of classical literature stems naturally, I think, from growing up with a mother who read to us, and I have such fond memories connected with those stories. That interest in children's literature just continued to grow over the years with my career in school librarianship.

I think that the reason for the emphases on art and music themes is my fine arts background. My first academic degree was in art education, but I also seriously considered pursuing a major in music. So, I am drawn to any pop-up that has very complex engineering or in which the original illustrations could be considered art, if they were separated from the pop-up format. I like the books that reflect art techniques other than just painting. I'm also intrigued by books with unusual shapes or formats.

Besides consideration of the quality of the artwork that's available in pop-up books, there are particular themes that I like to collect. I do enjoy traveling and whenever I am in a foreign country I search for pop-ups in that country's language to add to my collection. Also, I like to collect books that represent the travel experience.

Reaping the Benefits of Collecting

For me, the real benefit is the personal satisfaction that collecting gives me: the thrill when I find a new treasure for my collection, or the pleasure of taking a few minutes in a busy day or on a lazy, rainy afternoon and thumbing through an old favorite.

Pop-ups give me the chance to stay a kid in one aspect of my life when I have to be a responsible grown-up about everything else.

And. of course, it's always fun to discover a new paper engineer or artist whose work one likes, and to chase down another acquisition!

Besides the collaborating that Rhonda and I do on who will collect what, the best benefit of our networking orientation is not keeping our collections just to ourselves. We feel strongly that our collections should be shared with people who can learn from the various lessons that they hold—thus our books have seen quite a bit of handling during workshops and presentations, and that's fine! On reflection, we think that doing what is very natural to librarians, resource sharing, occurred quite easily to us, both professionally and personally. Thus, we've come to our latest shared endeavor, this book about pop-ups, for teachers and librarians.

REFERENCES

Zelinsky, Paul O. 1986. *Rumpelstiltskin*. New York: E.P. Dutton.

Zelinsky, Paul O. 1990. *The Wheels on the Bus*. Adaptation and illustration by Paul O. Zelinsky; paper engineering by Rodger Smith. New York: Dutton Children's Books.

Zelinsky, Paul O. 2000. *The Wheels on the Bus,* 10th anniversary edition. Adaption and illustration by Paul O. Zelinsky; paper engineering by Rodger Smith. New York: Dutton Children's Books.

3

The Enduring Popularity of the Pop-Up Book—and What it Means for This Book

WELCOME TO A WONDERFUL WORLD OF OPPORTUNITY!

Teachers, librarians, and lovers of books often speak of literature coming to life, moving from the written page and insinuating itself into the three-dimensional world of the reader. Pop-up books have the advantage of already existing in the three-dimensional world, in spite of their capture of picture and word on ordinary paper. Imagine a version of *Alice's Adventures in Wonderland* (Sabuda 2003) in which the rabbit hole is pulled out of the book so the reader can view Alice's descent, or a coffee table book in which Frank Lloyd Wright's most famous buildings spring to life as intricate miniatures of the originals (Thomson 2002). Little wonder that such creations awe those who see them, whether they're being seen for the first or the hundredth time. Little wonder that they offer an irresistible siren song for teachers and their students and for librarians and their clients!

In this chapter, we highlight some indicators that mirror the popularity of pop-up books. These facets of popularity have helped to shape the content of this book **in ways that we note in bold print at the end of each of the following sections.**

THEY ARE HOW OLD?!??!

With pop-up books, there is a not widely known but long and respectable history that is relevant to the book arts, to the publishing and printing industries, to marketing, and so on.

Pop-up books as a format have been dated back to the 13th century, with the works of Matthew Paris, who used the techniques for maps and for determining dates of holy days (Rubin n.d.). The first printed (published) pop-up books date back to the 16th century, but they were not for children. Instead, pop-ups were used for astronomical/astrological books and for a "landmark book" of human anatomy for "surgeons, barbers, medical students, and lay people" (Rubin n.d.). During the 18th century, Robert

Sayers's movable books were the first published specifically for children (Bohning and Radencich 1987). During the 19th century, because of such notables as Lothar Meggendorfer and Ernest Nister, the pop-up book enjoyed what many consider its golden age. There are some who believe that we are currently in a second golden age of pop-up books, populated by acclaimed paper engineers such as David Carter, Bruce Foster, Matthew Reinhart, Robert Sabuda, and many others. **This book provides information about a selection of the current notables, as well as about individuals whom we consider to be rising stars in the world of the pop-up book. Also, we highlight some of the individuals who were the pioneers in the history of pop-ups.**

A POP-UP BOOK FOR EVERYONE!

Increasingly, pop-up books are produced for a large variety of audiences, from the youngest child to adults and for every subject area. Also, any given pop-up book has multiple potential audiences, and increasingly publishers are aware of that fact. For instance, David Carter's *One Red Dot* (2004) and its sequels, *Blue 2* (2006), *Yellow Square* (2008), and *White Noise* (2009) are subtitled *A Pop-Up Book for Children of All Ages*. And, famous children's author/illustrator Maurice Sendak's first pop-up book *Mommy?* (2006) was packaged with a flyer that announced, "An Amazing Pop-up Book for Children and Adults Alike!" Thus, the potential appeal of pop-ups to every age means that they are perfect for libraries and for educational purposes. **This book will offer guidance on the age/reading levels of the pop-up books that we discuss, as designated by the arrangement of the activities in that chapter.**

THE VARIETY OF POP-UP BOOKS

Pop-up books offer an incredible variety of formats, including size. For instance, what appears at first glance to be the world's smallest pop-up book is entitled *Love* (Eisen 1997b). It's about two inches tall and one-and-one-half inches wide, and it has five tiny pop-up pages. Armand Eisen also produced the similarly sized *Angels* (1997a) pop-up. At the other end of the size spectrum is *The Life-Sized Pop-Up Alien Book* (Hawcock 1999), which folds out to become the alien figure, and *3-D Kid* (Culbertson and Margulies 1995), which unfolds to a full-size body and illustrates its major biological systems. But, the almost 18-inch tall *Giant Dinosaurs Pop-Up* (Williams 2010) is certainly in the contest for the tallest pop-up book. These are examples of the wide variety of pop-up books, and every year there are more pop-up books being published. **This book will describe the many varieties of pop-up books, beyond size, that are available to librarians and educators.**

Those varieties include content topics, which range from counting (Pelham and Pelham 2004) to historical structures such as the Statue of Liberty (Penick 1986) to phobias (Greenberg 1999). Also represented are the many consumer age levels, which go from preschooler, as in *Fuzzy Bear's Potty Book* (Bentley 2001), to young adult and adult interest, such as *Moon Landing: Apollo 11 40th Anniversary Pop-Up* (Platt and Hawcock 2008). That available diversity also includes many uses of language: the introduction of simple vocabulary words (*My First Jumbo Book of Letters* 2003); popular song lyrics (Browne 2002); the fanciful verse of Dr. Seuss (2003) and Lewis Carroll (Base 1996);

commentary of artists' work, such as that of M.C. Escher (1991); and explanations of the nature of the our larger world, as in *Universe* (Couper and Pelham 1985), and of the cultural history of the indigenous Southwest (Gallagher 2004).

Pop-up books also present a diversity of engineering techniques and materials; for instance, Sabuda's paper engineering for *The Wonderful Wizard of Oz* (Baum 2000) uses string and a plastic dowel-like structure to create motion for a cyclone and shiny metallic papers to evoke the fantastical emerald green city.

JUST HOW POPULAR ARE THEY???

Perhaps the most telling indicator of the pop-up book format's widespread popularity is that they're sold in Dollar General stores! The company's website has had a page listing six criteria that new products in their stores meet, and one criterion was "appeal to a broad segment of the population. They should have high sales and turnover potential" (Dollar General 2002). That statement pretty much says it all!

Another indicator of the popularity of pop-up books is that even the famous romance writer Barbara Cartland produced one back in 1984. It is, naturally, a fairy tale about a princess and prince who "lived happily ever after!"

Anything popular at a given moment seems to get turned into a pop-up book, especially if there's a movie or television series. For instance, there are pop-up books about: Bert and Ernie of Sesame Street (Children's Television Workshop 1981), *Santa Claus the Movie* (*Santa Claus the Movie* 1985), Garfield (Kraft 1989), the Teenage Mutant Ninja Turtles (*Teenage Mutant Ninja Turtles* 1990), Space Jam (*Space Jam Collector's Pop-Up* 1996), Batman and Robin (*Batman & Robin Pop-Up Book* 1997), Pokémon (*Pokémon* 1998), Wallace & Gromit (Aardman Animations 1998), Barbie (Rojany 1999), Scooby-Doo! (Cunningham 2005), SpongeBob SquarePants (Banks 2004; Pass 2005; Sollinger 2006), Harry Potter (Rowling 2001a, 2001b, 2002), Spider-man (*The Amazing Spider-Man Pop-Up* 2007), and Dora the Explorer (Burroughs 2007). And, of course, there seem to be countless Walt Disney pop-up books. There is even *The Pop-Up Book of Celebrity Meltdowns* (2006) and its sequel, *Even More Outrageous Celebrity Meltdowns* (2008), both deliberately styled to be reminiscent of a supermarket tabloid.

Not surprisingly, science fiction and fantasy have been perfect genres for the pop-up format. There are pop-up books about *Dinotopia* (Gurney 1993) and *Dune* (Silverman 1984) and *Star Trek* (Kurts 1996). There are several *Star Wars* pop-up books (Anderson and Moesta 1995, 1996; Reynolds 1998; Whitman 1997; Reinhart 2007). There is even a *Star Wars* pop-up comic book (Windham 1996)—talk about fusion! Too bad there was no *X-Files* television series pop-up book!

The very popular graphic novel and comic book format are now represented in the pop-up book world as well as in the movie world. For instance, Marvel has produced as series of the True Believers Retro Character Collection, with titles including *The Incredible Hulk Pop-Up* (2008), *The Amazing Spider-Man Pop-Up* (2007), and *The All-New All-Different X-Men Pop-Up* (2007). Similarly, DC Comics is represented in *DC Super Heroes: The Ultimate Pop-Up Book* (Reinhart 2010). Classic book titles, frequently translated to movies, are now available as pop-up graphic novels: Jules Verne's *20,000 Leagues Under the Sea* (Ita 2008) and Herman Melville's *Moby-Dick* (Ita 2007).

Another reflection of the popularity of the pop-up book is the fact that miniature pop-up books have been promotional items from fast food chains, specifically Braum's Ice Cream and Dairy Stores and Sonic. And, when Martha Stewart highlights pop-ups, as she has done repeatedly on her television show and on her website, with instructions, videos, and interviews (MarthaStewart.com 2007, n.d.a, n.d.b.; *Martha Stewart Living* 1999/2000, 2008, 2009, 2011), you know that this is popular stuff! However, undoubtedly there are some individuals who would point to the Wikipedia entry titled "Pop-Up Book" (Wikipedia 2011) as being the ultimate indicator of popularity.

Just the pop-up format itself is very popular. One example of the format's wide appeal is the greeting card that pops up. There are several producers of these, including Avalon's (Leap Year Publishing, Sonoma, California) line of thank you cards that were marketed in Dollar General stores, as well as a line by Gallant Greetings Corporation (Schiller Park, Illinois) sold in those same retail chain stores. PopShots, of Westport, Connecticut, has done a series of "slide cards." Major greeting card companies American Greetings (Cleveland, Ohio) and Hallmark (Kansas City, Missouri) market pop-up cards, some with sound. Pop-up cards are also international. Santoro Graphics, based in London, has done wonderful "swing cards" that are 3-D and move freely. There are pop-up cards made in Mexico, cards from England (produced by Paper D'Art and by Rococo and by Hunkydory), and pop-up postcards from the Czech Republic (a pop-up 3-D postcard and a 3-D System Magicard).

Cards are not the only non-book format of pop-ups that is popular. For several years, Universe Publishing and the Smithsonian Institution National Museum of National History produced an annual pop-up dinosaur calendar (Smithsonian Institution, National Museum of Natural History 2008). In a similar collaboration, Universe Publishing and the Metropolitan Museum of Art produced "The Pop-Up Ancient Egypt Calendar" (Metropolitan Museum of Art 2006). Borders Bookstores produced a special edition of a pop-up "Marvel Heroes Calendar" for 2009 (Marvel Comics 2008).

Then there's the phenomenon of the pop-up format now becoming an important part of scrapbooking, which is certainly a hugely popular craft. Instructions for pop-up techniques for scrapbooks appear in how-to books, such as one by Suzanne McNeill (1999). On the cable channel HGTV, which focuses on creative projects, there have been numerous episodes that feature pop-up scrapbook pages, including one for clapping hands (HGTV.com 2004) and a windmill pop-up page (HGTV.com n.d.). The popular website eHow offers instructions for several pop-up scrapbook pages, including a pop-up window (eHow n.d.).

In the 2002 movie *Master of Disguise* the plot progresses through the use of a giant pop-up book! At the time of the movie's release, its website home page was built around the pop-up model (*Master of Disguise* 2002). The 2011 remake of the 1981 *Arthur* movie has a heroine who finds success with her pop-up children's book, *MADhattan*, which she shares at a read-aloud session (*Arthur* 2011). Then there are pop-up advertisements, such as those cigarette magazine ads that featured the now infamous Joe Camel! And pop-up ads aren't restricted to print. Target stores had an ad on television (Target 2002), and it used the flap book format to advertise clothes. And then, there are those intrusive pop-up ads on websites, called, of course, pop-ups! **This book's Activities chapters have instructions for making pop-ups, using individualized ideas about content, including the messages, and format.**

REFERENCES

Aardman Animations. 1998. *Wallace & Gromit: A Close Shave.* Paper engineering by Damian Johnston. London: BBC Worldwide.

The All-New All-Different X-Men Pop-Up. 2007. 1st ed. True Believers Retro Character Collection #2. Design and paper engineering by Andy Mansfield; editing by Caroline Repchuk. Cambridge, MA: Candlewick Press.

The Amazing Spider-Man Pop-Up. 2007. 1st ed. True Believers Retro Character Collection #1. Design and paper engineering by Andy Mansfield; editing by Caroline Repchuk. Cambridge, MA: Candlewick Press.

Anderson, Kevin J., and Rebecca Moesta. 1995. *Star Wars: The Mos Eisley Cantina Pop-Up Book.* Book design by Lynette Ruschak; paper engineering by Chuck Murphy and Heather Vohs; sound chip production by Fisher & Co. Boston: Little, Brown.

Anderson, Kevin J., and Rebecca Moesta. 1996. *Star Wars: Jabba's Palace: Pop-Up Book.* 1st ed. Book design by Lynette Ruschak and Lisa Graff; paper engineering by James Diaz. New York: Little, Brown.

Arthur. 2011. Burbank, CA: Warner Brothers Pictures.

Banks, Steven. 2004. *SpongeBob Pops Up!* New York: Simon Spotlight/Nickelodeon.

Base, Graeme. 1996. *Lewis Carroll's Jabberwocky: A Book Of Brillig Dioramas.* Design by Graeme Base; retouching and color separation by Ross McCartney & Associates; production by Compass Productions. New York: Harry N. Abrams.

Batman & Robin Pop-Up Book. 1997. Ashland, OH: Landoll.

Baum, L. Frank. 2000. *The Wonderful Wizard of Oz.* Art by Robert Sabuda; additional design work by Matthew Reinhart. New York: Little Simon.

Bentley, Dawn. 2001. *Fuzzy Bear's Potty Book.* Design by Melanie Random; illustration by Krisztina Nagy; paper engineering by Dennis Meyer. Inglewood, CA: Intervisual Books.

Bohning, Gerry, and Margie Radencich. 1987. "Action Book Nursery Rhymes and Favorite Tales." *Reading Horizons* 27, no. 4: 276–81.

Browne, Anthony. 2002. *The Animal Fair: A Spectacular Pop-Up.* Paper engineering by Martin Taylor. Cambridge, MA: Candlewick Press.

Burroughs, Caleb. 2007. *Dora the Explorer Musical Pop-Up Treasury.* Illustration by Bob Roper and Zina Saunders. Lincolnwood, IL: Publications International.

Carter, David A. 2004. *One Red Dot: A Pop-Up Book for Children Of All Ages.* New York: Little Simon.

Carter, David A. 2006. *Blue 2: A Pop-Up Book for Children Of All Ages.* New York: Little Simon.

Carter, David A. 2008. *Yellow Square: A Pop-Up Book for Children Of All Ages.* New York: Little Simon.

Carter, David A. 2009. *White Noise: A Pop-Up Book for Children Of All Ages.* New York: Little Simon.

Cartland, Barbara. 1984. *Barbara Cartland's Princess to the Rescue.* London: Hamlyn Publishing Group, 1984.

Children's Television Workshop. 1981. *Bert and Ernie On the Go.* New York: Random House.

Couper, Heather, and David Pelham. 1985. *Universe.* [New York]: Random House.

Culbertson, Roger, and Robert Margulies. 1995. *3-D Kid: A Life-Size, Pop-Up Guide to Your Body and How It Works.* Design by Roger Culbertson and Robert Margulies; illustration by Robert Margulies; paper engineering by Roger Culbertson; medical consultation by Margaret M. Mahon; editorial by Jean Bunge and Roger Culbertson; production art by Cristina Camacho, Joe DiDomeico, and Takeshi Takahashi; packaging coordination by Claudia Bennett. New York: Scientific American Books for Young Readers, Imprint of W. H. Freeman & Company.

Cunningham, Scott. 2005. *Scooby-Doo! and the Hungry Ghost*. Illustration by Duendes del Sur. New York: Scholastic.

Dollar General. 2002. Product Selection Criteria. http://www.dollargeneral.com/DG_Merchandise/DG_Product_Selection_Criteria/dg_product_selection_criteria.htm (no longer available). Accessed August 1, 2007.

eHow. n.d. How to Make a Pop-Up Window for Your Scrapbook Page by Braniac. Accessed May 25, 2011.

Eisen, Armand. 1997a. *Angels: A Pop-Up Book*. Kansas City: Andrews & McMeel.

Eisen, Armand. 1997b. *Love: A Pop-Up Book*. Kansas City: Andrews & McMeel.

Escher, M.C. 1991. *The Pop-Up Book of M.C. Escher*. Production by Blaze International Productions; engineering by John J. Strejan; design by Bonnie Smetts Design. Petaluma, CA: Pomegranate Artbooks.

Even More Outrageous Celebrity Meltdowns: Pop-Up Parodies of Your Favorite Stars. 2008. Pop-ups by Kees Moerbeek; illustration by Mick Coulas; writing by Heather Havrilesky; creation by Melcher Media. New York: Melcher Media.

Gallagher, Derek. 2004. *Ancient Dwellings of the Southwest*. Illustration by Sally Blakemore; paper engineering by Eileen Banashek, Sally Blakemore, and Anthony Esparsen. Tucson, AZ: Western National Parks Association.

Greenberg, Gary. 1999. *The Pop-Up Book of Phobias*. 1st ed. Illustration by Balvis Rubess; pop-ups by Matthew Reinhart; production by Melcher Media. New York: HarperCollins.

Gurney, James. 1993. *Dinotopia: Pop-Up Book*. Pop-up art by Michael Welply; design by Jon Z. Haber; paper engineering by Rodger Smith. Atlanta: Turner Publishing.

Hawcock, David. 1999. *The Life-Sized Pop-Up Alien Book*. London: Madcap Books.

HGTV.com. 2004. Movement on Pages: Clap Your Hands Together by Sandi Genovese. http://img.hgtv.com/DIY/2004/01/05/Movement_On_Pages.pdf'. Accessed May 25, 2011.

HGTV.com. n.d. Windmill Pop-Up Scrapbook Page by Eric Erickson. http://www.hgtv.com/crafting/windmill-pop-up-scrapbook-page/index.html. Accessed May 25, 2011.

The Incredible Hulk Pop-Up. 2008. 1st ed. True Believers Retro Character Collection #3. Design and paper engineering by Andy Mansfield; editing by Caroline Repchuk. Cambridge, MA: Candlewick Press.

Ita, Sam. 2007. *Moby-Dick: A Pop-Up Book*. New York: Sterling.

Ita, Sam. 2008. *20,000 Leagues Under the Sea: A Pop-Up Book*. New York: Sterling.

Kraft, Jim. 1989. *Garfield and the Haunted Diner*. Creation by Jim Davis; illustration by Mike Fentz. New York: Grosset & Dunlap.

Kurts, Charles. 1996. *"These are the Voyages. . .": A Three-Dimensional Star Trek Album*. Illustration by Sonia R. Hillios, Nicholas Jainschigg, John Eaves, and Clark Schaffer; cover illustration by Nadre Davani; design and paper engineering by Chuck Murphy. New York: Pocket Books.

MarthaStewart.com. 2007. Reindeer pop-up card. http://www.marthastewart.com/article/on-todays-show-12–04–07?autonomy_kw=robert%20sabuda%20and%20October%2018%20 2002&rsc=header_5. Accessed May 25, 2011.

MarthaStewart.com. n.d.a. Pop-up books. http://www.marthastewart.com/article/pop-up-books?autonomy_kw=robert%20sabuda%20and%20October%2018%202002&rsc=header_1. Accessed May 25, 2011.

MarthaStewart.com. n.d.b. Vintage valentines. http://www.marthastewart.com/article/vintage-valentines?autonomy_kw=robert%20sabuda%20and%20October%2018% 202002&rsc=header_2. Accessed May 25, 2011.

Martha Stewart Living. 1999/2000. "Pop-Up Cards." http://www.marthastewart.com/267744/pop-up-cards. Accessed May 25, 2011.

Martha Stewart Living. 2008. "Pop-Up Card." http://www.marthastewart.com/277258/pop-up-card. Accessed May 25, 2011.

Martha Stewart Living. 2009. "Glittered Pop-Up Place Cards." http://www.marthastewart.com/272040/glittered-pop-up-place-cards. Accessed May 25, 2011.

Martha Stewart Living. 2011. "Pop-Up Card for Mother's Day." http://www.marthastewart.com/how-to/pop-up-card-for-mothers-day. Accessed May 25, 2011.

Marvel Comics. 2008. *Marvel Heroes: Special Edition 2009 Calendar.* Dayton, OH: MeadWestvaco.

Master of Disguise. 2002. Culver City, CA: Columbia Pictures; Revolution Studios. http://www.sonypictures.com/movies/masterofdisguise//.

McNeill, Suzanne. 1999. *The Scrap Happy Guide To: Peek & Pull.* Fort Worth, TX: Design Originals.

Metropolitan Museum of Art. 2006. *The Pop-Up Ancient Egypt Calendar 2007.* New York: Universe.

My First Jumbo Book of Letters: Learning Fun for Little Ones! 2003. Illustration by James Diaz and Melanie Gerth; production by White Heat. New York: Scholastic.

Pass, Erica. 2005. *SpongeBob SantaPants.* Illustration by Heather Martinez. New York: Simon Spotlight/Nickelodeon.

Pelham, Sophie, and David Pelham. 2004. *Counting Creatures: Pop-Up Animals from 1 to 100.* 1st ed. New York: Little Simon.

Penick, Ib. 1986. *The Story of the Statue of Liberty.* Paper engineering by Ib Penick; illustration by Joseph Forte. New York: Holt, Rinehart & Winston, by arrangement with Runcible Press.

Platt, Richard, and David Hawcock. 2008. *Moon Landing: Apollo 11 40th Anniversary Pop-Up.* Cambridge, MA: Candlewick Press.

Pokémon: Where Are You, Pikachu? 1998. New York: Golden Books.

The Pop-Up Book of Celebrity Meltdowns. 2006. Pop-ups by Bruce Foster; illustration by Mick Coulas; writing by Heather Havrilesky; creation by Melcher Media. New York: Melcher Media.

Reinhart, Matthew. 2007. *Star Wars: A Pop-Up Guide to the Galaxy.* New York: Orchard Books.

Reinhart, Matthew. 2010. *DC Super Heroes: The Ultimate Pop-Up Book.* 1st ed. New York: Little, Brown.

Reynolds, David West. 1998. *Star Wars X-Wing: A Pocket Manual.* Editing by Brendan Cahill and Allan Kausch; picture research by Susan Oyama; design and paper engineering by H.V. Simmons and J. McTeigue. Philadelphia, PA: Running Press.

Rojany, Lisa. 1999. *I Love You Because . . . Love, Barbie.* Illustration by Joann Owen Coy; paper engineering by Heashin Kwak and Sally Gabb; art direction by Allison Higa. New York: Golden Book.

Rowling, J.K. 2001a. *Harry Potter and the Sorcerer's Stone: A Deluxe Pop-Up Book.* Illustration by Jill Daniels; paper engineering by Rodger Smith. United States: Scholastic.

Rowling, J.K. 2001b. *Harry Potter Hogwarts School: A Magical 3-D Carousel Pop-Up.* Design by Willabel L. Tong; illustration by Joe Vaux; paper engineering by Renee Jablow. S.I.: Scholastic.

Rowling, J.K. 2002. *Harry Potter and the Chamber of Secrets: A Deluxe Pop-Up Book.* Illustration by Joe Vaux; design by Treesha Runnells; paper engineering by Dennis Meyer. Los Angeles, CA:Intervisual Books, 2002.

Rubin, Ellen. n.d. Pop-up and movable books in the context of history. The PopUpLady: Specializing in movable paper. http://www.popuplady.com/about01-history.shtml

Sabuda, Robert. 2003. *Alice's Adventures in Wonderland: A Pop-Up Adaptation of Lewis Carroll's Original Tale.* 1st ed. New York: Little Simon.

Santa Claus the Movie: Pop-Up Panorama Book. 1985. New York: Grosset & Dunlap.

Sendak, Maurice. 2006. *Mommy?* 1st ed. Art by Maurice Sendak; scenario by Arthur Yorinks; paper engineering by Matthew Reinhart. New York: Scholastic.

Seuss, Dr. 2003. *Oh, the Places You'll Pop Up!* 1st ed. New York: Random House.

Silverman, Maida. 1984. *Dune: A Pop-Up Panorama Book.* Illustration by Daniel Kirk. New York: Grosset & Dunlap.

Smithsonian Institution, National Museum of Natural History. 2008. *Pop-Up Dinosaur Calendar 2009.* New York: Universe Publishing.

Sollinger, Emily. 2006. *SpongeBob's Valentine's Surprise.* Illustration by Heather Martinez. New York: Simon Spotlight/Nickelodeon.

Space Jam Collector's Pop-Up. 1996. Ashland, OH: Landoll.

Target. 2002. Advertisement. NBC.

Teenage Mutant Ninja Turtles: Pop-Up Storybook. 1990. New York: Random House.

Thomson, Iain. 2002. *Frank Lloyd Wright in Pop-Up.* London: PRC Publishing.

Whitman, John. 1997. *Star Wars: The Death Star.* Paper engineering by James Diaz and Heather Simmons; illustration by Barbara Gibson. S.I.: Little, Brown.

Wikipedia. 2011. Pop-Up Book. http://en.wikipedia.org/wiki/Pop_up_book. Accessed May 25, 2011.

Williams, Rachel. 2010. *Giant Dinosaurs Pop-Up.* Editing by Ruth Martin; illustration by Kim Thompson; design and paper engineering by Andy Mansfield; devised and production by The Templar Company. Surrey, England: Templar Group.

Windham, Ryder. 1996. *Star Wars: Battle of the Bounty Hunters: The Pop-Up Comic Book!* 1st ed. Script by Ryder Windham; art by Christopher Moeller; lettering by Ellie de Ville; editing by Lynn Adair; paper engineering by Vicki Teague-Cooper. Milwaukie, OR: Dark Horse.

4

Taking Journeys through the History of Pop-Up Books: Web and Book Adventures

Oftentimes an interest in pop-up books quickly becomes an interest in the history of this wonderful format. Having a short list of resources about the history, the notables, and the trends to which one can refer students and library patrons, can be a time-saver for students and librarians. In addition, teachers and librarians who are preparing lessons or programs or workshops will find such a list useful in quickly finding dates, names, and interesting details to enhance the presentations. Also, the Internet offers great online exhibits of pop-up books that would often not be available to wide audiences and which can also be used as part of lessons or other presentations.

Thus, in this chapter is provided a list of websites that offer exhibits of pop-up books and their history. That section is followed by a listing of reproductions of historical pop-up books that are widely available—they represent the works of a sample of pop-up book creators who have had enduring name recognition.

WEB EXHIBITS OF POP-UP BOOKS AND THEIR HISTORY

Notable pop-up collector Ellen Rubin's website, The PopUp Lady: Specializing in Movable Paper (http://www.popuplady.com), is an excellent source for keeping up with online exhibits—once into the site, click on Links and use the left-hand bar to locate Interactive Websites and also Special Collections. Rubin's website is also a good place to see photographs of individual pop-up books, complete with movement! Click on the menu bar link to My Collections, and then use the left-hand menu.

Following are some favorite online exhibits of pop-up books. They also contain really good information about the history of pop-up books.

The Great Menagerie: The Wonderful World of Pop and Movable Books, 1811–1996. University of North Texas Libraries. http://www.library.unt.edu/rarebooks/exhibits/popup/main.htm.

This website accompanying a November 1997 to February 1998 exhibit in the Rare Book Room of the University of North Texas Willis Library offers views of, and information about, important pop-up books from the 19th and 20th centuries. Follow the instructions to click on the book cover illustrations and see short video clips of the inside of the books, with their wonderful pop-ups. Also online is the five-page exhibit catalog, listing the books.

Paper Engineering: Fold, Pull, Pop & Turn. Smithsonian Institution Libraries, National Museum of American History, Kenneth E. Behring Center. http://americanhistory.si.edu/exhibitions/exhibition.cfm?key=38&exkey=1508.

This June 14, 2010, through September 30, 2011, exhibit is captured on the Internet in a blog (http://smithsonianlibraries.si.edu/foldpullpopturn/) that includes photos of books in the exhibit and links to featured paper engineers

Picturing Childhood: Illustrated Children's Books from the University of California Collections, 1550–1990. University of California. http://unitproj.library.ucla.edu/special/child hood/index.htm.

One section of this online exhibit is devoted to movable and pop-up books, toys, and games. Click on the photographs of the items and see them in larger scale.

Pop Goes the Page: Movable and Mechanical Books from the Brenda Forman Collection. University of Virginia Library Special Collections. http://www.lib.virginia.edu/speccol/exhibits/popup/theme.html.

This digital selection is from the physical exhibit of a limited number of items from Dr. Brenda Forman's collection of over 800 pop-up books. The exhibit was from May 12, 2000, to August 18, 2000. With Quick Time software, the viewer can move the images in the books. This online exhibit also has substantial history about pop-up books and the many creators behind them, arranged by topical highlights from that history.

Pop-Up, Peek, Push, Pull . . .: An Exhibition of Movable Books and Ephemera from the Collection of Geraldine Roberts Lebowitz. Bienes Center for the Literary Arts, Broward County Library. http://www.broward.org/library/bienes/lii13900.htm.

This online resource provides a glimpse into an exhibit of 96 selections from a private collection of over 700 movable books, dating from 1901 to contemporary times. Click on the link that says Click Here to Enter!, after the exhibition guide stops rotating. The website is enriched by such resources as a statement from the collector, a short history of pop-up and movable books by expert and collector Ann Montanaro, and various indexes to the exhibit. The exhibition checklist describes all 96 selections and includes very nice color photos of some of the books.

Pop-ups! They're Not Just for Kids! Bowdoin College Library George J. Mitchell Department of Special Collections & Archives. http://library.bowdoin.edu/arch/exhibitions/popup/menu.shtml.

As is stated in the website's introductory text: "This online exhibition has been adapted from the public display at Hawthorne-Longfellow Library during spring semester 2011. It features works that demonstrate the wide diversity of pop-up books—for children and for adults." It provides glimpses of items from the donated 1,800 volume collection of Harold M. Goralnick, an alum of Bowdoin College in Maine.

REPRODUCTIONS OF HISTORICAL POP-UP BOOKS

Rubin's website has a readable overview of "pop-up and movable books in the context of history," which highlights not only individual creators of these marvels but also important corporate producers/distributors, such as Blue Ribbon Press, Hallmark

Cards, and Intervisual Books. Click on the menu bar link for Pop-up Books to access this link to history.

After encountering the history of how pop-ups came to be, individuals are often interested in seeing some of the historic examples of these works, and thanks to reproductions, that is possible.

During what is often called the golden age of the pop-up book, during the 19th century, two notables who created truly fabulous pop-ups were Lothar Meggendorfer and Ernest Nister. If someone owned original works from either of these two individuals, those books would be extremely valuable.

However, it is easy to find reproductions (not always exact facsimiles) of these and other historical and significant pop-ups. These historical reproductions can be used in a number of ways:

1. as an introduction to the history of the pop-up book and to the famous talented people who helped to create that history;
2. as examples of the many ways that pop-up books have been made over time;
3. as illustrations of 19th-century everyday activities, clothing, and so on;
4. as inspiration for individuals who are interested in entering the graphic arts field.

Following is a small sampling of notable reproductions that can be easily found and obtained. They are arranged alphabetically by last name of the producer/creator/artist. All of them are illustrated in color.

Lothar Meggendorfer

Lothar Meggendorfer was born in Germany in 1847 and was an illustrator. He created movable, or mechanical as they're often called, books with figures that become animated with a pull-tab, much like puppets.

The following book provides reproductions of movable pictures from three different Meggendorfer books. It also contains an introductory tribute, "The Genius of Lothar Meggendorfer," by famous children's illustrator/author Maurice Sendak. The unique cover of this book has a dancing figure on a stage, protected behind clear plastic, that can be moved by the reader. In addition, the last page of the book reveals, behind clear plastic, the paper-and-rivet construction that creates the movement of the illustrations.

The Genius of Lothar Meggendorfer. Design by David Pelham; illustration by Jim Deesing after Lothar Meggendorfer; paper engineering by Tor Lokvig. London: Jonathan Cape, 1985.

Ernest Nister

Ernest Nister was a publisher who worked in Germany and in London. The following list is a sampling of the long list of his 19th-century creations available as reproductions.

All of the following books are of poetry about Victorian childhoods, accompanied by pop-ups. Most of the pop-ups are circular revolving pictures (transformations) or carousels. However, *Moving Pictures Book* is unique for its lift-the-flaps that reveal not only a second picture, but a third one as well.

The Nister titles below are designed by Keith Moseley and are small books, five-by-six inches in size. They are part of a series of titles designed by Moseley.

Ernest Nister's Book of Christmas. New York: Philomel Books, 1991.
Favorite Animals. Design by Keith Moseley. New York: Philomel Books, 1989.
Good Friends. Design by Keith Moseley. New York: Philomel Books, 1989.
Keepsake Carousel. Honesdale, PA: Bell Books, 1992.
Land of Sweet Surprises. New York: Philomel Books, 1983.
Magic Windows. New York: Philomel Books, 1980.
Merry Magic-Go-Round. New York: Philomel Books, 1983.
Mother and Me. Design by Keith Moseley. New York: Philomel Books, 1990.
Moving Pictures. New York: Philomel Books, 1985.
Playtime Delights. New York: Philomel Books, 1993.
Rainbow Roundabout. New York: Philomel Books, 1992.
Surprising Pictures for Little Folks. Los Angeles: Intervisual Communications. 1983.
Wild Animal Stories. New York: Philomel Books, 1988.

Jakob Ferdinand Schreiber

Jakob Ferdinand Schreiber founded a printing firm in Germany in 1831. The J.F. Schreiber (now Esslinger Verlag J.F. Schreiber) firm is, per its website (http://www.es slinger-verlag.de/foreign/index.php), "one of the oldest and most renowned children's book publishers in Germany." The following book is a reproduction of a book published by Schreiber in 1884. It has six full-page, three-dimensional scenes of animals and performers that are revealed when the page is lifted by a tab. The scenes are "from a traveling menagerie show, popular during the late nineteenth century." The scenes are accompanied by verses describing the scenes and that were created for this reproduction.

The Great Menagerie: An Adaptation of the Antique Pop-Up Book. Text for this reproduction written by Anthea Bell. Harmondsworth, Middlesex, England: Penguin Books, 1979.

Walt Disney Studios

The following reproduction is of a pop-up book originally published in 1933. It is part of a series of Vintage Collection Walt Disney reproduction books. The text is well illustrated, including three pop-ups.

The "Pop-Up" Minnie Mouse. Story and illustration by the staff of the Walt Disney Studios. Franklin, TN: Dalmatian Press, 2006.

Julian Wehr

Julian Wehr was a 20th-century paper engineer whose first pop-up book was published in 1942. He would ultimately produce 30 books. He is noted for engineering the pop-ups' movement without the need for any gluing.

Reproductions of two of his books can be obtained from Wehr Animations. Wehr Animations is a project of Wehr's son. The website (http://www.Wehranimations.com) and the books note that income from the sale of the reproduction books is donated to charitable endeavors. The website includes moving images from the books. The following reproduction is a retelling of the famous fairy tale and is illustrated with two Wehr pop-ups as well as "regular" illustrations.

> *Snow White and the Seven Dwarfs.* Animation and illustration by Julian Wehr. Boulder: Wehr Animations, 2004.

MORE, MORE!

For information about contemporary giants in the world of pop-ups, see the Creators chapter of this book. Also, don't forget that it is possible to still obtain very reasonably priced original works by prolific individuals whose well-deserved acclaim has continued to grow after their deaths. Two of those individuals include 20th-century notables Ib Penick and Vojtěch Kubašta (see an online exhibit about Kubašta on the University of Virginia Library exhibit *Pop! Goes the Page* at http://www2.lib.virginia.edu/exhibits/popup/kubasta.html).

5

The Pop-Up Book Creators: A Selection of Contemporary Notable Paper Engineers and Rising Stars

This chapter is provided to highlight selected contemporary notable and rising star paper engineers, designers, and/or illustrators. They are also some of the individuals whose works have been included in this book. The one-stop-shop information provided here can serve several purposes.

For instance, one of the best ways to select pop-up books is to start becoming familiar with the paper engineers and designers whose works are compelling for the teacher or librarian and/or students and other readers with whom one works.

Also, when working with students and with program audiences, it's always a good practice to share some information about the authors and illustrators of the books being highlighted. Audiences want to know more about the creators of the books that they enjoy. And, for younger audiences, learning that someone has a career creating these works is an eye-opening experience as they contemplate their own career paths.

Usually information is fairly easy to find for those individuals who write and illustrate books. However, paper engineers and designers are just now beginning to get the recognition that they deserve—in the past and even today, their contributions to pop-up books were acknowledged in very small print on the back of title pages, if present at all, and their names, even now, are often not included in standard reference works. Also, as author/illustrator John Patience (who has pop-up books among his credits) has so succinctly noted on his website (http://www.patience.co.uk/john/gcse.shtml), his primary role is freelance illustrator. In other words, personal time spent in publicity and marketing endeavors is time away from studio work and creation.

This section is a starting point for those who want a quick introduction to some talented and prolific creators of unforgettable pop-up books. But, there are many other individuals who are not included in this sample who are also doing amazing work with pop-ups. Be on the lookout for them!

FORMAT OF ENTRIES

Name (surname and then first name of the creator)

Personal Data (individual's birth date and place where available, with other facts)

Career Highlights (educational background and career accomplishments)

Selected Works (selected works arranged by author's name and then by dates, emphasizing works that are well-known/recognized and those that are easily obtained; several of these individuals have collaborated, sometimes extensively, and so for those collaborative works, the citation will appear under one individual's name, with the multiple credits noted in the citation)

Awards and Honors (selected honors for pop-up books)

Did You Know? (great quotes by and about this individual)

Sources of Information (sources used for creating this entry and for further information, divided by reference sources, book sources, periodical sources, and websites, which include blogs and other digital spaces)

ARRANGEMENT OF ENTRIES

The arrangement of the creators' entries is alphabetical by their last names (surnames).

THE CREATORS

NAME: BANTOCK, NICK

Personal Data

Born July 14, 1949, in Stourbridge, England.
Moved to Vancouver, Canada in 1988.

Career Highlights

Went to art college in Maidstone, Kent; has a BA in fine art (painting).
Began working as a freelance illustrator at 23, producing book covers.
Besides his art and his books, he has written scripts for movies as well as a play based on his Griffin and Sabine book series.

Selected Pop-Up and Other Interactive Works

Bantock, Nick. 1990. *There Was an Old Lady: A Pop-Up Rhyme Retold and Illustrated by Nick Bantock*. New York: Viking Adult.

Bantock, Nick. 1990. *Wings: A Pop-Up Book of Things That Fly*. 1st ed. New York: Random House Books for Young Readers.

Bantock, Nick. 1991. *Griffin & Sabine: An Extraordinary Correspondence*. Illustration by Nick Bantock. San Francisco: Chronicle Books.

Bantock, Nick. 1992. *Sabine's Notebook: In Which the Extraordinary Correspondence of Griffin & Sabine Continues.* Illustration by Nick Bantock. San Francisco: Chronicle Books.

Bantock, Nick. 1992. *Solomon Grundy: A Pop-Up Rhyme.* New York: Viking.

Bantock, Nick. 1993. *The Golden Mean: In Which the Extraordinary Correspondence of Griffin & Sabine Concludes.* San Franciso: Chronicle Books.

Bantock, Nick. 1993. *Robin Hood: A Pop-Up Rhyme Book.* Illustration and design by Nick Bantock; paper engineering by Nick Bantock and Dennis K. Meyer. New York: Viking.

Bantock, Nick. 2001. *The Gryphon: In Which the Extraordinary Correspondence of Griffin & Sabine Is Rediscovered.* San Francisco: Chronicle Books.

Bantock, Nick. 2002. *Alexandria: In Which the Extraordinary Correspondence of Griffin & Sabine Unfolds.* San Franciso: Chronicle Books.

Bantock, Nick. 2003. *The Morning Star: In Which the Extraordinary Correspondence of Griffin & Sabine Is Illuminated.* San Franciso: Chronicle Books.

Bantock, Nick and Stacie Strong. 1992. *Runners, Sliders, Bouncers, Climber: A Pop-Up Look at Animals in Motion.* New York: Hyperion.

Carroll, Lewis. 1991. *Jabberwocky: A Pop-Up Rhyme from Through the Looking Glass.* Paper engineering by Nick Bantock and David K. Meyer. New York: Viking Penguin.

Carroll, Lewis. 1992. *The Walrus and the Carpenter: Another Pop-Up Rhyme from Through the Looking Glass.* Design and illustration by Nick Bantock; paper engineering by Nick Bantock and David K. Meyer. New York: Viking.

Coleridge, Samuel Taylor. 1993. *Kubla Khan: A Pop-UpPop-Up Version of Coleridge's Classic.* Illustration by Nick Bantock; design by Barbara Hodgson and Nick Bantock; paper engineering by Nick Bantock and Dennis K. Meyer. New York: Viking.

Awards and Honors

The 1998 British Academy of Film and Television Arts interactive sound and moving image awards for the CD-ROM version of the Griffin and Sabine series, "Ceremony of Innocence," which also received other international electronic media awards: http://www.nickbantock.com/Bantock/Ceremony_Innocence.html; http://www.bafta.org/awards-database.html?sq=ceremony+of+innocence.

Did You Know?

Bantock has said of his pop-up books using verse and nursery rhyme that they represent a "gallows chuckle," which has been characterized as rising from a "deeply rooted taste for zany black humor" (Hluchy 1992).

The idea for his interactive book series about Griffin and Sabine occurred when he responded to a day of junk mail by writing his own imaginary correspondence (*Something About the Author*).

Sources of Information

Periodicals

Hluchy, Patricia.1992."Thrills on the Page." *Maclean's* 105, no. 16 (April 20): 7–8.

Smith, Colleen. 2010. "Creators of the Popular Griffin and Sabine Saga to Exhibit Body of Work." *Denverpost.com.* http://www.denverpost.com/books/ci_15370745. Accessed on June 27, 2010.

Reference Source

Something About the Author. vol. 95, s.v. "Bantock, Nick."

Website

Nick Bantock's website: http://www.nickbantock.com.

NAME: BARON, ANDREW

Personal Data

His studio in Santa Fe, New Mexico, is named Popyrus Studio.

Career Highlights

Baron has said, "My experience includes everything from creating original paper designs and functional engineering, to editorial, pre-press production, production consulting, cost-reduction refinements and manufacturing support" (http://www.popy rus.com).

Selected Pop-Up Works

Child, Lauren. 2001. *My Dream Bed. Loads of Tabs and Flaps and Wheels and More!* Paper engineering by Andrew Baron. London: Hodder Children's.

Chu, Miyoko (with Cornell Lad of Ornithiology). 2008. *Birdscapes: A Pop-Up Celebration of Birdsongs in Stereo Sound.* Paper engineering by Gene Vosough, Renee Jablow, and Andy Baron; illustration by Julia Hargreaves. San Francisco: Chronicle Books.

Davenport, Meg, and Werenko, Lisa V. 1998. *Circus!: A Pop-Up Adventure.* Illustration by Meg Davenport; paper engineering by Andrew Baron and Sally Blakemore. New York: Little Brown.

Harris, John, and Calef Brown. 2005. *Pop-Up Aesop.* Written by John Harris; illustration by Calef Brown; editing by John Harris; design by Kurt Hauser; production coordination by Elizabeth Zozom; paper engineering by Arty Projects Studio; Sally Blakemore, and Eileen Banshek; engineering refinements and production by Andy Baron. Los Angeles: Getty Publications.

Tolkien, J.R.R. 1999. *The Hobbit: A 3-D Pop-Up Adventure.* Illustration by John Howe; paper engineering by Andrew Baron. New York: Harper Festival.

Zelinsky, Paul O. 2002. *Knick-knack Paddywhack! A Moving Parts Book.* Adaptation from the counting song and illustration by Paul Zelinsky; paper engineering by Andrew Baron. New York: Dutton Children's Books.

Awards and Honors

Knick-Knack Paddywhack!

American Library Association Notable Children's Book, All Ages, 2003: http://www.ala.org/ala/mgrps/divs/alsc/awardsgrants/notalists/ncb/ncbpastlists/2003ncblist.cfm.

Meggendorfer Prize 2004 (The Movable Book Society): http://www.movable booksociety.org/pdf/meggendorferprize.pdf.

Did You Know?

Baron has said, "By age twelve, I became intrigued with wind-up phonographs and soon my interests expanded to encompass antique clocks, vintage radios, brass cash registers, antique cars and other fascinations. The skills I cultivated in my machine restoration now enhance and inform my paper engineering" (http://www.popyrus.com).

Sources of Information

Website

Andrew Baron's website is: http://www.popyrus.com.

NAME: BATAILLE, MARION

Personal Data

Lives in Paris, France.

Career Highlights

Is a graduate of the Ecole Supérieure des Arts Graphiques de Paris.
She is an "artist, illustrator, costume designer, photographer, graphic designer and typographer" (Siouxwire.com 2008).

Selected Pop-Up Works

Bataille, Marion. 2008. *ABC3D*. 1st American ed. Book design by Marion Bataille; cover design by Michael Yuen. New York: Roaring Book Press.
Bataille, Marion. 2011. *10*. New York: Roaring Book Press.

Awards and Honors

ABC3D (2008)
Meggendorfer Prize 2010 (The Movable Book Society): http://www.movable booksociety.org/pdf/meggendorferprize.pdf.

Did You Know?

She is the first European to be awarded the Meggendorfer Prize.
ABC3D was originally a limited edition object (Bolle 2008). According to Bataille, "Z" was the letter that was the hardest to produce and "A" was the easiest (kidsthinkdesign n.d.).

Sources of Information

Periodicals

Bolle, Sonja. 2008. "The Pleasures of Learning One's ABCs: Marion Bataille's 'ABC3D' Offers an Exuberant Visual Exploration of the Alphabet." *Los Angeles Times*. http://www.latimes.com/features/books/la-caw-word-play19–2008oct19,1,3007832.story. Accessed October 19, 2008.

Websites

kidsthinkdesign: A Kids Design Collaborative Project. n.d. "Bataille: Winner of Meggendorfer Prize." http://kidsthinkdesign.org/books/meet.html.

Siouxwire.com. 2008. "Introducing Marion Bataille." http://www.siouxwire.com/2008/04/introducing-marion-bataille.html.

NAME: BLAKEMORE, SALLY

Personal Data

Born in 1947 in Odessa, Texas.

Career Highlights

University education includes North Texas State University and the University of Texas, Austin. Blakemore has a bachelor's of art degree in painting and sculpture.

Work experiences include type houses and ad agencies and various theater magazines, where she illustrated and designed, and a position as art production manager at *New York Magazine*. Was also the creative director for a design studio in New Orleans. Worked as art director for paper engineer James Diaz's White Heat company in Santa Fe (Olmon 2009).

Her studio is named Arty Projects Studio, and she started it in 1999 (Google Profile n.d.).

Selected Pop-Up Works

Davenport, Meg, and Werenko, Lisa V. 1998. *Circus!: A Pop-up Adventure*. Illustration by Meg Davenport; written by Meg Davenport and Lisa V. Werenko; paper engineering by Andrew Baron and Sally Blakemore. New York: Little Brown.

Gallagher, Derek. 2004. *Ancient Dwellings of the Southwest*. Illustration by Sally Blakemore; pop-up design and production by Arty Projects Studio, ; paper engineering by Eileen Banashek, Sally Blakemore, and Anthony Esparsen. Tucson, AZ: Western National Parks Association.

Harris, John, and Calef Brown. 2005. *Pop-Up Aesop*. Written by John Harris; illustration by Calef Brown; editing by John Harris; design by Kurt Hauser; production coordination by Elizabeth Zozom; paper engineering by Arty Projects Studio; Sally Blakemore, and Eileen Banshek; engineering refinements and production by Andy Baron. Los Angeles: Getty Publications.

Blakemore, Sally. 2009. *NASCAR Pop-Up: A Guide to the Sport*. 1st ed. Illustrations by Doug Chezem. Gibbs Smith.

Did You Know?

She plays in an AfroFusion marimba band and lists her occupation as "paper engineer/illustrator/book designer/musician" (Google Profile n.d.).

She bought her first pop-up book at the age of 33, in 1979: Tor Lokvig's *Haunted House*, by Jan Pieńkowski (Olmon 2009).

Her dyslexia and synesthesia always made reading and test-taking difficult, and she has said, "I find many children who have difficulty reading, as I did in school, can be lured into books that are illustrated novels and sculptural paper fantasies (Olmon 2009).

Sources of Information

Periodical

Olmon, Kyle. 2009. "Interview with Sally Blakemore." http://www.kyleolmon.com/work/ articles/blakemore.html. Abbreviated version of article was published in *Movable Stationery* 17, no.4 (November 2009): 1–2, 11–12.

Websites

Google Profile. n.d. https://profiles.google.com/artywildmakers#artywildmakers/about. YouTube video (6:20 minutes) of Blakemore's studio and work, including music and sound effects: http://www.youtube.com/watch?v=hUH5BAIyy9E.

NAME: CARTER, DAVID A.

Personal Data

Born March 4, 1957, in Salt Lake City, Utah.
Has collaborated on pop-up and interactive books with his wife, Noelle L. Carter.

Career Highlights

Attended Utah State University, studying illustration and art.

Worked in graphic design and advertising before working at Intervisual Communications, which is renowned for its pop-up book publication history.

In 1987, left a job in publishing for freelance work as a writer, illustrator, and paper engineer (*Something About the Author*, vol. 170).

Selected Pop-Up Works

Carter, David A. 2011. *Welcome to Bugland: A Fun Foldout World*. New York: Little Simon.
Carter, David A. 2010. *Counting: A Bugs Pop-Up Concept Book*. New York: Little Simon.
Carter, David A. 2010. *Opposites: A Bugs Pop-Up Concept Book*. New York: Little Simon.
Carter, David. 2009. *Blue2: A Pop-Up Book for Children of All Ages*. London: Tate Publishing.
Carter. David A. 2008. *Yellow Square: A Pop-Up Book for Children of All Ages*. New York: Little Simon.
Carter, David A. 2007. *600 Black Spots: A Pop-Up Book for Children of All Ages*. New York: Little Simon.
Carter, David A. 2009. *White Noise: A Pop-Up Book for Children of All Ages*. New York: Little Simon.
Carter, David A. 2004. *Birthday Bugs: A Pop-Up Party*. New York: Little Simon.
Carter, David A. 2004. *One Red Dot: A Pop-Up Book for Children of All Ages*. New York: Little Simon.
Carter, David A., and James Diaz. 1999. *The Elements Of Pop Up: A Pop Up Book for Aspiring Paper Engineers*. New York: Little Simon.
Carter, David A. 1998. *Bed Bugs: A Pop-Up Bedtime Book*. New York: Little Simon.
Carter, David A. 1988. *How Many Bugs in a Box? A Pop-Up Counting Book*. New York: Simon & Schuster. [Also available as a mini-edition (2006).]

Seuss, Dr. 2008. *Horton Hears a Who Pop-Up!* 1st ed. Pop-Ups by David A. Carter. New York: Random House.

Weeks, Sarah A., and David A. Carter. 1996. *Noodles: An Enriched Pop-Up Product.* New York: HarperFestival.

Carter. David. 1994. *Alpha Bugs.* New York: Little Simon. [Also available as a mini-edition (2006).]

Awards and Honors

Elements of Pop-Up: A Pop-Up Book For Aspiring Paper Engineers (1999)
> American Library Association Notable Children's Books, Older Readers 2000: http://www.ala.org/ala/mgrps/divs/alsc/awardsgrants/notalists/ncb/ncbpastlists/2000ncblist.cfm.

One Red Dot: A Pop-Up Book for Children of All Ages (2005)
> Bank Street Best of the Best Outstanding Books 1997–2008, Special Interests, Activities: http://edit.bankstreet.edu:8080/bookcom/best_special_interest.
> Meggendorfer Prize 2006 (The Movable Book Society): http://www.movable-booksociety.org/pdf/meggendorferprize.pdf.
> National Parenting Publications Awards Preschoolers & Kindergarteners Gold Award Winner 2005: http://www.parenthood.com/article-topics/nappa_2005_books_for_preschoolers_amp_kindergarteners.html/full-view.
> New York Public Library Recommended Reading, Children's Books 2005: http://kids.nypl.org/reading/recommended_2005.cfm.

600 Black Spots: A Pop-Up Book for Children of All Ages (2007)
> Bank Street Best of the Best Outstanding Books 1997–2008, Special Interests, Arts: http://edit.bankstreet.edu:8080/bookcom/best_special_interest.
> National Parenting Publications Awards Gold Award Winner 2006: http://www.parenthood.com/article-topics/nappa_gold_winners_2007_books.html/page/6.
> New York Times Best Illustrated Children's Books of 2007: http://query.nytimes.com/gst/fullpage.html?res=9D06E6DD1F3FF932A25752C1A9619C8B63.

White Noise (2009)
> National Parenting Publications Awards Honors Winner, Ages 12 & Up, 2009: http://www.parenthood.com/NAPPA/books09_12up.php.

Did You Know?

Carter has said, "discovering that link between my childhood curiosities and thrills and my books has something to do with where my ideas come from" (*Something About the Author,* vol. 114).

In response to a question about what interested him in paper engineering and pop-up art, he said, "I enjoy building as much as I do drawing and painting, and I saw the opportunity to do both in pop-up book making" (Harcourt Trade Publishers' website).

Sources of Information

Periodical

Henwood, Danny. 2000. "Pop-Up Laureate." *The Washington Times* (March 25): B6.

Reference Sources

Something About the Author. vol. 114, s.v. "Carter, David."
Something About the Author. vol. 170, s.v. "Carter, David."

Websites

David Carter's website (shared with Noelle L. Carter): http://www.popupbooks.com.
Harcourt Trade Publishers' website, "Interview with David A. Carter": http://biography.jrank.org/pages/2262/Carter-David-1957.html.

NAME: CARTER, NOELLE L.

Personal Data

Born January 31, 1961, in Los Angeles, California.

Is the daughter of renowned paper engineer Tor Lokvig and the wife of paper engineer David Carter, with whom she has collaborated on pop-up/interactive books.

Career Highlights

Attended California State University, Northridge, and studied graphic arts and illustration.

Worked as a production artist at Intervisual Communications, which is renowned for its pop-up book publication history.

Selected Pop-Up Works

Carter, David, and Noelle Carter. 2000. *The Nutcracker: A Pop-Up Adaptation of E.T.A. Hoffman's Original Tale.* New York: Little Simon.
Carter, Noelle. 1991. *My House: A Pop-Up Book.* New York: Viking.
Carter, Noelle. 2005. *Birthday Fun 1, 2, 3: A Counting Flap Book.* New York: Little Simon.
Carter, Noelle. 2004. *Where Is the Rainbow?: A Color Flap Book.* 1st ed. New York: Little Simon.
Carter, Noelle, and David Carter. 2003. *Little Mouse's Christmas: A Scratch-the-Scent and Lift-the-Flap Book.* Los Angeles: Piggy Toes Press.

Did You Know?

On the website that she shares with David A. Carter (http://www.popupbooks.com), she says that while working at Intervisual Communication she "learned much of the making of pop-up books with their creative director, Jim [James] Diaz."

On the same website, she notes that Intervisual Communication was where her father, Tor Lokvig, had worked as a paper engineer for many years.

Sources of Information

Website

Noelle Carter's website (shared with David A. Carter): http://www.popupbooks.com.

NAME: DIJS, CARLA

Selected Pop-Up Works

Dijs, Carla. 1987. *Who Sees You? In the Forest.* New York: Grossett & Dunlap.
Dijs, Carla. 1992. *Pretend You're a Whale: A Pop-Up Book.* New York: Little Simon.
Dijs, Carla. 1994. *How Many Fingers?* New York: Random House.
Dijs, Carla. 1995. *Hurry Home, Hungry Frog: A Pop-Up Book.* New York: Little Simon.
Dijs, Carla. 2002. *Halloween Colors: A Turn-the-Flap Book.* New York: Scholastic.
Moerbeek, Kees, and Carla Dijs. 1997. *When the Wild Pirates Go Sailing: A Pop-Up Adventure Book.* Kansas City, MO: Piggy Toes Press
Moerbeek, Kees, and Carla Dijs. 1998. *Look What I Can Do!* Brookfield, CT: Millbrook Press.
Thomas, Pamela. 2000. *Brooklyn Pops Up.* Text Pamela Thomas; project management Evan Kingsley and Beth D. Weinstein; designer Chani Yammer; concept Ann Montanaro, Ellen G.K. Rubin, and Robert Sabuda. New York: Little Simon.

Did You Know?

Carla Dijs resides in the Netherlands.

She has collaborated on many pop-up books with her husband, Kees Moerbeek. In *Brooklyn Pops Up* (2000), their facial images are reflected in an egg cream glass in the page spread of "Flavors of Brooklyn," which they engineered ("Trivia" 2009).

Sources of Information

Periodicals

"Trivia." 2009. *Movable Stationery* 17, no. 3 (August): 8.

NAME: FISCHER, CHUCK

Personal Data

After graduation, originally considered a career in acting.

Has said, "The most vivid memories of books I read as a child are of beautifully illustrated picture books that my sisters and I shared" (Peña 2007).

Career Highlights

Has a BA in advertising art from the University of Kansas.

Has had a successful career as a muralist and a product designer of home furnishings, including china, crystal, wallpaper, and fabric.

In 2005, was a visiting artist at the American Academy in Rome.

Selected Pop-Up Works

Fischer, Chuck. 2006. *Christmas in New York: A Pop-Up Book.* Paper engineering by Bruce Foster. New York: Bulfinch.

Fischer, Chuck. 2007. *Christmas Around the World: A Pop-Up Book.* Text by Anne Newgarden; paper engineering by Bruce Foster. New York: Little Brown.

Fischer, Chuck. 2008. *In the Beginning: The Art of Genesis.* Paper engineering by Bruce Foster; text by Curtis Flowers. New York: Little Brown.

Fischer, Chuck. 2009. *Angels: A Pop-Up Book.* Text by Curtis Flowers; paper engineering by Bruce Foster. New York: Little Brown.

Fischer, Chuck. 2010. *A Christmas Carol: A Pop-Up Book.* Paintings by Chuck Fischer; paper engineering by Bruce Foster. New York: Little Brown.

Did You Know?

When Fischer was first asked about creating a pop-up book, he "thought it was a great third dimension to my painting" (Peña 2007).

In considering similarities between his design projects, including pop-up books, he has said, "All of the design projects I accept begin with a lot of research. I love this part of the process and I use all resources available. I visit libraries, go to museums, and use the internet more than ever" (Peña 2007).

He has said of the pop-up book that it is a "format that lends itself to my illustrations and my sense of history and sense of place" (Hachette Book Group video).

Sources of Information

Periodicals

Fischer, Chuck. 2002. "Building a Pop-Up Book." *Movable Stationery* 10, no. 4 (November): 3.

Peña, Adie C. 2007. "Interview with Chuck Fischer." *Movable Stationery* 15, no. 1 (February):1, 2, 9–10.

Websites

Chuck Fischer's website: http://www.chuckfischer.com/index.htm.

Forum Network. "The White House: A Pop-Up Book." http://forum-network.org/lecture/white-house-pop-book.

Hachette Book Group video, Chuck Fischer virtual studio: http://www.hachettebookgroup.com/authors_Chuck-Fischer-(1065146).htm; after introduction, click on items in studio to hear explanation from the Fischer avatar: http://www.chuckfischer.com/interact.htm.

NAME: FOSTER, BRUCE

Personal Data

Has said that he "lived most of my life in the South—Louisiana as a young boy, Tennessee as a teen and young adult and Texas as an adult and father—although as a young child I did live briefly in L.A. and San Diego" (Hoffarth 2009).

Career Highlights

Studied pre-medicine and painting at the University of Tennessee, Knoxville.

Began his career designing pop-ups for books as a freelancer for Ottenheimer Publishers.

Designed the pop-ups that appear in the 2007 Oscar-nominated Walt Disney musical comedy *Enchanted*.

Selected Pop-Up Works

Aronson, Sarah. 2002. *The Princess and the Pea: A Pop-Up Book*. Illustration by Chris Demarest; adaptation by Sarah Aronson; paper engineering by Bruce Foster. New York: Little Simon.

Beer, Robert. 2004. *Tibetan Buddhist Altars*. Conception by Tad Wise; illustration by Robert Beer; paper engineering by Bruce Foster. Novato, CA: New World Library.

Beer, Robert. 2007. *Hindu Altars: A Pop-Up Gallery of Traditional Art & Wisdom*. Art by Pieter Weltevrede; paper engineering by Bruce Foster; conception by Tad Wise. Novato, CA: New World Library.

Colan, Kathleen. 2008. *Architectural Wonders*. Paper engineering by Bruce Foster; illustration by Dan Brown; text by Kathleen Murphy Colan. San Diego, CA: Thunder Bay Press.

East, Jacqueline. 2006. *A Three Dimensional Princess Palace*. Illustration by Jacqueline East; paper engineering by Bruce Foster. Los Angeles: Piggy Toes Press.

Eisner, Will. 2008. *The Spirit: A Pop-Up Graphic Novel*. Adapted by Bruce Foster; design and paper engineering by Bruce Foster. San Rafael, CA: Insight Editions.

Ewe, Olive. 2004. *Bee Mine*: A Pop-Up Book of Valentines. New York: Little Simon. 2004.

Havrilesky, Heather. 2006. *The Pop-Up Book of Celebrity Meltdowns*. Pop-ups by Bruce Foster; illustration by Mick Coulas; creation by Melcher Media. New York: Melcher Media.

Kee, Lucy. 2010. *Harry Potter: A Pop-Up Book: Based on the Film Phenomenon*. Paper engineering by Bruce Foster; art by Andrew Williamson; text by Lucy Kee. San Rafael, CA: Insight Editions.

Koontz, Robin. 2006. *Creepy Crawly Colors: A Pop-Up Book*. Paper engineering by Bruce Foster; book design by Aviva Presby. New York: Little Simon.

Koontz, Robin. 2006. *Up All Night Counting: A Pop-Up Book*. Paper engineering by Bruce Foster. New York: Little Simon.

Lewis, J. Patrick. 2005. *Galileo's Universe*. Poems by J. Patrick Lewis; illustration by Tom Curry; paper engineering by Bruce Foster. Mankato, MN: Creative Editions.

Mitchell, Al. 2007. *Lighthouses: A Pop-Up Gallery of America's Most Beloved Beacons*. Paper engineering by Linda Costello and Bruce Foster; illustration by Wendy Edelson. San Diego, CA: Thunder Bay Press.

Murray, Elizabeth. 2005. *Popped Art*. Pop-Ups designed by Bruce Foster. New York: Museum of Modern Art.

Rogers, Richard, Oscar Hammerstein, Howard Lindsey, and Russel Crouse. *The Sound of Music: A Classic Collectible Pop-Up*. Illustration by Dan Andreasen; paper engineering by Bruce Foster. New York: Little Simon.

Rojany-Buccieri, Lisa. 2008. *Sammy's Suitcase*. Paper engineering by Bruce Foster; illustration by Sachiko Yoshikawa. New York: Robin Corey Books.

Ruffner, Ginny. 2003. *Creativity: The Flowering Tornado: A Pop-Up Gallery*. Paper engineering by Bruce Foster. Montgomery, AL: Montgomery Museum of Fine Arts.

Ruffner, Ginny. 2008. *The Imagination Cycle*. Paper engineering and design by Bruce Foster. La Conner, WA: Museum of Northwest Art; Long Beach, CA: Long Beach Museum.

Schulz, Charles M. 2004. *Peanuts: A Pop-Up Celebration*. Art adaptation by Paige Braddock; paper engineering by Bruce Foster. New York: Little Simon.

Sports Illustrated Kids. 2009. *Wow! The Pop-Up Book of Sports*. Paper engineering by Bruce Foster. New York: Time.

White, George. 2007. *Christmas at the Zoo: A Pop-Up Winter Wonderland*. Illustration by Jason O'Malley; paper engineering by Bruce Foster; conception by George White. Mason, OH: Jumping Jack Press.

White, George. 2007. *Halloween at the Zoo: A Pop-Up Trick-or-Treat Experience*. Illustration by Jason O'Malley; paper engineering by Bruce Foster; concept by George White. Mason, OH: Jumping Jack Press.

Willard, Nancy. 1995. *Gutenberg's Gift: A Book Lover's Pop-Up Book*. Illustration by Bryan Leister; illuminated border on page two by Avraham Cohen; other illustrated borders by Samantha Carol Smith; paper engineering by Bruce Foster. Baltimore, MD: Wild Honey.

Did You Know?

Foster has said that "The Lord of the Rings" trilogy was his most influential childhood reading: "I would probably not be a designer if not for that book. Really" (http://www.paperpops.com).

He cites early influences on his work as being Kees Moerbeek and John Stejan; Moerbeek's *Topsy Turvy* "was the first pop-up book he owned" (Uria 2010).

He says that he sees the paper engineer, the writer, and the illustrator as "being equal partners in a pop-up book . . . but cooperative and collaborative artists, all working together" (Uria 2010).

Sources of Information

Periodicals

Hoffarth, Tom. 2009. "'Wow' con't: A Bruce Foster Q-and-A." *Farther off the Wall*. http://www.insidesocal.com/tomhoffarth/archives/2009/11/wow-cont-a-bruc.html. Accessed November 6, 2009.

Uria, Isabel. 2010. "Bruce Foster: Why He is a Paper Magic Master." *Movable Stationery* 18, no. 2 (May): 1–2.

Website

Bruce Foster's website: http://www.paperpops.com.

NAME: FRY, PATRICIA

Personal Data

Childhood and young-adult years were spent in Snowflake, Arizona, Mesa; Arizona; and Rainier, Washington.

Career Highlights

Has bachelor's degree (1989) is from Brigham Young University in elementary education.

Taught mathematics in kindergarten through sixth grade in New York City, and the first and second grades in Washington, D.C.

Became interested in designing children's books and completed a master's degree at Teacher's College in New York City. After graduation, she interned with the studio of Robert Sabuda and Matthew Reinhart (Olmon 2008).

Selected Pop-Up Works

Fry, Patricia. 2008. *The Nutcracker: A Pop-Up Book*. Adaptation from the classic tale by E.T.A. Hoffmann. New York: Katherine Tegen Books.

Did You Know?

Her first pop-up books were Robert Sabuda's *Mother Goose* and *Wizard of Oz*, which she acquired as an adult (Olmon 2008).

She has said that she thinks of the child when she designs a book, and, "It helps to have been surrounded by so many children over the years" (Olmon 2008).

Sources of Information

Periodicals

Olmon, Kyle. 2008. "The Next Generation of Pop-Up Artists: Patricia Fry." *Movable Stationery* 16, no. 3 (August): 1–3.

Websites

Patricia Fry's website: http://www.patriciafrybooks.com.

NAME: MOERBEEK, KEES

Personal Data

Resides in the Netherlands.

Selected Pop-Up Works

Havrilesky, Heather. 2007. *Even More Outrageous Celebrity Meltdowns*. Pop-ups by Kees Moerbeek; illustration by Mick Coulas. New York: Melcher Media.

King, Stephen. 2004. *The Girl Who Loved Tom Gordon: A Pop-Up Book*. 1st ed. Text adaptation by Peter Abrahams; illustration by Alan Dingman; paper engineering by Kees Moerbeek. London: Little Simon.

Moerbeek, Kees. 1992. *Hi Mom, I'm Home: Another Pop-Up Adventure*. Devised, design, and illustration by Kees Moerbeek. Los Angeles: Price Stern Sloan.

Moerbeek, Kees. 1993. *Boo Whoo? A Spooky Mix-and-Match Pop-Up Book*. Los Angeles: Price Stern Sloan.

Moerbeek, Kees. 2002. *The Diary of Hansel and Gretel*. New York: Little Simon.

Moerbeek, Kees. 2006. *Alfred Hitchcock: The Master of Suspense: A Pop-Up Book*. Paper engineering by Kees Moerbeek. London: Simon & Schuster.

Moerbeek, Kees. 2009. *Wicked the Musical: A Pop-Up Compendium of Splendiferous Delight and Thrillifying Intrigue; Based on the Hit Broadway Show*. Pop-ups by Kees Moerbeek; illustration by Greg Call. New York: Melcher Media.

Moerbeek, Kees. 2011. *Count 1 to 10: A Pop-Up Book*. New York: Abrams Books for Young Readers.

Moerbeek, Kees, and Carla Dijs. 1997. *Six Brave Explorers: A Pop-Up Book*. Los Angeles: Piggy Toes Press.

Sardegna, Jill. 2002. *You Monsters Are in Charge: A Boisterous Bedtime Pop-Up*. Illustration by Kees Moerbeek. New York: Little Simon.

Did You Know?

An "unconventional" project for which Kees Moerbeek did the paper engineering was a pop-up book for the Wendy Evans Joseph Architecture firm. It highlighted 10 of the firm's architectural projects (http://www.clearmag.com/tag/kees-moerbeek/).

NAME: OLMON, KYLE

Personal Data

Born outside Chicago, Illinois.

Career Highlights

Enrolled in the painting department at the University of Illinois-Champaign Urbana, and received a second degree in art history.

Studied under paper engineer Andrew Baron in Santa Fe and then worked in the studio of paper engineers Robert Sabuda and Matthew Reinhart.

Has taught a course at Pratt Institute on paper engineering (http://www.kyleolmon.com).

Selected Pop-Up Works

Olmon, Kyle. 2006. *Castle: Medieval Days and Nights*. 1st ed. Illustration by Tracy Sabin. New York: Orchard Books.

Olmon, Kyle, and Jacqueline Rogers. 2009. *Baby Signs*. Paper engineering by Kyle Olmon; art by Jacqueline Rogers. New York: Orchard Books.

Did You Know?

He says that he moved from making artist's books to pop-ups after being "reintroduced to the world of pop-up books" in a bookmaking course that he took as an exchange student in Australia and recalling "fond memories of dismantling pop-up books as an inquisitive child flooded back!" (http://www.kyleolmon.com).

Sources of Information

Website

Kyle Olmon's website: http://www.kyleolmon.com.

NAME: PIEŃKOWSKI, JAN MICHAL

Personal Data

Born in Warsaw, Poland, on August 8, 1936.

World War II took him and his parents to Great Britain in 1946, by way of Austria, Germany, and Italy. Formally started school in Britain, where he learned English (already knew Polish, German, and Italian) (Travis n.d.; *Fourth Book of Junior Authors and Illustrators* 1999).

His name is pronounced: yon pe en koff ski.

Career Highlights

At King's College, Cambridge, England, Pieńkowski planned to study architecture but instead read classics and English, receiving a BA in 1957 and an MA in 1961. It was at college that he began designing.

He co-founded the greeting card company Gallery Five.

He has done work in advertising, publishing, television graphics, and stage design.

His illustrations were commended for the Kate Greenaway Medal in 1971 (*The Golden Bird*; not a pop-up book) and received the medal in 1972 (*The Kingdom Under the Sea*; not a pop-up book).

Selected Pop-Up Works (Author, Illustrator)

Pieńkowski, Jan. 1986. *Little Monsters*. Paper engineering by Marcin Stajewski, James Roger Diaz, and David A. Carter. Los Angeles: Price Stern Sloan.

Pieńkowski, Jan.1989. *Oh My a Fly!* Paper engineering by Marcin Stajewski and Dennis K. Meyer. Los Angeles: Price Stern Sloan.

Pieńkowski, Jan. 1991. *Phone Book*. Text by Anne Carter and Jan Pieńkowski; paper engineering by Marcin Stajewski. Los Angeles: Price Stern Sloan.

Pieńkowski, Jan. 1996. *Botticelli's Bed & Breakfast*. Paper engineering by Rodger Smith and Helen Blamer, with special thanks to Hilary Sanders. New York: Simon & Schuster.

Pieńkowski, Jan. 2004. *The First Noel: A Christmas Carousel*. Illustration assistance by David Walser; paper engineering by Helen Balmer, with Lois Bulow Osborne. Cambridge, MA: Candlewick Press.

Pieńkowski, Jan. 2008. *Dinner Time*. Text by Anne Carter; paper engineering by Marcin Stajewski and James Roger Diaz. Cambridge, MA: Candlewick Press.

Awards and Honors

The Haunted House (1979)

> Kate Greenaway Medal in 1980: http://www.carnegiegreenaway.org.uk/green away/full_list_of_winners.php.

Did You Know?

Of his books, Pieńkowski has said, "The most important thing is that it must entertain me, then it's got a chance of entertaining someone else" (*Something About the Author*, vol. 58).

"He has always been attracted to comics, which were not available in Poland during his wartime childhood. . . . 'It seems to me that this form has enormous merits of impact and economy. Instead of describing one another, words and pictures are complementary and the narrative depends equally on both'" (*Fourth Book of Junior Authors and Illustrators* 1999).

Sources of Information

Reference Sources

Fourth Book of Junior Authors and Illustrators: Junior Authors Electronic (1978, updated 1999).
Something About the Author. vol. 58, s.v. "Pieńkowski, Jan Michal."
Something About the Author. vol. 131, s.v. "Pieńkowski, Jan Michal."

Websites

Jan Pieńkowski's website: http://www.janpienkowski.com.
Travis, Madelyn. n.d. "Something Extraordinary." BookTrust. http://www.booktrustchil drensbooks.org.uk/show/feature/search/Interview-with-Jan-Pienkowski.
Young, Kirsty. n.d. "Desert Island Discs: Jan Pienkowski." BBC Radio 4. http://www.jan pienkowski.com/latestnews/desertislanddiscs/index.htm.

NAME: REINHART, MATTHEW CHRISTIAN

Personal Data

Born September 21, 1971, in Cedar Rapids, Iowa.
Has collaborated on pop-up books with Robert Sabuda.

Career Highlights

Studied biology as an undergraduate at Clemson University.
Completed a two-year graduate program at Pratt Institute for Industrial Design.
Created models for the Nickelodeon television program *Blue's Clues*.
While at Pratt Institute, interned with paper engineer Robert Sabuda and began making pop-ups (Olmon 2009).

Selected Pop-Up Works

Greenberg, Gary. c1999. *The Pop-Up Book of Phobias*. 1st ed. Created by Gary Greenberg; illustration by Balvis Rubess; pop-ups by Matthew Reinhart. New York: Rob Weisbach Books.

Greenberg, Gary. 2001, c2001. *The Pop-Up Book of Nightmares*. Creation by Gary Greenberg; illustration by Balvis Rubess; pop-ups by Matthew Reinhart. New York: St. Martin's Press.

Reinhart, Matthew. 2002. *Animal Popposites: A Pop-Up Book of Opposites*. New York: Little Simon.

Reinhart, Matthew. 2005. *The Ark: A Pop-Up by Matthew Reinhart*. New York: Little Simon.

Reinhart, Matthew. 2005. *Cinderella: A Pop-Up Fairy Tale*. New York: Little Simon.

Reinhart, Matthew. 2006. *The Jungle Book: A Pop-Up Adventure*. New York: Little Simon.

Reinhart, Matthew. 2007. *Star Wars: A Pop-Up Guide to the Galaxy*. New York: Orchard Books.

Reinhart, Matthew. 2009. *A Pop-Up Book of Nursery Rhymes*. New York: Simon & Schuster.

Reinhart, Matthew. 2010. *DC Super Heroes: The Ultimate Pop-Up Book*. 1st ed. New York: Little Brown.

Sendak, Maurice. 2006. *Mommy?* 1st ed. Art by Maurice Sendak; scenario by Arthur Yorinks; paper engineering by Matthew Reinhart. Michael di Capua Books.

Awards and Honors

A Pop-Up Book of Nursery Rhymes (2009)
> National Parenting Publications Award Honors Award Winner, Infants & Toddlers 2009: http://www.parenthood.com/NAPPA/books09_infants_toddlers.php.

Star Wars: A Pop-Up Guide to the Galaxy (2007)
> Meggendorfer Prize (The Movable Book Society) 2008: http://www.movablebooksociety.org/pdf/meggendorferprize.pdf.

Did You Know?

The first pop-up book that Reinhart owned as a child was *Dinosaurs*, created by Intervisual Communications, which is renowned for its pop-up book publication history (Olmon 2009).

In discussing the topics of his pop-up books on nightmares and phobias, he has said. "Readers seem to love examining the darker sides of their lives even if it makes them uncomfortable" (Peña 2002).

In discussing his extensive collecting of Star Wars figures and Transformers figures, he has said. "Transformers epitomize change and evolution and I think that parallels the work we do—making paper transform into something amazing and new" (Olmon 2009).

Sources of Information

Periodicals

Olmon, Kyle. 2009. "In Conversation with Matthew Reinhart." *Movable Stationery* 17, no. 2 (May): 1, 2, 12–13.

Peña, Adie. 2002. "16 Questions with Robert and Matthew." *Movable Stationery* 10, no. 4 (November): 5–6.

Perrin, Martin. 2007. "Pop-Up Books and Scary Monsters." *Blueprint* no. 255 (June): 101–3, 105–6.

Reference Sources

Artist to Artist: 23 Major Illustrators Talk to Children About their Art: 94–97.
Something About the Author. vol. 161, s.v. "Reinhart, Matthew."

Websites

Barnes and Noble. "Meet the Writers: Video Interviews with Today's Top Writers. Matthew Reinhart." http://www.parenthood.com/article-topics/be_a_nappa_winner.html.
The Library of Congress. "Matthew Reinhart & Robert Sabuda: Book Fest 08." (27 minutes) http://www.loc.gov/today/cyberlc/feature_wdesc.php?rec=4393.
Matthew Reinhart's website: http://www.matthewreinhart.com.

NAME: SABUDA, ROBERT CLARKE

Personal Data

Born March 8, 1965, in Michigan.

Career Highlights

Earned a B.A. from Pratt Institute (summa cum laude), 1987.
Has collaborated on pop-up books with Matthew Reinhart.

Selected Pop-Up Works

Baum, L. Frank. 2001. *The Wonderful Wizard of Oz: A Commemorative Pop-Up.* Art by Robert Sabuda. New York: Little Simon.
DePaola, Tomie, Robert Sabuda, and Matthew Reinhart. 2008. *Brava, Strega Nona!: A Heartwarming Pop-Up Book.* New York: Putnam.
Lewis, C.S. 2007. *The Chronicles of Narnia Pop-Up: Based on the books by C.S. Lewis.* Paper engineering by Robert Sabuda; full-color art by Matthew Armstrong. New York: HarperCollins Children's Books.
Moore, Clement Clarke, and Robert Sabuda. 2002. *The Night Before Christmas.* New York: Little Simon.
Sabuda, Robert. 1994. *The Christmas Alphabet.* New York: Orchard Books. (Also available in a 2004 deluxe anniversary edition.).
Sabuda, Robert. 1996. *The 12 Days of Christmas.* New York: Little Simon. (Also available in a 2006 anniversary edition.)
Sabuda, Robert. 1997. *Cookie Count: A Tasty Pop-Up.* New York: Little Simon.
Sabuda, Robert. 1998. *ABC Disney Pop-Up.* New York: Disney Press. (Also available in a 2009 anniversary edition.)
Sabuda, Robert. 1999. *The Movable Mother Goose.* 1st ed. Additional design work by Matthew Reinhart. New York: Little Simon.

Sabuda, Robert. 2003. *Alice's Adventures in Wonderland: A Pop-Up Adaptation of Lewis Carroll's Original Tale.* 1st ed. New York: Little Simon.

Sabuda, Robert. 2004. *America the Beautiful.* New York: Little Simon.

Sabuda, Robert. 2005. *Winter's Tale: An Original Pop-Up Journey.* New York: Little Simon.

Sabuda, Robert. 2007. *Winter in White: A Mini Pop-Up Treat.* New York: Little Simon.

Sabuda, Robert. 2008. *Peter Pan: A Pop-Up Adaptation of J.M. Barrie's Original Tale.* New York: Little Simon.

Sabuda, Robert. 2010. *Beauty and the Beast: A Pop-Up Adaptation of the Classic Tale.* New York: Little Simon.

Sabuda, Robert, and Matthew Reinhart. 2001. *Young Naturalist Pop-Up Handbook: Beetles.* New York: Hyperion.

Sabuda, Robert and Matthew Reinhart. 2001. *Young Naturalist Pop-Up Handbook: Butterflies.* New York: Hyperion.

Sabuda, Robert, and Matthew Reinhart. 2005. *Encyclopedia Prehistorica: Dinosaurs: The Definitive Pop-Up.* Cambridge, MA: Candlewick.

Sabuda, Robert and Matthew Reinhart. 2006. *Encyclopedia Prehistorica: Sharks & Sea Monsters.* Cambridge, MA: Candlewick.

Sabuda, Robert and Matthew Reinhart. 2007. *Encyclopedia Prehistorica: Mega-beasts Pop-Up.* Cambridge, MA: Candlewick.

Awards and Honors

Alice's Adventures in Wonderland (2003)

American Library Association Notable Children's Book, All Ages, 2004: http://www.ala.org/ala/mgrps/divs/alsc/awardsgrants/notalists/ncb/ncbpastlists/2004ncblist.cfm.

America the Beautiful (2004)

Oppenheim Toy Portfolio Platinum Award: http://www.toyportfolio.com.

The Christmas Alphabet (2001; 2005)

Meggendorfer Prize (The Movable Book Society) 1998: http://www.movablebooksociety.org/pdf/meggendorferprize.pdf.

Cookie Count (1997)

Meggendorfer Prize (The Movable Book Society) 2000: http://www.movablebooksociety.org/pdf/meggendorferprize.pdf.

Parents Magazine All-Time Best Books for Toddlers: http://www.parents.com/fun/entertainment/books/best-toddler-books/?page=19.

Encyclopedia Prehistorica: Dinosaurs (2005)

American Library Association Notable Children's Book, Middle Readers, 2006: http://www.ala.org/ala/mgrps/divs/alsc/awardsgrants/childrensnotable/notablechibooks/ncbpastlists/index.cfm.

Bank Street Best of the Best Outstanding Books of 1997–2008, Special Interests—Science: http://edit.bankstreet.edu:8080/bookcom/best_special_interest.

Texas Bluebonnet List 2006–2007: http://txla.org/groups/tba/masters/masterlists06_07.html.

Winter's Tale (2005)

Oppenheim Portfolio Platinum Award 2006: http://www.toyportfolio.com.

The Wonderful Wizard of Oz (2001)

American Library Association Notable Children's Book, All Ages, 2001: http://www.ala.org/ala/mgrps/divs/alsc/awardsgrants/notalists/ncb/ncbpastlists/2001ncblist.cfm.

Meggendorfer Prize (The Movable Book Society) 2002: http://www.movable booksociety.org/pdf/meggendorferprize.pdf.

Did You Know?

In reference to the first pop-up book that he encountered (*The Adventures of Superpickle*), Sabuda said, "I loved reading and loved books, but this was different." He recalls, "This was art, and I said, 'I want to do this'" (Minzesheimer 2005).

He notes that "since childhood he has been able to see images in three dimensions. He credits some of the influence to his father, who was a mason and a carpenter" ("In the Studio" 1996).

In reference to his art, he has said, "I was always fascinated with movement, the how and the why" (Morrison 2005).

When asked about the greatest challenge in creating pop-ups, he responded: "Getting it to pop shut! I know most people would think that making it pop-up is the difficult part, but making it pop shut is the real challenge" (Pastor 2010).

Sources of Information

Periodicals

"In the Studio with Robert Sabuda." 1996. *Publishers Weekly* (November 25): 30–31.
Minzesheimer, Bob. 2005. "Sabuda's Creativity Pops Up." *USA Today* (December 20):7D.
Morrison, Jim. 2005. "The Wizard of Ahhhs." *American Way* (November 1): 72, 74, 78.
Pastor, Pam. 2010. "Paper Engineers." *Philippine Daily Inquirer,* March 13. http://lifestyle. inquirer.net/super/super/view/20100313–258305/Paper-engineers.
"Q&A: Robert Sabuda." 2000 *School Library Journal* 46, no. 10 (October): 19.

Reference Sources

Something About the Author. vol. 81, s.v. "Sabuda, Robert."

Websites

Barnes and Noble. "Meet the Writers: Video Interviews with Today's Top Writers. Robert Sabuda." http://media.barnesandnoble.com/?fr_story=d19696f7e28fb15602c2a386298 b1c5e74e2a569&rf =sitemap.
Robert Sabuda's website: http://www.robertsabuda.com.

NAME: SANTORO, LUCIO AND MEERA

Personal Data

In 1983, art directors Lucio and Meer Santoro founded Santoro London, which specializes in paper engineering, including "swing cards" and pop-up books as well as other products (http://www.santorographics.com/paperengineering/santoro. html).

Santoro London's Paper Engineering Studio has produced three pop-up book titles, which use the swing design in the pop-ups.

Selected Pop-Up Works

Santoro, Lucio, and Meera Santoro. 2007. *Journey to the Moon: A Roaring, Soaring Ride! A Pop-Up Book with Revolutionary Pop-Up Technology.* New York: Little Simon.

Santoro, Lucio, and Meera Santoro. 2008. *Predators: A Pop-Up Book with Revolutionary Technology.* New York: Little Simon.

Santoro, Lucio, and Meera Santoro. 2010. *Wild Oceans: A Pop-Up Book with Revolutionary Technology!* New York: Little Simon.

Source of Information

Website

The Santoro London company website is: http://www.santorographics.com/paperengineering/santoro.html.

6

Using Pop-Ups in Activities and Programs, with How-To Instructions (Introduction and Elementary Grades)

This section begins Chapter 6-8, which describe how pop-up books can be used in the classroom or library or homeschool setting to both catch the attention of children or young adults and deliver content that challenges the learner. The activities provided are not "the end of the story" but rather the beginning—they are examples of approaches that can easily be extended to other pop-up book titles.

One of the most appealing aspects of pop-up books is the ease with which they can enhance interdisciplinary curricula. A number of the activities provided will suggest ways in which these wonderful books can be used to connect disciplines. For instance, the pop-up book *Galileo's Universe* (Lewis 2005) is written in verse, which makes it a logical selection in a language-arts study of poetry, but it can easily be adapted for use in activities for history. A pop-up book with a religious theme, such as one about Noah's ark (Reinhart 2005), can be used with a math lesson that centers on measurement, or with a science lesson that focuses on animals of the world.

The activities provided can be easily revised by a teacher-librarian as needed to accommodate the educational needs of children and young adults and the unique aspects of a variety of class and instructional settings. Also, changes can be readily made to accommodate the requirements of state and local curriculum standards. Modifications to the activities will enable the teacher-librarian to meet individual student needs and interests.

These activities are also easily incorporated into programming for public library settings.

HOW TO BEGIN AN ACTIVITY OR PROGRAM USING POP-UP BOOKS

The term "paper engineer" is not generally known to most audience members of any age. So, the first time that a pop-up is introduced in the classroom or library or homeschooling setting, take time to explain how a paper engineer differs from a traditional author or illustrator. Show the audience several examples of pop-up books, ranging from the very simple to the very complex and also representing work by different paper engineers. Audiences of all ages will discover that the style of these creators of motion is as varied as the artwork of well-known illustrators with whom they are already familiar.

Reading the book aloud before launching any activity is a very effective way to introduce a lesson or a program. Be sure to show each pop-up, opening the pages slowly so that everyone can observe the movement as the picture unfolds. The students will begin to anticipate what is about to happen, and excitement will build for the time when they can participate.

If the book that is being used is too complex or lengthy to share each detail, then giving a booktalk is an effective way to start. Just as with a non-pop-up book, give an overview or plot synopsis, providing the audience with just enough drama to leave them wanting more. As part of the booktalk, show some of the more spectacular pop-ups in the book, so that everyone will be eager to see the rest of the book. Allow time before beginning any activities for everyone to examine the book. Depending on the time frame allowed for a classroom lesson, choose either to pass the book around or to have each student look at it as she completes other work, before or after school, and so on. Keeping a checklist of who has completed this part of the assignment will provide an alert that everyone is ready to move forward.

In educational settings, pop-up books lend themselves easily to creative writing activities and to serving as inspiration for students to make their own pop-up cards or books. Even when not so indicated in the following activities, teachers-librarians are encouraged to always consider these two options.

WHY WERE THESE BOOKS CHOSEN FOR THE ACTIVITIES?

The pop-up books around which the following activities and programs are built were selected according to one or more of these criteria:

- the books are easily obtainable from local bookstores or online booksellers; the book around which the activity is built is currently available new; other pop-up books that are cited are available either new or used;
- the books are quality representations of a particular theme or format;
- the books illustrate the works of many of the best-known and acclaimed paper engineers;
- the books have high potential for ease of use in teaching curriculum areas;
- the books possess the "ah" factor; that is, experience has shown that these books always capture the interest of a wide range of audiences, who literally say, "Ahhh"!

THE ORGANIZATION OF EACH ACTIVITY

Following is a key to the organization of the activities. Items with asterisks are included in every activity; items without asterisks are included only when appropriate. What should be added to these activities, if required in the teaching situation, are references to state and local curriculum standards. The full text of these standards is usually easily available on websites provided by state departments of education and/or local coordinators. Some examples of portals to those resources include the following:

Education World. National standards; state standards. http://www.educationworld.com/standards/state/toc/index.shtml.

Macmillan McGraw Hill. Departments of education/curriculum standards: general and national information for all subjects. http://macmillanmh.com/common/teacher/staffdev/natstan.php3.

SEQUENTIAL ARRANGEMENT OF THE ACTIVITIES

The activities are arranged by three grade levels (lower to higher):

Elementary (kindergarten, 1, 2, 3, 4, 5)
Middle (6, 7, 8)
Secondary (9, 10, 11, 12)

The arrangement within these three groups is by grade levels of the activity. Where an activity would fit several grade levels, it is grouped with the lower grade level.

FORMAT OF THE ACTIVITIES

*Theme (s) of the Activity

Provided are topics that are the focus of the activity.

*Title of the Pop-Up Book to be Used for the Activity

Titles and, where available, subtitles are provided for all books used in the activities.

Paper Engineer(s) and/or Designer(s)

With very few exceptions, names of paper engineers and/or designers are provided for pop-up books around which the activities are built.

Author(s)

Authors for pop-up books are those individuals who write the text (narrative) for them. Sometimes they are not credited in pop-up books.

Illustrator(s)

For pop-up books, if an illustrator is credited, that individual's name is provided. For pop-up books, an illustrator creates the illustrations, whatever the original format, but that individual might not be the paper engineer.

*Publisher, Copyright Date

The name of the publisher and the copyright date are provided for all books.

*Annotation

For each pop-up book used in the activities, information about the book's content that will be important for teachers-librarians is highlighted. For fiction, this overview is a synopsis of the plot and characters. For nonfiction, the overview identifies the main focus of the book. However, the teacher-librarian is the best judge for determining if the activity needs to be limited or extended to be appropriate for his students.

*Major Curriculum Areas for the Activity

For every activity, appropriate major curriculum areas are recommended, drawn from the following list.

Careers
Fine Arts
Health and Physical Education
Language Arts
Literature
Math
Music
Science
Social Studies (including history and geography)

*Activity Overview

For each activity, the teacher-librarian is provided with general information that introduces the opportunities for instruction using the pop-up book that is being highlighted.

*Description of Activity

For each pop-up book that is highlighted, provided are several strategies built around the curriculum areas listed for the pop-up book, with emphasis on opportunities to build critical thinking skills. Also, for some activities, provided is an extension for student learning that can be used beyond the classroom by the individual student or in the classroom if time allows.

*Additional Resources

For each activity, this section provides a list of additional resources that may be incorporated by the teacher-librarian and/or used by the student in this activity, arranged by heading: They might include other pop-up books than the one designated for the activity, books that use interactive engineering other than pop-ups, books without pop-ups or other interactivity, DVDs, and web resources. Any multiple titles that appear under a heading are arranged alphabetically by title. One consideration for inclusion of DVDs and regular books was the likelihood that those titles would be available in libraries or could be easily obtained.

Each listing of additional resources is a basic list that can also be expanded with other resources with which the teacher-librarian is already familiar. Classroom teachers and other instructors will find their school library media specialists and their public library children's librarians, young adult librarians, or youth services librarians to be helpful team members for identifying additional, appropriate resources.

Template(s)

Templates and instructions for making pop-ups and other activities are provided for certain activities.

REFERENCE LIST

Lewis, J. Patrick. 2005. *Galileo's Universe*. Illustration by Tom Curry; paper engineering by Bruce Foster. Mankato, MN: Creative Editions.

Reinhart, Matthew. 2005. *The Ark: A Pop-Up*. New York: Little Simon.

ELEMENTARY (GRADES K, 1–5)

THEME: Animal Dinnertime

TITLE: *Dinner Time*

PAPER ENGINEERS: Marcin Stajewski and James Roger Diaz

AUTHOR: Anne Carter

ILLUSTRATOR: Jan Pieńkowski

PUBLISHER, COPYRIGHT DATE: Candlewick Press, c1981, 2007

ANNOTATION:

"A frog was sitting on a log, catching flies"—and thus begins the story that ends with the shark in triumph. Each two-page spread of an animal provides a pop-up of its mouth which opens and closes.

MAJOR CURRICULUM AREAS:

Science
Social Studies

ACTIVITY OVERVIEW:

As humans, how do we help and work with the animals that share this world with us? This activity opens the dialog with children about our various relationships with animals, starting with ideas about how animals get their food. The activity can serve as a very basic introduction to environmental stewardship.

DESCRIPTION OF ACTIVITY:

1. This book has pop-ups of a variety of animals: frog, vulture, gorilla, tiger, crocodile, and shark. In a sequence similar to the "farmer takes a wife" and the "gingerbread boy," each animal consumes the last. The book has an amusing disclaimer in the front: "The creatures portrayed in this book are no reflection on any real animals, living or dead." While sharing the pop-up book with the students, frame critical thinking questions about animals for the students. Do these animals live in the same environments? If not usually found in the same place, in what situation would all of these animals be together (such as the zoo or circus or in this book or in the movies)? What do the children think that these animals would regularly eat? Would the animals be eating the same or different foods (compare and contrast)?

2. Discuss with the children that the animals in the book are wild. In contrast, what animals do the children see living very close to or with them (domesticated animals)? How do those animals get their food? What do they eat? How do the children or their families or friends help those animals to be fed?

3. Discuss with children what animals live on the farm and what they eat. What do such animals provide for the children to eat (milk, eggs)? Who helps to feed these animals?

4. Take a trip to the library so each child can select, check out, and read a book about an animal. Have the child share the book with someone at home by reading the book to that person.

ADDITIONAL RESOURCES:

Other Pop-Up Books

TITLE: *Pizza! A Yummy Pop-Up*

PAPER ENGINEERS: Helen Balmer and Martin Taylor

AUTHOR: Jan Pieńkowski

ILLUSTRATOR: David Walser (assistant illustrator)

PUBLISHER, COPYRIGHT DATE: Candlewick Press, c2001

ANNOTATION: The characters in this book are animals, and a king's visit spurs the making of a special pizza, with both familiar ingredients, such as tomatoes and cheese, and surprising ones, such as snails, caterpillars, and tadpoles—the preferred foods of various animals. The simple text comes to life with bold pop-ups reminiscent of the clarity of coloring-book drawings.

Books without Interactivity

TITLE: *The Berenstain Bears' Trouble with Pets* (**fiction**)

AUTHORS: Stan Berenstain and Jan Berenstain

ILLUSTRATORS: Stan Berenstain and Jan Berenstain

PUBLISHER, COPYRIGHT DATE: Random House Books for Young Readers, c1990

TITLE: *What Do Animals Eat?* (**informational**)

ILLUSTRATORS: Ute Fuhr and Raoul Sautai

PUBLISHER, COPYRIGHT DATE: Cartwheel Books, c2002

DVD

TITLE: *Elmo's World: Pets!* (2006); 50 minutes (**fiction, informational**)

DISTRIBUTOR: Sesame Street

ANNOTATION: Multiple episodes of *Sesame Street*, all about relationships with pets and their care, are included on this video which stars the familiar characters.

Website

TITLE; AGENCY: *Pets*; Sesame Street

URL: http://www.sesamestreet.org/parents/topicsandactivities/topics/pets

ANNOTATION: The *Sesame Street* website page for parents has five short (similar to YouTube) online videos featuring children (one is animated). They include the topics of taking care of pets, pets at the vet, animal babies, kids talking about caring for pets, and a kitty's relationship with her child. Each video is accompanied by a question that might be discussed with a child.

THEME: Basic Anatomy and Lifelong Health

TITLE 1: *Blood and Goo and Boogers, Too: A Heart-Pounding Pop-Up Guide to the Circulatory and Respiratory Systems*

AUTHOR: Steve Alton

ILLUSTRATOR: Nick Sharrat

PUBLISHER, COPYRIGHT DATE: Dial Books for Young Readers, c2009

ANNOTATION:

The presentation of this book, with its honest approach to "goo and boogers," is sure to appeal to young readers.

TITLE 2: *Chewy, Gooey, Rumble, Plop! A Deliciously Disgusting Plop-Up Guide to the Digestive System*

AUTHOR: Steve Alton

ILLUSTRATOR: Nick Sharrat

PUBLISHER, COPYRIGHT DATE: Dial Books for Young Readers, c2007

ANNOTATION:

Follow the journey of food through the digestive system, from ingestion to elimination.

MAJOR CURRICULUM AREAS:

Health and Physical Education
Language Arts
Science (Biology)

ACTIVITY OVERVIEW:

Maintenance of lifelong health begins in childhood. This activity reinforces for children the practices that can be used to keep good health, starting with an understanding of basic anatomy, with its interrelated systems, and bodily processes. It also provides children the opportunity to plan and implement a project of disseminating information products developed from their own research.

DESCRIPTION OF ACTIVITY:

1. Share the two pop-up books with the children, introducing them to the important systems of circulation and digestion. Discuss with them what makes the presentation of the information in these books appealing to children.
2. Have prepared slips of paper with various body organs (lungs, heart, eyes, etc.) and have teams of children draw one.
3. The teacher-librarian will collaborate to help children understand how to judge the credibility of information. Each team, using library print and digital

resources, will investigate how to keep that organ healthy and collect information for further use, including citing sources.

4. After the research process, provide the team members with steps that they will need to follow to design and illustrate (using the computer is a good option) an informational, one-page brochure for their age group about good practices to maintain the health of the assigned organ (brain, heart, lungs, etc.). The brochure will need to include citations. Ask the children who might review the brochure to make sure that it is accurate, emphasizing to them the need to have correct information regarding health. As part of the planning process, have the children consider appropriate ways to disseminate that brochure (at a parent-teacher organization meeting, in the school nurse's office, on a school website, on a classroom blog, etc.).

EXTENSIONS

1. Distribute copies of the children's informational brochures.
2. Have the children brainstorm information that they already have about health. Then, have the children investigate, through library research, selected ideas to see if they can verify or debunk them.

ADDITIONAL RESOURCES:

Other Pop-Up Books

TITLE: *Alive: The Living Breathing Human Body Book*

PAPER ENGINEER: Ian Smith

AUTHOR: Richard Walker

AWARD ALERT: Richard Walker is the recipient of a 2002 Royal Society Prize for Science Books, a British recognition for general and children's science writing. Also, another of his books was nominated in 2005.

PUBLISHER, COPYRIGHT DATE: DK Children, c2007

TITLE: *Human Body: Bring the Body to Life*

PAPER ENGINEER: Andy Mansfield

AUTHORS: Emily Hawkins and Sue Harris

ILLUSTRATORS: Kim Thompson; front cover illustration Steve Kingston

PUBLISHER, COPYRIGHT DATE: Templar Company, c2007

ANNOTATION: Pop-ups and flaps add dimension to explanations of physical functions: breathing, digestion, dreaming, moving, hearing, seeing, and so on.

TITLE: *Human Body: An Interactive Guide to the Inner Workings of the Body*

AUTHOR: Steve Parker

ILLUSTRATORS: Sebastian Quigley and Steve Weston

PUBLISHER, COPYRIGHT DATE: Barron's Educational Series, 2008

ANNOTATION: A variety of interactive techniques, including pop-ups, guide the reader through exploration of the remarkable aspects of bones.

TITLE: *Human Body*

PAPER ENGINEER: Powerplay Books

ILLUSTRATOR: Patrick Girouard

PUBLISHER, COPYRIGHT DATE: Igloo, c2008

ANNOTATION: Pop-ups, flaps, and pull tabs guide the reader through explanations of muscles, the heart, digestion, waste removal, and so on.

TITLE: *3-D Kid: A Life-Size Pop-Up Book to Your Body and How it Works*

PAPER ENGINEER: Roger Culbertson

AUTHORS: Roger Culbertson and Robert Margulies

PUBLISHER, COPYRIGHT DATE: Scientific American Books for Young Readers, 1995

ANNOTATION: Its life-size dimensions makes this unusual book a real attention-getter for children.

Other Books with Interactivity

TITLE: *The Human Body: A Magic Skeleton Book*

AUTHOR: Janet Sacks

ILLUSTRATORS: Ian Smith; cross sections Peter Bull

PUBLISHER, COPYRIGHT DATE: Sterling Publishing, c2003

ANNOTATION: Pull tabs transform clear, black-and white-drawings into color illustrations with organs and bones highlighted. The storyline follows a class learning about biology as students go through their daily school schedule.

Books without Interactivity

TITLE: *Bones: Skeletons and How They Work* (**informational**)

AUTHOR: Steve Jenkins

ILLUSTRATOR: Steve Jenkins

PUBLISHER, COPYRIGHT DATE: Scholastic, c2010

ANNOTATION: By Caldecott Honor Book Award recipient (2004) Steve Jenkins, this book highlights all aspects of skeletons (human, animal, prehistoric, etc.), including such interesting facts as how bones influenced the design of the Eiffel Tower.

TITLE: *First Human Body Encyclopedia* (**informational**)

AUTHOR: Penny Smith (senior editor)

ILLUSTRATOR: Peter Bull; digital illustrator Pilar Morales

PUBLISHER, COPYRIGHT DATE: DK Publishing, c2005

ANNOTATION: This liberally illustrated introductory encyclopedia to the human body is arranged by categories such as heart and blood, lungs and breathing, reproduction, communication, fighting disease, communication, staying healthy, and so on.

TITLE: *Germs Make Me Sick* (**informational**)

AUTHOR: Melvin Berger

ILLUSTRATOR: Marylin Hafner

PUBLISHER, COPYRIGHT DATE: HarperCollins, c1985, 1995

ANNOTATION: This title is part of the "Let's Read-and-Find-Out-Science" book series and offers an easily understood explanation of how viruses and bacteria cause illnesses and how the body resists them.

TITLE: *The Magic School Bus Inside the Human Body* (**informational**)

AUTHOR: Joanna Cole

ILLUSTRATOR: Bruce Degen

PUBLISHER, COPYRIGHT DATE: Scholastic, c1989

DVDs

TITLE: *Germs Make Me Sick* (an episode of the PBS *Reading Rainbow* television series); 30 minutes (**fiction, informational**)

DISTRIBUTOR: GPN Educational Media

ANNOTATION: What are germs, and how do our bodies fight them? In addition to the book being read, in this episode there is an animated feature about germs, a visit to a farm to see how microorganisms help agriculture, and LeVar Burton's viewing of germs in a microscope.

TITLE: *The Magic School Bus Human Body* (2005); 30 minutes per episode (**fiction, informational**)

DISTRIBUTOR: Warner

ANNOTATION: In this animated DVD, there are three episodes of *The Magic School Bus* television series on the topics about the digestive system; the circulatory system; and bones, muscles, and joints.

THEME: Basic Concepts—Alphabet

TITLE: *Alphabet*

PAPER ENGINEER: Matthew van Fleet

AUTHOR: Matthew van Fleet

ILLUSTRATOR: Matthew van Fleet

PUBLISHER, COPYRIGHT DATE: Simon & Schuster Books for Young Readers, c2008

ANNOTATION:

Move through the alphabet with smiling creatures (animals and insects) from "scaly green Alligators" to "Zorillas." Flaps (including one of giraffes that folds out and above the book) and pull *and* push tabs provide the motion, while touch-and-feel additions promote interactivity with the reader. The accompanying 21-inch A-to-Z poster provides small pop-ups under each block letter. The poster's pop-ups are also the key to the search for the three creatures and the plants on each page that illustrate a letter of the alphabet. The two-and three-letter descriptions of the creatures also capture rhymes, action words, and opposites.

MAJOR CURRICULUM AREAS:

Fine Arts (Art)
Language Arts
Math

ACTIVITY OVERVIEW:

A pop-up book designed to be manipulated by children; other manipulatives provided to them by the teacher are used for teaching the alphabet and encouraging children to see artistic possibilities in the everyday.

DESCRIPTION OF ACTIVITY:

1. Share the book with the children, pointing out the bold "A," and so on, highlighted on each page. Encourage them to predict what the next letter will be on the subsequent page or behind the flap. While sharing the book, help them to understand what the symbols (arrow) for push and pull mean. While continuing with the activity, help them to see that alphabetical symbols are similar as "helps" to the arrow symbols in the book.
2. Display the book's accompanying poster with the pop-ups. As each block is turned, return to the book and help them to locate the other creatures that begin with "A," and so forth.
3. Use the manipulatives (see Figure 6.1 at the end of this theme) of circle and rectangle shapes to demonstrate how these shapes can be used to create the first few capital letters for the alphabet. Help the children to identify the geometric shapes as circles and rectangles. Then, allow the children to assist you in moving the manipulatives to shape each letter, continuing down the alphabet.
4. Have the children first trace the circles and rectangle shapes and next draw them freehand. Then, have the children use their drawn freehand circle and rectangle shapes as patterns to help them write alphabetical letters.
5. Help each child to identify the letter that starts her or his name. Help the children to see that others also have names that start with those same letters.

EXTENSION

Have sets of manipulatives of the circles and the rectangles made from different textures, such as sandpaper, felt, and so on. After sharing the touch and feel aspects of the book with the children, help them to think of adjectives that describe the textures of the manipulatives. Use the book to help them see that many of its adjectives start with the same letter as the creatures. Encourage them to identify the alphabetical letter that begins the names of the adjectives they have brainstormed to describe the textured manipulatives.

ADDITIONAL RESOURCES:

Other Pop-Up Books

TITLE: *ABC Disney*

PAPER ENGINEER: Robert Sabuda

AUTHOR: Robert Sabuda

ILLUSTRATOR: Robert Sabuda

PUBLISHER, COPYRIGHT DATE: Disney Press, c1998

ANNOTATION: Each double-page spread of white background has four hand-size flaps that open to reveal pop-ups of Disney characters whose names correspond with the alphabetical letters. The color and illusion of texture for the flaps and pop-ups comes from the original hand-painted paper that was used in their creation.

TITLE: *A is for Animals: 26 Pop-Up Surprises: An Animal ABC by David Pelham*

PAPER ENGINEER: David Pelham

ILLUSTRATOR: David Pelham

PUBLISHER, COPYRIGHT DATE: Simon & Schuster Children's Publishing Division, c1991

ANNOTATION: Color blocks, with the capital and lower-case letters printed on them, are actually flaps that turn to show animals with names that start with those letters.

TITLE: *The Bible Alphabet: A Pop-Up Book*

PAPER ENGINEER: Keith Moseley

COVER AND INTERIOR DESIGNER: Michael J. Young

PUBLISHER, COPYRIGHT DATE: Ottenheimer Publishers, c1998

ANNOTATION: A flap for each alphabetical letter reveals a pop-up of people, events, and symbols from the Old and New Testament.

TITLE: *Elemenopee: The Day L, M, N. O, P Left the ABC's*

PAPER ENGINEER: Renee Jablow

AUTHOR: Pamela Hall

DESIGNER: Treesha Runnells

PUBLISHER, COPYRIGHT DATE: Piggy Toes Press, c2003

ANNOTATION: Two-page spreads of pop-ups capture the escape of these important letters from the alphabet, who are reacting to teasing from the other letters who call them ELEMENOPEE. When they return, the lesson is: "Never again was there ever a letter who thought it was smarter, more important, or better."

TITLE: *Giant ABC Pop-Up Book*

PAPER ENGINEER: Keith Moseley

AUTHOR: Jo Goodberry

PUBLISHER, COPYRIGHT DATE: Backpack Books, c2005

ANNOTATION: In this oversized and colorful pop-up book, flaps and pop-ups link letters of the alphabet with a variety of words, from choir to helicopter to wagon.

Other Books with Interactivity

TITLE: *The Hidden Alphabet*

AUTHOR: Laura Vaccaro Seeger

ILLUSTRATOR: Laura Vaccaro Seeger

PUBLISHER, COPYRIGHT DATE: Roaring Book Press, c2003

ANNOTATION: Full-page-sized black flaps with cut-outs lift to match the flap word with alphabet letters formed from part of the cut-out illustration.

TITLE: *The Spinning Alphabet Book*

AUTHOR: Betty Ann Schwartz

ILLUSTRATOR: Michelle Berg

PUBLISHER, COPYRIGHT DATE: HarperFestival, c2006

ANNOTATION: This is a book of spinning wheels, one for each letter of the alphabet. As each wheel is turned, it points to a picture of something that starts with that letter and has its name printed below it.

Books without Interactivity

TITLE: *On Market Street* (**fiction, informational**)

AUTHOR: Arnold Lobel

ILLUSTRATOR: Anita Lobel

PUBLISHER, COPYRIGHT DATE: Greenwillow Books, c1981

ANNOTATION: In this Caldecott Award Honor Book (1982), a shopping trip along Market Street results in a child buying an item for each letter of the alphabet. Notable for the delightful and intricate illustrations.

TITLE: *SuperHero ABC* (**fiction, informational**)

AUTHOR: Bob McLeod

ILLUSTRATOR: Bob McLeod

PUBLISHER, COPYRIGHT DATE: HarperCollins, c2006

ANNOTATION: In this graphic-novel-format approach to the ABC's, each letter of the alphabet is illustrated with a super hero whose name matches the letter, as do most of the words in the descriptions of super powers and of the action.

DVD

TITLE: *Barney Animal ABCs* (2008); 56 minutes (**informational**)

DISTRIBUTOR: PBS Kids

NOTE: In English and Spanish

ANNOTATION: Barney helps the viewers learn their ABCs.

Website

TITLE; AGENCY: *Letter of the Day Game*; Sesame Street

URL: http://pbskids.org/sesame/#

ANNOTATION: Play with an animated Cookie Monster and identify letters that start words.

Alphabet Manipulatives

Instructions:

For each set of manipulatives, cut out:

- 2 small circles of the same size
- 1 large circle
- 2 copies of a rectangle
- 3 copies of a shorter rectangle

The dimensions may be of any size. Relative proportion is what makes them work.

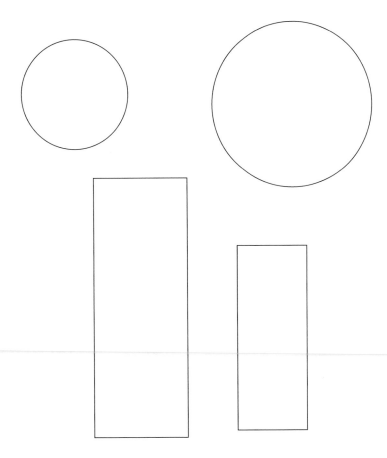

These eight shapes can be used to create any alphabetical letter.

Figure 6.1. Alphabet Manipulatives.

From *Pop-Up Books: A Guide for Teachers and Librarians* by Nancy Bluemel and Rhonda Taylor. Santa Barbara, CA: Libraries Unlimited. Copyright © 2012.

Sample letters:

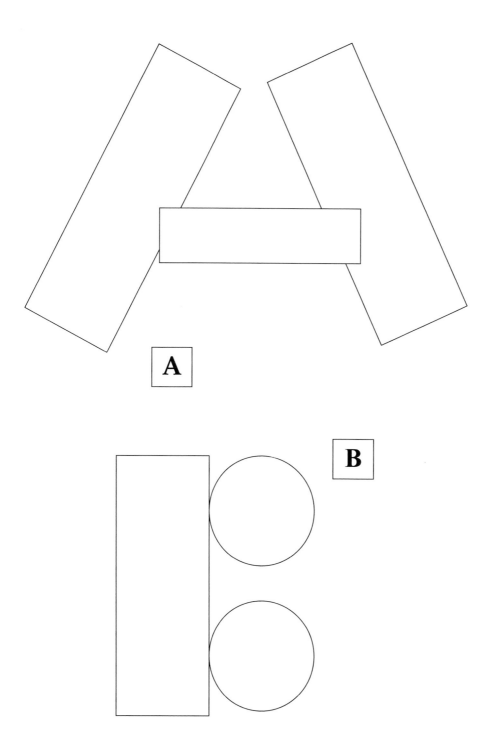

A

B

THEME: *Basic Concepts—Colors*

TITLE: *Creepy Crawly Colors: A Pop-Up Book*

PAPER ENGINEER: Bruce Foster

AUTHOR: Robin Koontz

PUBLISHER, COPYRIGHT DATE: Little Simon, c2006

ANNOTATION:

While not quite nine inches tall, this book packs a big visual punch in its use of bright colors for the pop-ups covering double-page spreads and moving beyond the book. It is sure to entrance younger readers. Also of particular appeal to this age group are the "creepy, crawly" creatures, such as a "red octopus" and a "yellow slug." Rhymes in the description of the creatures add rhythm to the text, and pull tabs contribute to the sense of motion.

MAJOR CURRICULUM AREAS:

Art
Language Arts
Science (Animals)

ACTIVITY OVERVIEW:

This book's use of color identification with animals that aren't the standard "cow, pig, etc." can be used not only for teaching that basic concept but also for thinking about the many creatures with which a child is familiar and has yet to know. It is also a useful tool for building a foundation on which children can build ideas about where animals live, and eventually, why they live there.

DESCRIPTION OF ACTIVITY:

1. Share the pop-up book with the children. As each creature and its color(s) are introduced, ask the children if they have ever seen such a creature. Then, follow that conversation with discussion of which animals they already know that match these colors.
2. The book introduces facts about where the different colors of animals live. Discuss with the children what other animals live in these environments ("wave" and "tide" = ocean; "log" = on the ground, etc.).
3. Discuss with children: If they were going to draw these animals, what colors would they use and why? Children may use handouts with animals to color or they may draw and color their own animals. Ask children to share their animals and talk about the colors that they used and why.

> **EXTENSION**
>
> Bring a variety of fresh vegetables and fruits, including variations of colors (such as white and purple eggplants) to class. Have the children identify the colors of these edibles. Discuss how important fruits and vegetables are for health.

ADDITIONAL RESOURCES:

Other Pop-Up Books

TITLE: *Applebee's Colors: A Cat and Mouse Pop-Up Book*

PAPER ENGINEER: David Pelham

PUBLISHER, COPYRIGHT DATE: Running Press Kids, c2006

ANNOTATION: This six-and-half-inch book stars Applebee the cat and the mice, who work with cans of paint that splash out from the double-page spreads. The only words are the names of the colors on the cans.

TITLE: *Hungry Monsters: A Pop-Up Book of Colors*

AUTHOR: Matt Mitter

ILLUSTRATOR: Jo Brown

PUBLISHER, COPYRIGHT DATE: Reader's Digest Children's Books, c2008

ANNOTATION: This board book, with pop-ups, is perfect for introducing younger readers to colors.

TITLE: *A Pop-Up Color Book: Creature Colors*

AUTHOR: Jonathan Emmett

PUBLISHER, COPYRIGHT DATE: Backpack Books, c2005

ANNOTATION: The two-page spreads focus on animals, who demonstrate colors and adjectives.

TITLE: *Red, Stop! Green, Go!: An Interactive Book about Colors Based on Go, Dog, Go!*

AUTHOR: P. D. Eastman

ILLUSTRATORS: P. D. Eastman; new illustrations Peter Anthony Eastman

PUBLISHER, COPYRIGHT DATE: Random House Children's Books, c1961, 1989, 2004

ANNOTATION: Flaps, wheels, and tabs add motion to the adaptation of the classic *Go, Dog, Go!* in which dogs of every color race to a party.

TITLE: *Who's under that Hat?*

PAPER ENGINEER: David A. Carter

AUTHOR: Sarah Weeks

ILLUSTRATOR: David A. Carter

PUBLISHER, COPYRIGHT DATE: Red Wagon Books, c2005

ANNOTATION: Hats are the flaps that can be lifted to reveal animals. The text describes the animal that is hiding beneath the "red hat" or the "purple hat," and so on.

TITLE: *Yummy Colors*

PAPER ENGINEER: Americhip Studios

DESIGNER: Pamela Natarantonio

PUBLISHER, COPYRIGHT DATE: Cartwheel Books, c2007

ANNOTATION: This book's illustrations are photographs that reflect the diversity of children and of human-sized vegetables, all posed together to match the color of the children's clothing with the color of the vegetable. Pull tabs pop-up cards that show other foods and fruits and vegetables of that same color.

Other Books with Interactivity

TITLE: *Color Zoo*

AUTHOR: Lois Ehlert

ILLUSTRATOR: Lois Ehlert

PUBLISHER, COPYRIGHT DATE: St. Martin's Press, c2006

ANNOTATION: This cleverly constructed book combines color, zoo animals, and geometric shapes. Each animal's face is composed of several preceding solid-color pages with geometric cut-outs, and as each page is turned, a different animal is created. The animal names are the only text in the book (other than a prefatory poem about this zoo).

> **AWARD ALERT:** This is a Caldecott Honor Book (1990) and thus also an American Library Association Notable Children's Book (1990). It is also a 1990 Horn Book Fanfare Best Book of the Year.

TITLE: *Colors*

PAPER ENGINEER: Robert Crowther

PUBLISHER, COPYRIGHT DATE: Candlewick Press, c2001

ANNOTATION: Each double-page spread of this book is a solid color, unbroken by text or illustrations. Right-hand-page tabs reveal the name of the color. Left-hand-page tabs and flaps reveal creatures and objects (with their names) that are that color.

TITLE: *Colors Flip Flap Book*

ILLUSTRATOR: Nadeem Zaidi

PUBLISHER, COPYRIGHT DATE: Hyperion Books for Children, c2006

ANNOTATION: This Baby Einstein™ book has a very interesting approach to movement. On the right-hand pages there are flaps (next to pictures of various creature and objects) that can be flipped over to reveal the name of the color and hide the pictures behind the color. The left-hand pages describe what the pictures have in common.

TITLE: *Lemons Are Not Red* (**informational**)

AUTHOR: Laura Vaccaro Seeger

ILLUSTRATOR: Laura Vaccaro Seeger

PUBLISHER, COPYRIGHT DATE: Roaring Book Press, c2004

ANNOTATION: From an individual who has multiple recognitions of Caldecott Honor Awards and ALA Notable Children's Books is this simple book of bright colors. Turning the pages with cut-outs reveal the correct color cut-out of the object, such as lemons, carrots, and so on.

TITLE: *Rainbow Trucks: A Very First Lift the Flap Colors Book*

AUTHOR: Roger Priddy

PUBLISHER, COPYRIGHT DATE: St. Martin's Press, c2006

ANNOTATION: Part of the appeal of this sturdy flap book is its topic: vehicles such as tractors, ambulances, and dump trucks. Flaps and tabs add more information about the orange, yellow, green, and so on, vehicles. When opened, the flaps that constitute the half-circle pages form a rainbows at the top.

Books without Interactivity

TITLE: *Little Blue and Little Yellow* (**fiction, informational**)

AUTHOR: Leo Lionni

ILLUSTRATOR: Leo Lionni

PUBLISHER, COPYRIGHT DATE: HarperTrophy, c1995

ANNOTATION: Little Blue and Little Yellow play together, and then one day they greet each other with a hug and there's green!

TITLE: *Mouse Paint* (**fiction, informational**)

AUTHOR: Ellen Stoll Walsh

ILLUSTRATOR: Ellen Stoll Walsh

PUBLISHER, COPYRIGHT DATE: Red Wagon Books, Harcourt, c1989

ANNOTATION: Put three mice, a white piece of paper, and blue, yellow, and red paint jars together and watch what happens!

DVD

TITLE: *Barney Colors are Fun!*; 53 minutes (**fiction, informational**)

DISTRIBUTOR: PBS Kids

ANNOTATION: Colors are explored in real life contexts, such as a magic show and cave paintings.

Website

TITLE; AGENCY: *Color Me Hungry*; Sesame Street

URL: http://pbskids.org/sesame/#/games

ANNOTATION: Learn to eat by colors; Grover has the player click on the appropriately colored fruits and vegetables and move then into the colored bins. Grover explains the advantages of each food as he names it.

THEME: Basic Concepts—Counting

TITLE: *Salamander Rock: A Pop-Up Counting Adventure*

AUTHOR: Matt Mitter

ILLUSTRATOR: Karen Viola

PUBLISHER, COPYRIGHT DATE: Reader's Digest Children's Books, c2008

ANNOTATION: The storyline is written in verse and is a tale of a party of woodland animals and insects as well as a counting book, from 1 to 10. The book is unique in the construction of the pop-ups, which are foam pieces used for the salamanders' and caterpillars' bodies. Also, thinking questions are on each page, such as "How many striped moths can you find?"

MAJOR CURRICULUM AREAS:

Language Arts
Math (Counting, Prediction)

ACTIVITY OVERVIEW:

The pop-up book for this activity is an excellent example of a resource that combines counting, new vocabulary words, and critical thinking questions—which are also the foci of the activity.

DESCRIPTION OF ACTIVITY:

1. First, share the book with the children, reading it through as a story. At the middle of the book, ask them what they think (predict) will happen at the end of the story.
2. Share the book with the children a second time, emphasizing the numbers in it; at each page, ask them the book's questions about the various counts.
3. Have prepared a set of questions about "how many" objects there are in the classroom (up to 10).
4. Have on hand a disposable camera. Have the children assist in identifying and/or arranging numbers of items in the classroom (such as one teacher at his desk, two children reading together, six pairs of shoes on three children's feet, four computers, etc.). Then, take pictures of those "counts." Use the pictures to make a class book. Help each child provide a short explanation under one picture of the count and what is being portrayed.

ADDITIONAL RESOURCES:

Other Pop-Up Books

TITLE: *Applebee's Numbers: A Cat and Mouse Pop-Up Book*

PAPER ENGINEER: David Pelham

AUTHOR: David Pelham

ILLUSTRATOR: David Pelham

PUBLISHER, COPYRIGHT DATE: Running Press Kids, c2005.

ANNOTATION:

This is one of the Applebee cat pop-up books about concepts. As Applebee moves through his day, increasing numbers (1 through 10) of mice pop-up in unexpected places. Small flaps ask the reader to find the same number of other items on the page (such as three apples).

TITLE: *Counting Creatures: Pop-Up Animals from 1 to 100*

PAPER ENGINEERS: Sophie Pelham and David Pelham

ILLUSTRATOR: David Pelham

PUBLISHER, COPYRIGHT DATE: Little Simon, c2004

ANNOTATION: Each double-page spread has flaps with numbers that turn to reveal intricate pop-ups of creatures with names that start with the letter that corresponds to the first letter of each number's name. So, it can be used to work with both numbers and words. After the number 20, the counts are in 10s to 100.

Other Books with Interactivity

TITLE: *One Yellow Lion*

PAPER ENGINEER: Matthew van Fleet

AUTHOR: Matthew van Fleet

ILLUSTRATOR: Matthew van Fleet

PUBLISHER, COPYRIGHT DATE: Dial Books for Young Readers, c1992

ANNOTATION: This flap book combines concepts of numbers, colors, and animals. On each double-page spread, the left-hand page has the word for a number and an adjective. The right-hand page has a colored number; when the flap is turned, part of the number becomes part of the animal(s) that match the color.

Books without Interactivity

TITLE: *Anno's Counting Book* (**fiction, informational**)

AUTHOR: Mitsumasa Anno

ILLUSTRATOR: Mitsumasa Anno

PUBLISHER, COPYRIGHT DATE: Crowell, c1975

ANNOTATION: A winter scene comes to life as the pages are turned, and one house, two trees, and so on, are added.

TITLE: *Chicka Chicka 1 2 3* (**fiction, informational**)

AUTHORS: Bill Martin Jr. and Michael Sampson

ILLUSTRATOR: Lois Ehlert

PUBLISHER, COPYRIGHT DATE: Simon & Schuster, c2004

ANNOTATION: Rhyme is used to narrate this book in which numbers race to the top of a tree.

DVDs

TITLE: *Chicka Chicka 1 2 3: And More Counting Fun* (2009); 69 minutes (**fiction, informational**)

DISTRIBUTOR: Scholastic

ANNOTATION: Includes Bill Martin Jr. and Michael Sampson's book *Chicka Chicka 1 2 3* as well as three other number books.

TITLE: *Barney's Numbers! Numbers!*; 30 minutes (**fiction, informational**)

DISTRIBUTOR: PBS Kids (http://shop.pbskids.org/)

ANNOTATION: Barney looks for missing numbers.

Website

TITLE, AGENCY: *Count von Count* (Sesame Street)

URL: http://www.sesamestreet.org/muppets/count-von-count

ANNOTATION: This website stars Sesame character Count von Count and offers links to videos, online games, and printable coloring pages that focus on counting. Also provided are parent tips with questions to assist children with learning.

THEME: Basic Concepts—Opposites

TITLE: *Animal Popposites: A Pop-Up Book of Opposites*

PAPER ENGINEER: Matthew Reinhart

ILLUSTRATOR: Matthew Reinhart

AWARD ALERT: Matthew Reinhart received a 2008 Meggendorfer Prize, recognizing the paper engineering in the pop-up book *Star Wars: A pop-up guide to the galaxy*. The prize is given biennially by The Movable Book Society.

PUBLISHER, COPYRIGHT DATE: Little Simon, c2002

ANNOTATION:

This book is just about seven inches tall, and each double-page spread has two flaps. Each flap, labeled with an adjective, lifts to reveal a pop-up creature that characterizes the opposite (such as small/big). The illustration on the flap is carried over to the background of the pop-up.

MAJOR CURRICULUM AREAS:

Fine Arts (Art)
Language Arts
Math (Prediction)
Science (Nature: Animals)

ACTIVITY OVERVIEW:

The pop-up book is a fun and colorful introduction to words and concepts about opposition.

DESCRIPTION OF ACTIVITY:

1. Introduce the children to the idea of opposites. Then, share the pop-up book with the children. At each page, read the adjective and then lift the flap to reveal the opposite; then read that adjective to them. Depending on the age of the children, help them to identify the creature that is portrayed on the flap and then the one that is revealed on the pop-up.
2. On a second reading of the book (start at the back of the book, to be opposite!), ask the children to predict what the opposite will be (as small/big).
3. Work with the children to reinforce their understanding of opposites, using lists of common opposites. Then, have each of the children draw a picture of a creature that they like/know. Let children share their creatures and talk about them.

4. Display the pictures and discuss with the children the different possible concepts in that picture that could be opposites. For instance, a picture of a dog could be a small/large dog, a barking/quiet dog, and so on.

EXTENSION

Help the children create a simple flap to be added to their own pictures so that they can represent both sides of an opposite (see Figure 6.2 at the end of this theme). For younger children, assist them in adding the labeling words for the opposites.

ADDITIONAL RESOURCES:

Other Pop-Up Books

TITLE: *Snappy Little Opposites: A Big and Small Book of Surprises*

PAPER ENGINEER: Richard Hawke

DESIGNER: Janie Louise Hunt

AUTHOR: Donald Steer

PUBLISHER, COPYRIGHT DATE: Silver Dolphin Books, c2000

ANNOTATION: Rhymes about various animals introduce the idea of opposites. The simple, colorful illustrations translate nicely into pop-ups.

Other Books with Interactivity

TITLE: *Black? White? Day? Night!: A Book of Opposites*

AUTHOR: Laura Vaccara Seeger

ILLUSTRATOR: Laura Vaccara Seeger

PUBLISHER, COPYRIGHT DATE: Neal Porter Book, Running Book Press, c2006

ANNOTATION: Each of the book's pages are a solid color, full-page flap with a single word and a cut-out rectangle. The flaps lift to reveal a full-size scene and the opposite word. A great book for encouraging not only concept development but also for leading children to create their own stories of the scenes.

> **AWARD ALERT:** Seeger's book was a 2007 American Library Association Notable Children's Book and a 2006 Bank Street College of Education Best Book, among other recognitions.

TITLE: *Opposites*

PAPER ENGINEER: Robert Crowther

PUBLISHER, COPYRIGHT DATE: Candlewick Press, c2005

ANNOTATION: Flaps, wheels, and tabs are the mechanisms that move the action of a variety of opposites, ranging from thin and thick sandwiches to the up and down of a carnival ride.

TITLE: *Opposnakes*

AUTHOR: Salina Yoon

PUBLISHER, COPYRIGHT DATE: Little Simon, c2009

ANNOTATION: Flaps reveal the opposite (such as quiet/loud) of the snakes in clothing, who stretch the length of the opened book.

Books without Interactivity

TITLE: *Exactly the Opposite* **(informational)**

AUTHOR: Tana Hoban

ILLUSTRATOR: Tana Hoban

PUBLISHER, COPYRIGHT DATE: Greenwillow Books, c1990

ANNOTATION: Photographs of everyday scenes are used to illustrate the concept of opposites: tied/untied, up/down, push/pull, and so on.

DVD

TITLE: *Elmo's World: Opposites* (2008); 54 minutes **(fiction, informational)**

DISTRIBUTOR: Sesame Street

ANNOTATION: The video has multiple episodes of Elmo and his friends encountering opposites.

A Simple Flap

Steps:

1. Each child will need **one 8 ½ x 11-inch piece of paper (white or color),** which may be turned either portrait (tall) or landscape (wide).

2. Each child will also need **one 5 ½ x 8 ½-inch piece of paper (white or color).** Two of these pieces result from cutting an 8 ½ × 11-inch piece of paper in half.

3. The child should place the smaller piece of paper on the larger one and trace around it with a pencil. The smaller piece of paper may be placed anywhere on the larger one. The illustration that the child will create (whether drawn or glued from a cut-out) must fit within that penciled rectangle.

4. The child's illustration will be matched with an "opposite" illustration that the child will create on the smaller piece of paper.

5. After the child creates an illustration on the larger paper, she will **glue** down (glue only one edge) the smaller paper flap that will "cover" the illustration on the large piece of paper. The illustration on the smaller flap should be showing on top.

6. Once the glue is dry, assist the child in folding back the smaller flap so that it covers and uncovers the picture on the larger piece of paper.

7. Assist the child as needed in labeling (with crayola or marker) the words for the two opposite pictures.

Figure 6.2. A Simple Flap

From *Pop-Up Books: A Guide for Teachers and Librarians* by Nancy Bluemel and Rhonda Taylor. Santa Barbara, CA: Libraries Unlimited. Copyright © 2012.

Step 3: Picture on the larger paper

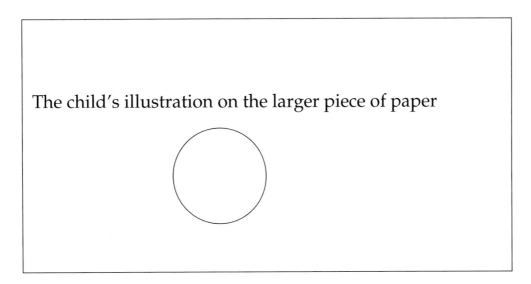

The child's illustration on the larger piece of paper

Step 4: Picture of an opposite illustration on the smaller paper (the flap)

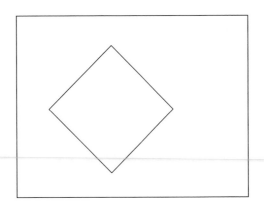

Steps 5, 6, 7: Glue the smaller piece of paper on top of the larger one to create the flap and hide the picture underneath

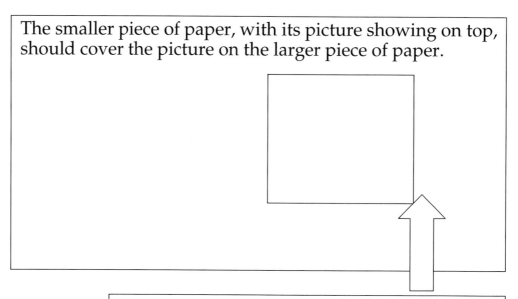

The smaller piece of paper, with its picture showing on top, should cover the picture on the larger piece of paper.

Place a thin line of glue on the underside of the smaller piece of paper (on one side only), so that the glue will hold the smaller piece of paper to the larger one. When the glue is dry, this flap can be folded back and creased. Then, the flap can be repeatedly opened and closed, hiding and revealing the picture underneath.

Label the pictures with their "opposite" names.

Website

TITLE; AGENCY: *Animal Opposites*; Enchanted Learning **(informational for teacher)**

URL: http://www.enchantedlearning.com/crafts/books/animalopposites/

ANNOTATION: Coloring book pages can be printed from the website. They use animals to demonstrate opposites.

TITLE; AGENCY: *Opposite Word (38 Pairs)*; Charles Kelly and Lawrence Kelly **(informational for teacher)**

URL: http://www.manythings.org/vocabulary/lists/2/words.php?f=opposites

ANNOTATION: The list of opposite word pairs is supplemented with online games, puzzles, and quizzes that provide a review of the list (see the pull-down menu).

THEME: Basic Concepts—Shapes

TITLE: *The Very Hungry Caterpillar Pop-Up Book*

AUTHOR: Eric Carle

PUBLISHER, COPYRIGHT DATE: Philomel, c2009

ANNOTATION:

Celebrating the 40th anniversary of the original publication of this beloved classic by re-creating it as a pop-up is a wonderful idea!

MAJOR CURRICULUM AREAS:

Fine Arts (Art)
Math (Shapes)

ACTIVITY OVERVIEW:

Learning to identify shapes in what they see in their lives is a basic skill on which children will build more advanced math skills.

DESCRIPTION OF ACTIVITY:

1. Introduce children to basic shapes (circle, square, etc.). Share the pop-up book with the children as a story and so they can enjoy the pop-ups. Then, return to the beginning of the book and, as the pages are turned, ask the children to find shapes in the various illustrations and pop-ups (for instance, the caterpillar's body is made of circles).

2. Have foam of various colors cut into shapes and provide each child with multiples of several shapes. Have the children glue the shapes onto pages to create pictures of their own (which can be guided as animals, or seasons, and so on, depending on scheduling of the activity).

3. Have the children share their pictures, identifying first what shapes they used and the story behind their creations.

ADDITIONAL RESOURCES:

Other Pop-Up Books

TITLE: *My First Book of Shapes*

AUTHOR: Chuck Murphy

ILLUSTRATOR: Chuck Murphy

PUBLISHER, COPYRIGHT DATE: Scholastic, c1992

ANNOTATION: Mice are the silent characters that interact with the objects representing the geometric shapes exposed by the flaps. The last flap reveals a multilevel pop-up of all of the shapes and those mice.

TITLE: *Noodles*

PAPER ENGINEER: David A. Carter

AUTHOR: Sarah Weeks

PUBLISHER, COPYRIGHT DATE: HarperFestival, c1996

ANNOTATION: Bug-eyed characters created from a variety of pasta types pop-up and slide across the pages of this book. Rhyming text gives each its own personality. The back of the book provides the names of the various pasta types, with pronunciation.

Other Books with Interactivity

TITLE: *Make a Change Shapes*

PAPER ENGINEER: Geff Newland

ILLUSTRATOR: Margot Thompson

PUBLISHER, COPYRIGHT DATE: Millbrook Press, c1999

ANNOTATION: Flaps and wheels transform geometric shapes into objects or creatures. The only text in the book is the names of the shapes and the names of the objects or creatures.

TITLE: *Shapes*

PAPER ENGINEER: Robert Crowther

AUTHOR: Robert Crowther

ILLUSTRATOR: Robert Crowther

PUBLISHER, COPYRIGHT DATE: Candlewick, c2002

ANNOTATION: Each page is actually the shape that is being identified. Tabs and flaps transform the shapes into familiar objects, and the only text is the shapes and familiar objects. Each shape is a solid color.

TITLE: *Shapes Flip Flap Book*

ILLUSTRATOR: Nadeem Zaidi

PUBLISHER, COPYRIGHT DATE: Hyperion Books for Children, c2006

ANNOTATION: Part of the Baby Einstein™ series, this book uses flaps that flip over to transform everyday objects into geometric shapes. Each flap asks: What is this shape? The left-hand pages have the flaps, and the right-hand pages illustrate the question that match the shapes, such as, "Are there shapes you take out when it's time to play?"

Books without Interactivity

TITLE: *The Shape of Me and Other Stuff* (**fiction**)

AUTHOR: Dr. Seuss

ILLUSTRATOR: Dr. Seuss

PUBLISHER, COPYRIGHT DATE: Random House Books for Young Readers, c1973

ANNOTATION: Illustrations in silhouette and classic Seuss rhyming teach children to see the shapes not only of "me" but also bees and keys, and so on.

DVD

TITLE: *Barney Shapes and Colors All Around* (2011); 51 minutes (**fiction, informational**)

DISTRIBUTOR: PBS Kids (http://shop.pbskids.org)

ANNOTATION: Besides colors, shapes in a child's room are explored.

Website

TITLE; AGENCY: *Telly's Shape Garden*; Sesame Street

URL: http://pbskids.org/sesame/#

ANNOTATION: Telly's garden has many shapes; interact with the animated character to match the shape on the seed packet with the garden sign.

THEME: Basic Concepts—Words

TITLE: *Super Snappy Words*

ILLUSTRATOR: Derek Matthews

PUBLISHER, COPYRIGHT DATE: Millbrook Press, c2002

ANNOTATION:

In this book, a word is highlighted at the bottom of each page. It also provides questions for leading discussions. Rhymes and animal characters enhance the presentation.

MAJOR CURRICULUM AREAS:

Language Arts
Literature

ACTIVITY OVERVIEW:

The pop-up book is an introduction to help children expand their vocabularies of objects in their everyday lives.

DESCRIPTION OF ACTIVITY:

1. Share the pop-up book with the children, highlighting for them the written word at the bottom of each page. Use the questions in the book for leading discussion with the children about the book.
2. Have prepared printed words of common objects in the classroom or library on signs that can be temporarily posted on the objects. Have the children identify the object and then label it with the sign. As the game progresses, give the children a choice of signs to post on a given object.
3. During a recess or break time, rearrange the signs so that they label the wrong objects. Have the children help you decide what the correct labels should be.
4. Ask the children to name favorite books that they like to have read aloud to them. Collaborate with the librarian to select several titles suggested by the

children. Read each of the books to them. After reading each book, go back through it with the children and have them identify the various objects in the illustrations.

EXTENSION

Each day, have each child create a three-by-five card that he can add to a file kept at his desk. On one side should be a word that the child learned or particularly liked that day. On the other side, the child might provide an illustration, even a pop-up! On a regular basis, have the children, in pairs, go through their cards together and help each other learn the words.

ADDITIONAL RESOURCES:

Other Pop-Up Books

TITLE: *My First Jumbo Book of Letters*

PAPER ENGINEER: James Diaz

AUTHOR: Melanie Gerth

PUBLISHER, COPYRIGHT DATE: Cartwheel, c2003

ANNOTATION: A variety of interactive elements, including pop-ups, add extra appeal to a book that links words to letters.

Books without Interactivity

TITLE: *Amelia Bedelia* (**fiction**)

AUTHOR: Peggy Parish

ILLUSTRATOR: Fritz Siebel

PUBLISHER, COPYRIGHT DATE: HarperCollins, c1963, 1991, 1992

ANNOTATION: This is the book that introduced the now-classic character of Amelia Bedelia, who appears in multiple titles. Amelia is the housekeeper who interprets all instructions literally. Image the results of saying "dust the furniture"!

TITLE: *Piggies in the Pumpkin Patch* (**fiction**)

AUTHOR: Mary Peterson and Jennifer Rofé

ILLUSTRATOR: Mary Peterson

PUBLISHER, COPYRIGHT DATE: Charlesbridge Publishing, c2010

ANNOTATION: Follow the rhyming adventures of the piggies playing in the pumpkin patch.

DVD

TITLE: *Sesame Street: Do the Alphabet* (1999); 45 minutes (**informational**)

DISTRIBUTOR: Sesame Street

ANNOTATION: Baby Bear, aided by Big Bird and the Sesame Street gang, learns his alphabet.

Website

TITLE; AGENCY: *Sesame Street Games.* Sesame Street

URL: http://pbskids.org/sesame/#/Games

ANNOTATION: Click on "Alphabet Soup" to watch an interactive video, requiring responses from the child about creating words using the alphabet letters in Cookie Monster's soup.

THEME: Celebrations—Birthdays

TITLE: *The Magical World of Teddies: Gilbert's Birthday Surprise: A Pop-Up Book*

AUTHORS: Sue Whiting and Stuart Martin

PUBLISHER, COPYRIGHT DATE: Book Company Publishing PTY Limited, c2002

ANNOTATION:

This title is part of a series, "The Magical World of Teddies," about the teddy bears of Teddy Town. On Gilbert's birthday, he follows rhyming clues on pop-up cards to find treats (including a piñata) that celebrate his special day; the clues end in a surprise party with all of his friends.

MAJOR CURRICULUM AREAS:

Art
Language Arts
Social Studies

ACTIVITY OVERVIEW:

Children look forward to birthday events, and this book introduces the idea of surprises as well as celebrations and games

DESCRIPTION OF ACTIVITY:

1. Share with the students the pop-up book about Gilbert's birthday celebration. Then ask the children how they celebrate their birthdays. Ask them if they have friends who celebrate their birthdays in other ways.
2. Have children construct interactive cards with a picture and/or message for a special person (see Figure 6.3 at the end of this theme).
3. Have children share what their favorite birthday party games are and make a flip chart list of them. Have children vote on one game that they will play together at recess that day. Assist them in understanding the concept of a majority vote.

ADDITIONAL RESOURCES:

Other Pop-Up Books

TITLE: *Christopher Bear's Birthday Party*

AUTHOR: Emma Borghesi

ILLUSTRATOR: Pete Smith

PUBLISHER, COPYRIGHT DATE: Borghesi & Adam, c2000

ANNOTATION: Isabel bear delivers all of the invitations to a surprise party for Christopher, and the book's one pop-up comes at the end, at the birthday celebration. The tiny invitations fit into mailboxes in the book.

TITLE: *Happy Birthday to You!*

AUTHOR: Dr. Seuss

ILLUSTRATOR: Dr. Seuss

PUBLISHER, COPYRIGHT DATE: Random House Children's Books, c2003

ANNOTATION: In this mini-book, there's a big celebration for "your Day of all Days," and Dr. Seuss's illustrations make great pop-ups that fit the occasion!

TITLE: *The Teddy Bears' Picnic*

DESIGNER: Katy Rhodes

AUTHOR: Jimmy Kennedy

ILLUSTRATOR: Fran Thatcher

PUBLISHER, COPYRIGHT DATE: Barron's, c2001

ANNOTATION: The 1947 song "The Teddy Bear's Picnic" finds new life in a pop-up book. All of the teddy bears are celebrating with a special gathering in the woods.

Books without Interactivity

TITLE: *A Birthday Basket for Tia* (**fiction**)

AUTHOR: Pat Mora

ILLUSTRATOR: Cecily Lang

PUBLISHER, COPYRIGHT DATE: Macmillan, c1992

ANNOTATION: Cecilia's great-aunt is having a very special birthday, and she prepares a special basket of memories as a gift.

TITLE: *It's My Birthday* (**fiction**)

AUTHOR: Helen Oxenbury

ILLUSTRATOR: Helen Oxenbury

PUBLISHER, COPYRIGHT DATE: Candlewick, 1994

ANNOTATION: A child who draws on animal friends for the ingredients to make the birthday cake.

DVD

TITLE: *Happy Birthday Clifford!* (2007); 90 minutes (**fiction**)

DISTRIBUTOR: PBS Kids (http://shop.pbskids.org/)

ANNOTATION: The video has four party-related *Clifford the Big Red Dog* episodes, including "The Best Party Ever," in which Clifford assists with a birthday party for his friend Emily Elizabeth.

Websites

TITLE; AGENCY: *Rosita's Fiesta*; Sesame Street

URL: http://pbskids.org/sesame/#/games

ANNOTATION: The interactive online game features animated Sesame Street characters at Rosita's birthday fiesta. The viewer must click on the appropriate number of party favors for the guests.

Interactive Cards

Steps:

1. Each child will need **one 8 ½ × 11-inch sturdy piece of paper (white or color), one letter-size plain white envelope,** and **one 5 ½ × 2 ¾-inch piece of paper (white or color)**. Point out to the children that the smaller piece of paper is 1/6 of an 8 ½ × 11-inch piece of paper.
2. The child should use **markers or crayons** to write a message to a special person. The message goes on the smaller piece of paper.
3. The child will fold the 8 ½ × 11-inch piece of paper in half, so that it becomes a 5 ½ by 8 ½-inch piece of paper. This piece of paper will form the card.
4. The child will place **glue** on the front of the envelope (where normally an address would go). The envelope is then glued to the inside of the card, lengthwise, so that when the card is opened, the envelope is revealed.
5. After the glue dries, the envelope is ready for the message to be inserted. The envelope flap is left free, so that the message may be repeatedly removed and returned to the envelope.
6. The outside of the card, the envelope, and the inside of the card may be decorated by the child, using **markers, crayons, glue, stickers, glitter, and so on.**

Figure 6.3. Interactive Cards

THEME: Celebrations—Easter

TITLE: *Kirby the Easter Dog: A Pop-Up Easter Egg Hunt*

PAPER ENGINEER: Renee Jablow

AUTHOR: George White

ILLUSTRATOR: Holli Conger

PUBLISHER, COPYRIGHT DATE: Jumping Jack Press, c2007

ANNOTATION:

Kirby thinks he is the Easter dog; the pop-ups are notable for their complex movement.

MAJOR CURRICULUM AREAS:

Fine Arts (Art)
Math (Counting)

ACTIVITY OVERVIEW:

The content and the art in *Kirby the Easter Dog* and similar Easter pop-up books are good springboards for counting activities and art projects.

DESCRIPTION OF ACTIVITY:

1. While sharing the not-so-typical storyline in *Kirby the Easter Dog*, encourage the children to count the Easter eggs and to predict the outcome.
2. Use the pop-up *Easter Bugs* (see the Additional Resources section) as a way to introduce children to art techniques. Begin by asking them how they might replicate the patterns on the Easter egg flaps that hide the pop-ups, using materials such as water-colors, crayons, jewels, stick-on dots, and so on. Have each child decorate a paper cut-out egg duplicating one of the art techniques in the book.
3. After sharing their decorated paper eggs, show the children how to fold up the bottom of the flap and glue it to a piece of paper (see Figure 6.4 at the end of this theme). Then, have each child draw a surprise picture behind her egg. The pages can be put together into a class book, with *Easter Bugs* as the inspiration.

EXTENSION

Share the rhyming text of *Easter Bugs* (see the Additional Resources section) with the children. Have older children write rhymes to accompany their decorated Easter eggs.

ADDITIONAL RESOURCES:

Other Pop-Up Books

TITLE: *Easter Bugs*

AUTHOR: David A. Carter

PAPER ENGINEER: David A. Carter

ILLUSTRATOR: David A. Carter

PUBLISHER, COPYRIGHT DATE: Intervisual Books, c2001

ANNOTATION: Who knew there were bugs hiding behind Easter eggs? This pop-up is typical of Carter's other bug books.

TITLE: *Easter Egg Hunt Pop-Up Fun Happy Snappy Book*

ILLUSTRATOR: Derek Matthews.

PUBLISHER, COPYRIGHT DATE: Silver Dolphin Books, 2006

ANNOTATION: Each page of this study pop-up book for younger kids features a creature associated with spring, such as a bunny, lamb, butterfly, and so on.

TITLE: *The Royal Easter Tea Party*

AUTHOR: Megan E. Bryant

ILLUSTRATOR: Claudine Gévry

ANNOTATION: Princess bunnies have a garden tea party, but it is the large sparkly Easter eggs on each two-page spread that steal the show. Pull the top up, and a surprise comes out of the egg.

Other Books with Interactivity

TITLE: *Clifford's First Easter: A Lift-the-flap Book*

AUTHOR: Norman Bridwell

ILLUSTRATOR: Norman Bridwell

PUBLISHER, COPYRIGHT DATE: Scholastic, c1995

Easter Egg Flap

Steps:

1. There should be **one egg (from the template) on sturdy white paper** for each child and **one 8 ½ × 11-inch of paper (color or white)** per child. Depending on skill, the eggs may be cut out by the children or be pre-cut.
2. The child should decorate one side of the egg with **markers, crayolas, paints, glitter, fabric, stickers, and so on.** This decorated side should not be the side of the egg with the solid line and the "glue" directions.
3. After eggs are dry, assist the child in deciding where on the paper the egg will be located. The child will cover the designated "glue" section on the back of the egg with glue.
4. The egg is placed (glue side down) on the paper and the glue is allowed to dry.
5. Assist the child in carefully folding up the egg, so that the crease allows movement of the egg.
6. The child will place a "surprise" (such as a message or a small sticker or drawing created by the child) under the egg flap. The surprise must fit under the flap (i.e., be totally covered by it).

Figure 6.4. Easter Egg Flap

From *Pop-Up Books: A Guide for Teachers and Librarians* by Nancy Bluemel and Rhonda Taylor. Santa Barbara, CA: Libraries Unlimited. Copyright © 2012.

Easter egg:

GLUE

_____

ANNOTATION: In this flap book Clifford gets into the fun of decorating eggs—using his tail for a paintbrush! It makes a nice introduction for discussing different ways to paint Easter eggs.

Book without Pop-Ups

TITLE: *Arthur's Jelly Beans* (**fiction**)

AUTHOR: Marc Brown

ILLUSTRATOR: Marc Brown

PUBLISHER, COPYRIGHT DATE: LB Kids, c2004

ANNOTATION: The popular character of Arthur the Aardvark attends a spring fling, and whoever finds the most jelly beans in the big hunt will win the chocolate egg. Will it be Arthur?

Website

TITLE; AGENCY: *Easter*; Enchanted Learning (**informational for teacher**)

URL: http://www.enchantedlearning.com/crafts/easter/

ANNOTATION: The site has worksheets for counting, words, and so on, that use egg and Easter motifs.

THEME: Celebrations—Grandparents' Day

TITLE: *Knitted by Grandma*

PAPER ENGINEERS: Jacqui Crawford

AUTHOR: Ruth Hearson

PUBLISHER, COPYRIGHT DATE: Dial Books for Young Readers, c2000

ANNOTATION:

This book, with a variety of tabs, flaps, folds, and pop-ups, is about a wonderful week that is spent with a grandma, who extends a special talent (knitting) to encompass the world with leg warmers, cardigans, and so on.

MAJOR CURRICULUM AREAS:

Fine Arts (Art)
Language Arts
Social Studies

ACTIVITY OVERVIEW:

This activity provides the opportunity for children to reflect on the important role of grandparents and other older adults in their lives.

DESCRIPTION OF ACTIVITY:

1. Share the pop-up book with the children. Afterward, ask the children what was special about the week that this little girl spent with her grandma. Ask the children what special skill(s) the grandma in the story has. Discuss what special skills their own grandparents have.
2. Brainstorm with the children what questions they would like to ask their grandparent(s) or senior friend(s) if they could ask about that person's childhood. Capture the questions so that the each of the students has a copy.
3. Invite a grandparent, who can serve as a model of an older adult who is active and engaged in interesting activities, to be a guest in the class and to be interviewed by the children. When the guest arrives, remind the students of the questions that they had previously compiled.

EXTENSION

The children will take home the list of questions so that, with the assistance of an adult in the home, the child can interview a grandparent or senior friend in person, on the telephone, or by e-mail.

ADDITIONAL RESOURCES:

Other Pop-Up Books

TITLE: *Jungle Adventure*

PAPER ENGINEER: Helen Balmer

ILLUSTRATOR: Helen Balmer

PUBLISHER, COPYRIGHT DATE: Simon & Schuster, c1993

ANNOTATION: A summer vacation with Gramps becomes a remarkable adventure in the jungle.

TITLE: *Just You and Me, Grandpa: A Pop-Up Story About a Special Day*

AUTHOR: Marcy Heller

ILLUSTRATOR: Joanna Yardley

PUBLISHER, COPYRIGHT DATE: Reader's Digest Association, c 1994

ANNOTATION: Grandpa and Tommy share a special day fishing.

TITLE: *Let's Make Noise at the Ballpark*

PAPER ENGINEER: Americhip Studios

AUTHORS: Lisa Rojany Buccieri and Debra Mostow Zakarin

ILLUSTRATOR: Marcela Cabera

DESIGNER: Willabel Tong

PUBLISHER, COPYRIGHT DATE: Silver Dophin Books, c2006

ANNOTATION: Twins and their Grandpa attend a baseball game; the book accompanies the pop-up action with sounds.

TITLE: *My Grandma Lives in Gooligulch*

PAPER ENGINEERS: John Baker and Keith Moseley

AUTHOR: Graeme Base

ILLUSTRATOR: Graeme Base

PUBLISHER, COPYRIGHT DATE: Doublebase Pty. Ltd., c1983, 1995

ANNOTATION: In the Australian outback, Grandma takes an amazing vacation, and the rhyming text does it justice.

Books with Other Interactivity

TITLE: *Grandpa and Me: A Lift-the-flap Book*

AUTHOR: Karen Katz

ILLUSTRATOR: Karen Katz **PUBLISHER, COPYRIGHT DATE:** Little Simon, c2004.

ANNOTATION: A child and her grandparent share a special occasion making pizza.

TITLE: *My Granny's Purse*

AUTHOR: P. Hanson

PUBLISHER, COPYRIGHT DATE: Workman Publishing, c2003

ANNOTATION: This board book (with flaps) is actually a replica of granny's purse, and each item is a reminder of the relationship between the child and the grandparent.

TITLE: *My Grandpa's Briefcase*

AUTHOR: P. Hanson

PUBLISHER, COPYRIGHT DATE: Workman Publishing, c2005

ANNOTATION: Along the model of this author's *My Granny's Purse* (and also with flaps), *My Grandpa's Briefcase* reflects the easy relationship between grandchild and grandparent.

Books without Interactivity

TITLE: *Me with You* (**fiction**)

AUTHOR: Kristy Dempsey

ILLUSTRATOR: Christopher Denise

PUBLISHER, COPYRIGHT DATE: Philomenon, c2009

ANNOTATION: Rhymes tell the story of a bear granddaughter and grandfather, who are "a rare and special two," and the activities that they share.

TITLE: *The Patchwork Quilt* (**fiction**)

AUTHOR: Valerie Flournoy

ILLUSTRATOR: Jerry Pinkney

PUBLISHER, COPYRIGHT DATE: Dell Books for Young Readers, c1985

ANNOTATION: Tanya's mother and grandmother collaborate on making a quilt pieced from the family's old clothes. When the grandmother becomes ill, Tanya and her mother work to complete it.

TITLE: *Song and Dance Man* (**fiction**)

AUTHOR: Karen Ackerman

ILLUSTRATOR: Stephen Gammell

PUBLISHER, COPYRIGHT DATE: Knopf Books for Young Readers, c2003

ANNOTATION: Three children's grandfather was a vaudeville "song and dance" man, and one special day he shares his performance skills with them.

TITLE: *Spot and His Grandma* (**fiction**)

AUTHOR: Eric Hill

ILLUSTRATOR: Eric Hill

PUBLISHER, COPYRIGHT DATE: Putnam Juvenile, c2008

ANNOTATION: Spot the puppy spends special time with his grandma, including time for reading together.

DVD

TITLE: *The Patchwork Quilt* (1985; an episode of the PBS *Reading Rainbow* television series); 30 minutes (**fiction, informational**)

DISTRIBUTOR: GPN Educational Media

ANNOTATION: Grandma's special quilt uses patchwork to keep memories. In addition to the book being read, in this episode there is a song about families illustrated with pictures of families and kids who quilt, and LeVar Burton visits a family-owned grocery store.

Website

TITLE; AGENCY: *National Grandparents Day*; National Grandparents Day Council (**informational for teacher**)

URL: http://www.grandparents-day.com

ANNOTATION: Grandparents' Day is the first Sunday after Labor Day. This website explains the history of this national day of recognition and provides information about various competitions honoring grandparents, as well as information and resources for teachers.

THEME: Celebrations—Halloween and Scary Things

TITLE: *Haunted House*

PAPER ENGINEER: Tor Lokvig

AUTHOR: Jan Pieńkowski

ILLUSTRATORS: Jan Pieńkowski and Jane Walmsley (assistant illustrator)

PUBLISHER, COPYRIGHT DATE: Dutton Children's Books, c1979

ANNOTATION:

A doctor who is summoned to make a house call at a haunted house meets a most unusual patient.

AWARD ALERT: This acclaimed pop-up book was a 1979 Kate Greenaway Award winner. Established by the [British] Library Association, the Greenaway medal for illustration is equivalent to the Caldecott award in the United States.

MAJOR CURRICULUM AREAS FOR ACTIVITY:

Math (Prediction)
Social Studies (Celebrations, Emotions—Fear)

DESCRIPTION OVERVIEW:

The plot of *Haunted House* is a wonderful kick-off for Halloween-themed activities, although the book never uses the term Halloween. It's also a useful device for talking about fears with young children.

DESCRIPTION OF ACTIVITY:

1. Ask the children if they are afraid of anything and discuss the fact that different people are afraid of different things. Then share the pop-up book *Haunted House*, asking the children to identify the scary things on each page.
2. Stop before the end of the book and ask the children to predict how they think the story in *Haunted House* will end. Discuss with the children what they should do when they're scared, and help them to understand strategies for dealing with fears.

EXTENSIONS

1. Ask the children when they pick Halloween costumes, what kind do they pick? Are they scary, funny, beautiful, based on a favorite character, and so forth? Why do the children want those costumes?

2. Have the children draw pictures that they can share with classmates, friends, and/ or family, of their costumes; have them also provide explanations of the costumes.

ADDITIONAL RESOURCES:

Other Pop-Up Books

TITLE: *The Beastly Pageant: A Monster Pop-Up Book*

PAPER ENGINEER: Bruce Foster

AUTHOR: P. Z. Mann

ILLUSTRATOR: Lisa Berrett

PUBLISHER, COPYRIGHT DATE: Paradise Press, Inc., c1995

ANNOTATION: Three double-page spreads of pop-ups tell the story of the beastly pageant when Boris dresses in costume as a human boy.

TITLE: *I'm Going to Eat You: A Spooky Pop-Up Flap Book*

AUTHOR: Matt Mitter

ILLUSTRATOR: Jimmy Pickering

PUBLISHER, COPYRIGHT DATE: Reader's Digest, c2006

ANNOTATION: The boy in his bed is very worried—everything seems determined to eat him! The pop-ups are hidden behind flaps.

TITLE: *I'm Not Afraid of Halloween! A Pop-Up and Flap Book*

PAPER ENGINEER: William C. Wolff

AUTHOR: Marion Dane Bauer

ILLUSTRATOR: Rusty Fletcher

PUBLISHER, COPYRIGHT DATE: Little Simon, c2006

ANNOTATION: Trick-or-treating can bring scary costumes to the door. The book has a surprise ending.

TITLE: *I'm Not Scared*

AUTHOR: Jan Pieńkowski

ILLUSTRATOR: Jan Pieńkowski

PUBLISHER, COPYRIGHT DATE: Barnes and Noble by arrangement with Reed International Books, c1997

ANNOTATION: I'm not scared, or am I? The book displays pop-ups created in the very recognizable Pieńkowski style.

TITLE: *In a Dark, Dark Wood: An Old Tale with a New Twist*

PAPER ENGINEER: David Carter

AUTHOR: David A. Carter

ILLUSTRATOR: David Carter

PUBLISHER, COPYRIGHT DATE: Simon & Schuster, c1991

ANNOTATION: In a dark, dark wood in a dark, dark house, there is a surprise waiting to pop out at the end.

TITLE: *Mommy?*

PAPER ENGINEER: Matthew Rinehart

AUTHOR: Maurice Sendak

ILLUSTRATOR: Maurice Sendak

PUBLICATION, COPYRIGHT DATE: Michael Di Capua Books, Scholastic, c2006

ANNOTATION: The toddler in blue pajamas looks everywhere for his mommy in a house of werewolves, vampires, and so on. The surprise ending, hidden behind a flap, will delight young readers. The pages are filled with pop-ups.

TITLE: *Skeleton in the Cupboard*

AUTHOR: David Pelham

ILLUSTRATOR: David Pelham

PUBLISHER, COPYRIGHT DATE: Dutton Children's Books, c1998

ANNOTATION: A skeleton lives in the cupboard (closet). Will he come out?

Other Books with Interactivity

TITLE: *Help, Mama, Help! A Touch-and-Feel Pull-Tab Pop-Up Book*

PAPER ENGINEER: Shonagh Rae

AUTHOR: Shen Roddie

ILLUSTRATOR: Frances Cony

PUBLISHER, COPYRIGHT DATE: Little, Brown, c1995

ANNOTATION: A yellow chick plans to camp out by himself, but nightfall brings scary thoughts.

TITLE: *I Don't Want to Sleep Tonight*

DESIGNER: Brown Wells & Jacobs

AUTHOR: Deborah Norville

ILLUSTRATOR: Richard O'Neill

PUBLISHER, COPYRIGHT DATE: Golden Books, c[1999?]

ANNOTATION: Flaps are used in this story of a little girl whose room becomes a very scary place at night.

Books without Interactivity

TITLE: *A Beasty Story* (**fiction**)

AUTHOR: Bill Martin Jr.

ILLUSTRATOR: Steven Kellogg

PUBLISHER, COPYRIGHT DATE: Voyager Books, Harcourt, c1999

ANNOTATION: Four mice track a scary beast into a "dark, dark" house. What will they find?

TITLE: *Franklin and the Thunderstorm* (**fiction**)

AUTHOR: Paulette Bourgeois

ILLUSTRATOR: Brenda Clark

PUBLISHER, COPYRIGHT DATE: Scholastic, c1998

ANNOTATION: Well-known children's book character Franklin the Turtle is frightened of thunderstorms, and his friends try to reassure him.

TITLE: *Where the Wild Things Are* (**fiction**)

AUTHOR: Maurice Sendak

ILLUSTRATOR: Maurice Sendak

PUBLISHER, COPYRIGHT DATE: Harper Collins, c1963

ANNOTATION: In Sendak's now-classic children's book, Max's mischief gets him sent to bed, where his bedroom is transformed into a forest, an ocean, a boat, and a land of wild things.

DVD

TITLE: *Sesame Street: A Magical Halloween Adventure* (1969, 2004); 60 minutes (**fiction**)

DISTRIBUTOR: Sesame Street

ANNOTATION: The *Sesame Street* characters enjoy Halloween and other fall activities.

Website

TITLE; AGENCY: *Read a Face*; Sesame Street

URL: http://www.sesamestreet.org/games

ANNOTATION: This online game is about facial expressions and feelings, including angry and scary. Includes film clips of the *Sesame Street* characters dealing with these feelings.

THEME: Celebrations—National Holidays: Thanksgiving

TITLE: *Macy's on Parade: A Pop-Up Celebration of Macy's Thanksgiving Day Parade*

PAPER ENGINEER: Pamela Pease

CONSULTING PAPER ENGINEER: Andrew Baron

DESIGNER: Pamela Pease

AUTHOR: Pamela Pease

ILLUSTRATOR: Pamela Pease

PUBLISHER, COPYRIGHT DATE: Paintbox Press, c2002

ANNOTATION:

Follow the pop-up parade on its journey; there is a small map included that traces the route. This annual celebratory event ends with Santa's sleigh hovering above the book.

MAJOR CURRICULUM AREAS:

Social Studies (Celebrations)

ACTIVITY OVERVIEW:

Seasons and observances of Thanksgiving focus on those things for which one is thankful and provides an opportunity to discuss the celebrations of different families and communities.

DESCRIPTION OF ACTIVITY:

1. Share with the children the origins of Thanksgiving (proclamation by President Lincoln to honor the end of the Civil War; see the website in Additional Resources in this section). Point out that people observe this holiday in many ways, including the fact that many (not all) people do not have to go to work or school. Then, share the pop-up book with them. Explain the significance of the parade to children who might not be familiar with it.
2. Have the children think quietly to themselves about what they have done or will do when the Thanksgiving holiday arrives. Are there special things that their families or communities always do (which can include activities ranging from watching football or other special programs on television to traveling for visits to family or friends to helping out with community meal sharing to simply staying home from school and work)?
3. Help the children to make a list of the many different things that people do on this holiday. Point out that the holiday is often one in which people do

something for other people. Have each of the children think of a nice thing that they might do for someone else during the holiday—discuss with them that being helpful can be a small but meaningful endeavor.

ADDITIONAL RESOURCES:

Other Pop-Up Books

TITLE: *Thanksgiving in the Barn: A Pop-Up Book*

AUTHORS: Nadine Bernard Westcott and Gene Vosough

ILLUSTRATOR: Nadine Bernard Westcott

PUBLISHER, COPYRIGHT DATE: Little Simon, c2004

ANNOTATION: Discover what goes on in the barn at Thanksgiving.

Other Books with Interactivity

TITLE: *Happy Thanksgiving, Biscuit!*

AUTHOR: Alyssa Satin Capucilli

ILLUSTRATOR: Pat Schories

PUBLISHER, COPYRIGHT DATE: HarperCollins, c1999

ANNOTATION: Lift the flaps to see what Biscuit is doing! How will he spend his first Thanksgiving?

Books without Interactivity

TITLE: *Clifford's Thanksgiving Visit* (**fiction**)

AUTHOR: Norman Bridwell

ILLUSTRATOR: Norman Bridwell

PUBLISHER, COPYRIGHT DATE: Scholastic, c1993

ANNOTATION: For Thanksgiving, Clifford the Big Red Dog goes to visit his mother, while his friend Emily Elizabeth and her family visit her grandparents.

TITLE: *Giving Thanks: A Native American Good Morning Message* (**informational**)

AUTHOR: Chief Jake Swamp

ILLUSTRATOR: Erwin Printup Jr.

PUBLISHER, COPYRIGHT DATE: Lee & Low, 1995

ANNOTATION: The Mowhawk good morning message offers thanks for many blessings, including those of the natural world.

TITLE: *Thanks to the Animals* (**fiction**)

AUTHOR: Allen Sockabasin

ILLUSTRATOR: Rebekah Raye

PUBLISHER, COPYRIGHT DATE: Tilbury House, c2005

ANNOTATION: When Joo Tum and his family travel to their winter home, the baby falls from the sled. The forest animals gather to protect him. Passamaquoddy names for the animals are provided.

DVD

TITLE: *Giving Thanks: A Native American Good Morning* Message (episode from the PBS *Reading Rainbow* television series); 30 minutes (**fiction, informational**)

DISTRIBUTOR: GPN Educational Media

ANNOTATION: The book illustrates a traditional Iroquois morning message of thanks for blessings. In addition to the book being read, in this episode LeVar Burton visits a cranberry farm, a Pueblo family of potters, and children planting trees in New York.

Website

TITLE; AGENCY: Proclamation of Thanksgiving. Abraham Lincoln Online; Rhoda and Lowell Sneller (**informational for teacher**)

URL: http://showcase.netins.net/web/creative/lincoln/welcome.htm

ANNOTATION: This site has the background and text of President Abraham Lincoln's 1863 Proclamation of Thanksgiving as a national day of observance.

THEME: Celebrations—Special Times with Parents

TITLE: *Hop on Pop-Up!*

AUTHOR: Dr. Seuss

PUBLISHER, COPYRIGHT DATE: Random House, c2002

ANNOTATION:

This mini-pop book suggests ways to be kind to pop (but hopping on him is *not* one of them!).

MAJOR CURRICULUM AREAS:

Fine Arts (Art)
Social Studies (Celebrations)

ACTIVITY OVERVIEW:

Hop on Pop can be used to introduce special days that provide the opportunity for children to recognize and offer appreciation to parents and other important adults in their lives. Activity 3 could be adapted and revised for honoring people in the children's school lives, such as the school nurse or principal.

DESCRIPTION OF ACTIVITY:

1. Read the pop-up book to the children. Discuss what the characters in the book are doing with their father—things that they think would be fun for him. Ask the children: What fun things do you like to do? This book is in rhyme—ask the children if they liked this; are rhymes fun?.
2. Ask the children, if they had a whole day to spend all by themselves with a parent, what would they want do for special activities? Have each child draw a picture illustrating that special day.
3. Show children how to make a simple pop-up card (see Figure 6.9 in "THEME: Time to Rhyme"). Have each child create a card with a message from the child to accompany the picture as a gift for the parent. For older children, ask them to create a rhyme to put in the card.

EXTENSION

Each child can design a pop-up appreciation card for someone outside of the school environment, such as a Sunday-school teacher, scout leader, neighbor, and so on.

ADDITIONAL RESOURCES:

Other Pop-Up Books

TITLE: *Because I Love You So Much*

AUTHOR: Guido van Genechten

PUBLISHER, COPYRIGHT DATE: Tiger Tales, c2005

ANNOTATION: Snowy the polar bear knows many things, but he also has many questions for his mother, including one about love.

TITLE: *Mama Loves Me*

PAPER ENGINEER: Mara Van Fleet (format)

AUTHOR: Mara Van Fleet

ILLUSTRATOR: Claudine Gévry

PUBLISHER, COPYRIGHT DATE: Reader's Digest Children's Book, c2005

ANNOTATION: The "pop-up" that ties together the plot of this book is the blue elephant's trunk (fabric) that runs loops through the book. The pop-up at the end illustrates the baby and its mom settling in for the evening.

Books without Interactivity

TITLE: *Guess How Much I Love You?* (**fiction**)

AUTHOR: Sam McBratney

ILLUSTRATOR: Anita Jeram

PUBLISHER, COPYRIGHT DATE: Candlewick, 1995

ANNOTATION: In this 1996 ALA Notable Children's Book, Big Nutbrown Hare and Little Nutbrown Hare share a bedtime game of "Guess How Much I Love You?"

TITLE: *I Like Noisy Mom Likes Quiet: A Mother's Day Story* (**fiction**)

AUTHOR: Eileen Spinelli

ILLUSTRATOR: Lydia Halverson

PUBLISHER, COPYRIGHT DATE: Ideals Children's Books, c2006

ANNOTATION: Little Raccoon likes noise, but Mama Raccoon likes quiet. Little Raccoon makes Mother's Day very special for her.

TITLE: *Mama, Do You Love Me?* (**fiction**)

AUTHOR: Barbara M. Joosse

ILLUSTRATOR: Barbara Lavallee

PUBLISHER, COPYRIGHT DATE: Chronicle Books, c1991

ANNOTATION: An Alaskan Inuit daughter asks: "Mama, do you love me?" **NOTE:** This book is also available in a Spanish version: *¿Me quieres, mamá?* It is translated by Diego Lasconi, Chronicle Books, 1998.

TITLE: *Papa, Do You Love Me?* (**fiction**)

AUTHOR: Barbara M. Joosse

ILLUSTRATOR: Barbara Lavallee

PUBLISHER, COPYRIGHT DATE: Chronicle Books, c2005

ANNOTATION: In Africa, a Maasai son asks "Papa, do you love me?"

TITLE: *A Perfect Father's Day* (**fiction**)

AUTHOR: Eve Bunting

ILLUSTRATOR: Susan Meddaugh

PUBLISHER, COPYRIGHT DATE: Sandpiper, 1993.

ANNOTATION: Young Susie has thought of the perfect outings to help her Dad celebrate a "perfect Father's Day."

TITLE: *I Love My Daddy Because* (**fiction**)

AUTHOR: Laurel Porter-Gaylord

ILLUSTRATOR: Ashley Wolff

PUBLISHER, COPYRIGHT DATE: Dutton Juvenile, c1991

ANNOTATION: Animal fathers care for their young ones in ways that human fathers take care of their children. **NOTE:** This book is also available in a Spanish version: *Quiero a mi papá porque.*

THEME: Celebrations—Valentine's Day

TITLE: *Never Too Little to Love*

AUTHOR: Jeanne Willis

ILLUSTRATOR: Jan Fearnley

PUBLISHER, COPYRIGHT DATE: Candlewick Press, c2005

ANNOTATION:

Soft watercolors are used to tell the story of Tiny Too Little, a mouse who is creative in trying to be tall enough to kiss his friend, a giraffe. Flaps in the book build his climb upward to the pop-up finale.

MAJOR CURRICULUM AREAS:

Language Arts (Rhymes)
Literature (Poetry)
Social Studies

ACTIVITY OVERVIEW:

Valentine's Day offers the opportunity to explore with children the idea that true friendship doesn't have to fit "into a box." And, true friends help you and don't demand that you be perfect.

DESCRIPTION OF ACTIVITY:

1. While sharing the pop-up book, ask the children how the giraffe helps out her friend.
2. Make a list on a flip chart of words, suggested by the children, that describe good friends.
3. Talk with the children about rhymes, which are used in many valentines sent to friends. Some children might be able to recite to you the following popular short poem. But, if not, share it with them.

   Roses are red,
   Violets are blue,
   Sugar is sweet,
   And so are you.

Then, work with the children to come up with rhyming words to go with the list of words about good friends that they suggested.

4. Assist children in creating their own rhymes about friends, drawing from the list of rhyming words.

5. The teacher, together with the class, can create an e-card about friendship, including verses from the children, to send to another class in the school or to a pen-pal class in another community. Digital clip art can be used to add illustrations to the rhymes.

EXTENSION

Show the children the technique in the pop-up book of using flaps to reveal a picture. Assist children in creating a simple valentine flap to use with their rhymes in individual cards (see Figure 6.5 at the end of this theme).

ADDITIONAL RESOURCES:

Other Pop-Up Books

TITLE: *Bee Mine: A Pop-Up Book of Valentines*

PAPER ENGINEER: Bruce Foster

AUTHOR: Olive Ewe

ILLUSTRATOR: David Moreton

PUBLISHER, COPYRIGHT DATE: Little Simon, c2004

ANNOTATION: Animal motif valentines fold open to show the pop-up animals and fun messages.

TITLE: *Clifford, I Love You Pop-Up*

AUTHOR: Norman Bridwell

ILLUSTRATOR: Norman Bridwell

PAPER ENGINEER, COPYRIGHT DATE: Scholastic, c1994

ANNOTATION: Sometimes Clifford the big red dog is good, and sometimes he is not so good. But in this pop-up board book, Clifford finds that his human friend, Emily Elizabeth, is a true friend.

TITLE: *Love Bugs: A Pop-Up Book*

PAPER ENGINEER: David Carter

AUTHOR: David Carter

ILLUSTRATOR: David Carter

PUBLISHER, COPYRIGHT DATE: Little Simon, c1995

ANNOTATION: The book is a heart shaped candy box, and then love bugs pop up to bring valentine greetings.

Books without Interactivity

TITLE: *Arthur's Valentine* (**fiction**)

AUTHOR: Marc Brown

ILLUSTRATOR: Marc Brown

PUBLISHER, COPYRIGHT DATE: Little Brown Books for Young Readers, 1988

ANNOTATION: Arthur the Aardvark receives a valentine from a secret admirer, and his classmates tease him about it.

TITLE: *Junie B. Jones and the Musy Gushy Valentime* (**fiction**)

AUTHOR: Barbara Park

ILLUSTRATOR: Denise Brunkus

PUBLISHER, COPYRIGHT DATE: Random House, c1999

ANNOTATION: Popular children's book character Junie B. Jones receives a "mushy gushy valentime." Who is the secret admirer?

DVD

TITLE; AGENCY: *Barney: Be My Valentine* (2010); 52 minutes (**fiction**)

DISTRIBUTOR: Lyons

ANNOTATION: Barney and his friends celebrate Valentine's Day.

Valentine Flap

Steps:

1. There should be **one heart on sturdy red paper (duplicated from the template)** for each child. There should also be **one 8 ½ × 11-inch piece of paper (color or white)** per child. Depending on skill, the hearts may be cut out **with scissors** by the child or be pre-cut.

2. The heart should be cut in half down the center. Assist the child in folding the heart in half to create a crease that can be cut.

3. The child should position the two heart halves on the preferred spot on the paper. Then, assist the child as needed in placing **glue** on the back of the heart halves, in the designated "glue section." The heart halves are then placed one at a time, glue side down, on the paper. Assist as needed in helping the child to line up the two halves to recreate a whole heart.

4. After the glue dries, assist the child as needed in carefully folding up the two sides of the heart to create creases that allow the two sides of the heart to open.

5. Assist as needed to help the child write his or her rhyme, with **crayons or markers,** on the paper under the heart. Remind the child that the rhyme should fit under the heart.

Figure 6.5. Valentine Flap

heart:

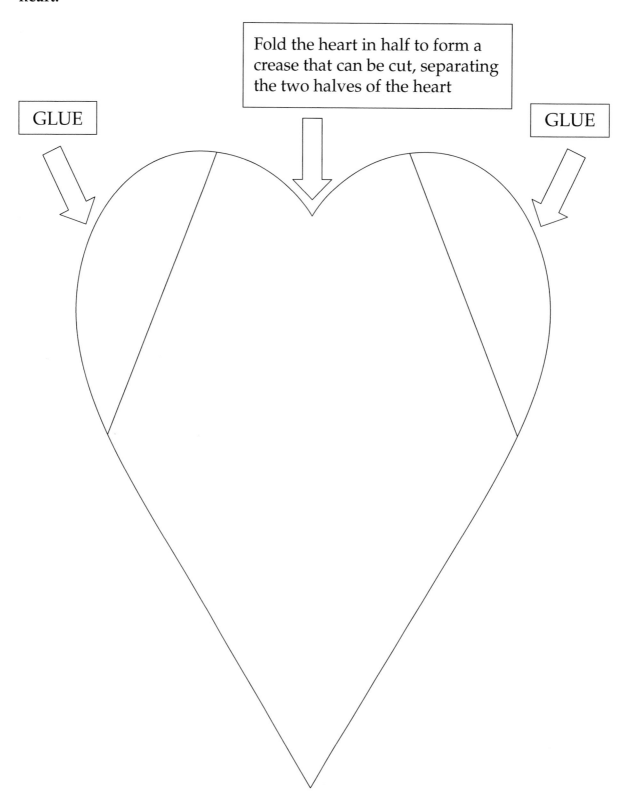

Fold the heart in half to form a crease that can be cut, separating the two halves of the heart

GLUE

GLUE

TITLE; AGENCY: *Winnie the Pooh: A Valentine for You, Special Edition* (2010); 60 minutes (**fiction**)

DISTRIBUTOR: Walt Disney

ANNOTATION: Winnie and friends look for Smitten the love bug; video also has two other stories on it.

Website

TITLE; AGENCY: *Sesame Street. PBS Kids*; PBS

URL: http://pbskids.org/sesame/

ANNOTATION: Click on the link for "Send an E-card" to walk through steps for sending either a "thank you" or a "friendship" card.

TITLE; AGENCY: *WordWorld: Where Words Come Alive: Frog's Rhyming Machine*; PBS Kids

URL: http://pbskids.org/wordworld/characters/game_frm.html

ANNOTATION: Click the button on Frog's machine, and a word appears for rhyming. Three bubbles with potential answers are generated by the machine, and Frog prompts the user through correct and incorrect responses.

THEME: Celebrations—Winter Observances

CONTRIBUTOR TO ACTIVITY: Gayle Baar (see Appendix for information on this contributor)

TITLE: *Cookie Count: A Tasty Pop-Up*

PAPER ENGINEER: Robert Sabuda

AUTHOR: Robert Sabuda

ILLUSTRATOR: Robert Sabuda

PUBLISHER, COPYRIGHT DATE: Little Simon, c1997

ANNOTATION:

Ten glorious pop-ups count and rhyme through delicious cookie types, ending with the most astounding gingerbread house.

MAJOR CURRICULUM AREAS:

Language Arts (Rhymes)
Literature Math (Counting)
Social Studies (Celebrations, Diversity, Food)

AWARD ALERT: Robert Sabuda received the 2000 Meggendorfer Prize, recognizing the paper engineering in this pop-up book. The prize is given biennially by The Movable Book Society.

PART 1: Celebrating with Food

ACTIVITY OVERVIEW:

This activity encourages children to reflect on special celebrations in their own lives and to learn about the diversity of observances, both individual/family and community.

DESCRIPTION OF ACTIVITY:

1. Share the pop-up book with the children, asking them before you start to be aware of rhymes and of the types of cookies.
2. After sharing the book, discuss with them the types of cookies that they know about (some children may have allergy or other constraints) or that they have eaten. Make a list of the cookies and discuss categories into which the cookies might be grouped. With the children, graph those groups.
3. Make another list of sources of cookies that the children have enjoyed: made at home, purchased, given to them by grandparents, eaten at a party, and so on. With the children, graph these groups and then let them take a count of how many children in the class have had these various experiences (pointing out that since some will have multiple experiences, the total number of experiences will be larger than the class size).
4. Bring an assortment of cookie-cutters to class. Include different shapes as well as cutters associated with various winter celebrations (such as stars, snowflakes, and other seasonal symbols). Children can describe the various shapes using either geometric terms or their own words. Children can discuss which cutters are familiar to them as represented in cookies that they have eaten or as symbols that they see in the wintertime.

EXTENSIONS

1. Have children identify their favorite December-centered or winter celebration books. Select some to share, and as they are shared, discuss how food is used in that book—as in Dr. Seuss's *How the Grinch Stole Christmas* and the theft of the holiday food, which is presented in the narrative and in the illustrations.

2. To reinforce counting and one-to-one communication, have each child create a "cookie" to pop off a large bulletin board display outside the library. In addition to the math implications, the children are also learning to follow directions, color, fold, and create their three-dimensional cookies, and count the delicious results.

PART 2: Sharing and Our Community Helpers

DESCRIPTION OF ACTIVITY:

1. Discuss with children the fun that there is in sharing things, including food, such as cookies. Point out, per the back cover of the pop-up book, that Robert Sabuda's dedication in his book says, "For my nieces Morgan and Paige—welcome to the world, girls!" so the book is shared with his nieces and also with all of the children who read it.
2. Brainstorm with the children the individuals with whom food or special meals is shared during times of winter season special celebrations (such as Christmas, or Hanukkah, or Kwanzaa), including dinners or parties or special treats: houseguests, family members (as well as extended family members), nursing-home residents, military personnel, college students, international visitors, and so on.
3. Discuss with children the fact that many people in their lives and communities help them. Have the class compose a rhyme, story, explanation, and so forth, of a cookie or other special treat in their lives. Help the children to collect these into short books that can be sent to helpers identified by the class (such as the local fire station) as a thank you or as a greeting to someone far from home. Help them to compose an introduction to the books and to create and include a pop-up illustration use (see Figure 6.9 in "THEME: Time to Rhyme").

EXTENSION

Children often assist in taking, preparing, or sharing food with community helpers, nursing homes, military personnel, college students, older family members, international visitors, and so on. Ask them to share these experiences.

ADDITIONAL RESOURCES:

Other Pop-Up Books

TITLE: *Hanukkah! A Three-Dimensional Celebration*

PAPER ENGINEERS: David Hawcock, Jerome Bruandet, and Mat Johnstone

AUTHOR: Sara Freedland

ILLUSTRATOR: Sue Clarke

PUBLISHER, COPYRIGHT DATE: Tango Books, c1991

ANNOTATION: Pop-ups and pages in muted shades of gold, yellow, and reds are a background for information about the history, traditions, and celebrations of Hanukkah.

TITLE: *A Kwanzaa Celebration*

PAPER ENGINEER: Robert Sabuda

AUTHOR: Nancy Williams

ILLUSTRATOR: Robert Sabuda

PUBLISHER, COPYRIGHT DATE: Little Simon, c1995

ANNOTATION: The joyous movements of a Kwanzaa celebration dance from the pages. The book is illustrated with hand-cut paper, and the technique marries bright colors with the illusion of muted texture.

TITLE: *The Story of Hanukkah: A Lift-the-flap Rebus Book*

PAPER ENGINEERS: Jose R. Seminario and Ariel Apte

DESIGNER: Leslie McGuire

AUTHOR: Lisa Rojany

ILLUSTRATOR: Holly Jones

PUBLISHER, COPYRIGHT DATE: Intervisual Books, c1993

ANNOTATION: Flaps and pop-ups illustrate the rebus that explains the Festival of Lights.

TITLE: *Pop-Up Firefighters, Police Officers, and EMTs to the Rescue*

ATUHOR: Calvert Gamwell

PAPER ENGINEERING: Carrie Jordan

ILLUSTRATOR: Carrie Jordan

PUBLISHER, COPYRIGHT DATE: Carah Kids, c2001

ANNOTATION: Each double-page pop-up focuses on one type of community helper (firefighters, police officers, and EMTs) in the vehicle specific to the profession.

Other Books with Interactivity

TITLE: *Emergency Rescue!*

AUTHOR: Lori Froeb

ILLUSTRATOR: Thomas LaPadula

PUBLISHER, COPYRIGHT DATE: Reader's Digest Children's Books, c2002

ANNOTATION: This oversized Tonka board book has moving parts for the emergency rescue vehicles: digger, fire truck, helicopter, and helicopter.

Other Books with Interactivity

TTLE: *Gingerbread Baby*

AUTHOR: Jan Brett

ILLUSTRATOR: Jan Brett

PUBLISHER, COPYRIGHT DATE: Putnam Juvenile, c2003

ANNOTATION: This cheerful board book of a gingerbread boy's adventures has a flap at the end.

TITLE: *Gingerbread Friends*

AUTHOR: Jan Brett

ILLUSTRATOR: Jan Brett

PUBLISHER, COPYRIGHT DATE: Putnam Juvenile, c2008

ANNOTATION: Who can resist this most delicious-looking and energetic of gingerbread boys? The book has a special fold-out surprise.

DVD

TITLE: *Max & Ruby: Everybunny Loves Winter* (2010); 99 minutes (**fiction**)

DISTRIBUTOR: Nickelodeon

ANNOTATION: Four episodes from the television series follow Max and Ruby as they enjoy winter activities, including building a snow bunny, making a gingerbread house, and prepare for Christmas.

Website

TITLE; AGENCY: *Winter Celebrations*; National Geographic Kids (**informational for teacher**)

URL: http://kids.nationalgeographic.com/kids/stories/peopleplaces/winter-celebrations

ANNOTATION: The web page has a list with short descriptions of December and January celebrations/observances around the world. There are also links to supporting resources such as a snowflake puzzler, winter sports, and a Kwanzaa recipe.

THEME: Daily Activities and Time

TITLE: *Nutsy the Robot Goes to Bed*

PAPER ENGINEER: Corinna Fletcher

AUTHOR: Mark Shulman

ILLUSTRATOR: Katie Boyce

PUBLICATION, COPYRIGHT DATE: Brighter Child, c2006.

ANNOTATION:

Wheels, flaps, and pull tabs move Nutsy the Robot Boy through his daily routine, until he's off to bed (a simple pop-up). The front cover of the book has pull components that transform it into Nutsy.

MAJOR CURRICULUM AREAS:

Math (Sequencing, Time)
Social Studies (Daily Activities)

ACTIVITY OVERVIEW:

This activity helps children to understand sequencing and the relationship between analog and digital versions of time.

DESCRIPTION OF ACTIVITY:

1. Read the pop-up book to the children, moving the parts as the day unfolds, and as the book is shared, discuss with them the sequence that Nutsy is following (What is first? What is next? etc.).
2. Discuss with the children their routine on school days, from the morning until the evening. Help them to notice the contrast in routines among the children. Also help them to compare similarities in routine. Help them to understand that there is an order to these activities.
3. Share a diagram of an analog clock with movable hands (brad in the center) with the children. Work with them through the times that this clock will show them.
4. Have a digital clock and an analog clock. Have the children watch the movements of both through several minutes. Discuss with them the relationship between the numbers on the analog clock and the numbers on the digital clock.

5. Discuss with the children what times they do various things during their school day (What time they get home? What time the school bus comes for them? When they eat lunch? When school is over for the day? When they go to bed? etc.). Have each child draw a picture of something that they do the same time on each school day.

6. Make a simple timeline on butcher paper that can be placed around the wall. On it, have the times of the day pictured with an analog face and a digital clock face. Help the children attach their pictures to match the times. Help them compare and contrast the differences and similarities that they see among this group of children.

ADDITIONAL RESOURCES:

Other Books with Pop-Ups

TITLE: *Learn About Time*

PAPER ENGINEER: Jose Seminario

DESIGNER: Treesha Runnells

ILLUSTRATOR: David Sim

PUBLISHER, COPYRIGHT DATE: Intervisual Books, c2002

ANNOTATION: This small book uses pop-ups, tabs, and flaps to illustrate the daily activities of a blue rabbit and a brown bear: breakfast time, playtime, fun time, and so on. A small clock face on each face is a flap that hides the time for each activity.

TITLE: *Sam's Pop-Up Schoolhouse*

AUTHOR: Yves Got

ILLUSTRATOR: Yves Got

PUBLISHER, COPYRIGHT DATE: Chronicle Books, c2002

ANNOTATION: This pop-up carousel opens to reveal school classrooms and the playground.

TITLE: *Super Sue*

AUTHOR: Cressida Cowell

ILLUSTRATOR: Russell Ayto

PUBLISHER: Candlewick Press, 2003

ANNOTATION: The rhyming text of this pop-up book recounts Sue's daily activities at home.

TITLE: *Too Many Shoes!*

AUTHOR: Keith Faulkner

ILLUSTRATOR: Stephen Holmes

PUBLISHER, COPYRIGHT DATE: Backpack Books, c2006

ANNOTATION: A blue spider is faced with the dilemma of what shoes to wear each day. The pop-ups are the shoes, and a blue shoe lace on the cover can be used to lace them.

Other Books with Interactivity

TITLE: *Just a Snowy Day*

AUTHOR: Mercer Mayer

PUBLISHER, COPYRIGHT DATE: HarperFestival, c1983

ANNOTATION: Pull tabs and touch-and-feel additions enhance the daily routine of Little Critter's snowy day.

TITLE: *Little Pirate Goes to Bed*

AUTHOR: Lawrence Schimel

ILLUSTRATOR: Sara Rojo

PUBLISHER, COPYRIGHT DATE: Innovative Kids, 2007

ANNOTATION: In this flap book, small pirates also have daily routines.

TITLE: *Time*

PAPER ENGINEERS: Roger Priddy, Joanna Bicknell, Robert Tainsh, and Louisa Beaumont

AUTHORS: Sarah Kappely and Andrea Pinnington

ILLUSTRATOR: Richard Brown (pictures)

PUBLISHER, COPYRIGHT DATE: St. Martin's Press, c2002

ANNOTATION: This book is arranged by the activities that a child would have through the day and includes seasons. Flaps reveal the answers to questions related to the activities.

TITLE: *Twinkle, Twinkle, Little Star*

AUTHOR: Alison Boyle

ILLUSTRATOR: Liz Pichon

PUBLISHER, COPYRIGHT DATE: Sterling, 2000

ANNOTATION: Lift-the-flaps and a large fold-out at the end illustrate the story of the evening star looking for the little bear who is her friend and who usually watches her each evening.

Books without Interactivity

TITLE: *The Clock Struck One: A Time-telling Tale* (**fiction**)

AUTHOR: Trudy Harris

ILLUSTRATOR: Carrie Hartman

PUBLISHER, COPYRIGHT DATE: Millbrook Press, c2009

ANNOTATION: Rhyming verses tell the story of a cat chasing a mouse through each hour of the day.

TITLE: *Good Night, Gorilla* (**fiction**)

AUTHOR: Peggy Rathmann

ILLUSTRATOR: Peggy Rathmann

PUBLISHER, COPYRIGHT DATE: Putnam Juvenile, c1994

ANNOTATION: Each night, the zoo's watchman says "goodnight, gorilla" as he passes that cage. Then, one night the animals follow him home.

TITLE: *Goodnight, Moon* (**fiction**)

AUTHOR: Margaret Wise Brown

ILLUSTRATOR: Clement Hurd

PUBLISHER, COPYRIGHT DATE: Harper & Brothers, c1947

ANNOTATION: Poetry captures the young rabbit's nightly ritual of bidding goodnight to everything in his world.

DVDs

TITLE; AGENCY: *Elmo's World: Wake up with Elmo!* (2002); 50 minutes (**fiction**)

DISTRIBUTOR: Sesame Street

ANNOTATION: Learn along with Elmo as he brushes his teeth, gets dressed, and so on.

TITLE: *Good Night, Gorilla . . . and more Great Sleepytime Stories* (2008); 61 minutes (**fiction**)

DISTRIBUTOR: Scholastic

ANNOTATION: Besides Peggy Rathmann's book *Good Night, Gorilla*, the animated video has five other stories, including Audrey Wood's *The Napping House*.

Website

TITLE; AGENCY: *Elmo's Cupcakes*; Sesame Street

URL: http://pbskids.org/sesame/#/games

ANNOTATION: This short online animated video follows the routine of Elmo with a babysitter on the day that his mom returns to work. It includes a collage game, in which the viewer clicks and moves objects on to the paper.

THEME: Dinosaur Investigator

CONTRIBUTOR TO ACTIVITY: Merry Graves (see Appendix for information on this contributor)

TITLE: *The Dinosaur Museum*

PAPER ENGINEERS: Keith Moseley and Alan Brown

AUTHOR: Jen Green

ILLUSTRATOR: Sebastian Quigley

PUBLISHER, COPYRIGHT DATE: National Geographic Society, c2008

ANNOTATION:

This intricate, information-dense book covers the Triassic, Jurassic, and Cretaceous Periods. It is cleverly organized as a visit through a museum of dinosaurs, including the lab.

MAJOR CURRICULUM AREAS:

Fine Arts
Language Arts
Science
Mathematics

ACTIVITY OVERVIEW:

Dinosaurs are the perfect "hook" to entice students into practicing effective strategies for research to find the answers to their own questions. Use this book to introduce Big Six research to students: This activity will take six to eight class periods of thirty minutes and is usually spread out over a two-week period.

DESCRIPTION OF ACTIVITY:

1. Share the pop-up book, which uses a museum tour as a way to deliver information about dinosaurs. Point out to the students that the lab is one place where questions are generated and answers are found and that the exhibits provide answers to common questions.
2. Students listen to selected pages from the book to initiate and generate questions for research about dinosaurs: What did they look like? What did they eat? Where did they live? How did they move? Who were their predators? What do their names mean?
3. Students write questions on their Big Six chart (see Figure 6.6 at the end of this theme). For younger children, charts are made with a sheet of manila paper (twelve-by-eighteen inches).
4. As a class discussion activity, the teacher and students examine each question, underline the key words, and add synonyms that will help them access the answers from the sources.
5. Students examine the table of contents and the index of a sample book and discover how to find the page with the answer using keywords and synonyms recorded on their Big Six work charts.
6. Students review note taking using the "Trash & Treasure" technique: Using a sample paragraph, students will circle answers to a question and mark

through extraneous material. Then the teacher will demonstrate where to record answers on the students' papers.

7. Students spend three to four days taking notes from sources provided and recording them on their Big Six charts.
8. Students write a summary of information for each question. This summary is used when creating the product for the unit.
9. Students make and deliver visual presentations based on the knowledge gathered. For example: The students who research stegosaurus can create a picture of the dinosaur, with its bony plates, eating plants while its predator looms in the background. Additional information could be written on rocks, plants, and so forth, in the picture. Or, the student could create a diorama showing this information. Using the computer, students can compose an informative book using KidPix or even PowerPoint. They can develop a brochure for their own dinosaur museum. Students can give an oral presentation about their dinosaur. If three or four students researched the same dinosaur, each can present a fact or two, and the teacher can record the presentations. These videos can be added to the class web page.

ADDITIONAL RESOURCES:

Other Pop-Up Books

TITLE: *Dinosaur Skeletons*

PAPER ENGINEER: Keith Moseley

AUTHOR: John Malam

ILLUSTRATOR: Bob Cremins

PUBLISHER, COPYRIGHT DATE: Dell Publishing, c1991

ANNOTATION: This book is unique in its presentation: The pop-ups are white skeletons set against the color illustrations of the various types of dinosaurs.

TITLE: *Dinosaurs*

DESIGNER: Mike Sund

AUTHOR: Dylan M. Nash

ILLUSTRATOR: Bryn Barnard

PUBLISHER, COPYRIGHT DATE: Intervisual Books, c2007

ANNOTATION: Flaps, wheels, pop-ups, and pull-out tabs are used to present dinosaurs. Each two-page spread covers a topic such as the Cretaceous Period, fossils, extinction, and so on.

TITLE: *Dinosaurs in the Round*

AUTHOR: Jen Green

ILLUSTRATOR: Luis V. Rey

PUBLISHER, COPYRIGHT DATE: Design Eye Publishing, c2008

ANNOTATION: This book unfolds into a dramatic pop-up diorama of dinosaurs of the Triassic, Jurassic, and Cretaceous periods. An accompanying booklet provides information about the various dinosaurs.

TITLE: *Extreme Dinosaurs*

DESIGNER: Andy Jones

AUTHOR: Robert Mash

ILLUSTRATOR: Stuart Martin

PUBLISHER, COPYRIGHT DATE: Atheneum Books for Young Readers, c2007

ANNOTATION: Tabs, flaps, and a Velociraptor pop-up enhance this coverage, which is organized by clever topics: sprinters and plodders, oddballs, super heavyweights, and so on. It also has an Extreme Hall of Fame, with a table of the smallest, longest, biggest, and so forth, dinosaurs.

TITLE: *Pop-Up Dinosaur Danger*

PAPER ENGINEER: Nick Denchfield

AUTHOR: Macmillan Children's Books

ILLUSTRATOR: Anne Sharp

PUBLISHER, COPYRIGHT: Macmillan Children's Books, c2006

ANNOTATION: The dinosaur pop-ups in this book are rip-roaring! Short paragraphs provide the name with pronunciation, and important facts about the dinosaur. The arrangement is by dinosaur behavior (attackers, defenders, etc.), and there are also charts of comparison for the dinosaurs in each grouping.

Books with other Interactivity

TITLE: *Dinosaur Hunters*

PAPER ENGINEER: Alan Brown

AUTHOR: Jen Green

ILLUSTRATOR: Bob Nicholls (cover); Bob Nicholls (interior), Gian Paolo Faleshini, Martin Sanders, Gary Slater, Keith Williams, Joe Tucciarone, and Ray and Corinne Burrows

PUBLISHER, COPYRIGHT DATE: Running Book Publishers, c2007

ANNOTATION: Flaps and specimen tags and a "secret drawer" enhance this informative presentation of "the lost world of dinosaurs."

TITLE: *Dinosaurs*

AUTHOR: Stephanie Stansbie

ILLUSTRATORS: Robert Nicholls, James Robins, and Roar Publishing

PUBLISHER, COPYRIGHT: Little, Brown, c2008

ANNOTATION: The format is the handbook of a retiring paleontologist. Flaps, envelopes, and an accompanying chart bring interactivity to the abundant facts about dinosaurs.

Books without Interactivity

TITLE: *The Dinosaurs of Waterhouse Hawkins: An Illuminating History of Mr. Waterhouse Hawkins, Artist and Lecturer* (**informational**)

AUTHOR: Barbara Kerley

ILLUSTRATOR: Brian Selznick

PUBLISHER, COPYRIGHT DATE: Scholastic, c2001

ANNOTATION: Benjamin Waterhouse Hawkins was a Victorian artist who created life-size dinosaur models, including for the Smithsonian Institution.

TITLE: *I Like Dinosaurs* (**informational**; this is a series of books, each one about a different dinosaur)

AUTHOR: Michael William Skrepnick

ILLUSTRATOR: Michael William Skrepnick

PUBLISHER, COPYRIGHT DATE: Enslow Elementary, c2005

ANNOTATION: The series includes Tyrannosaurus Rex, Diplodocus, Sinosauropteryx, and Triceratops.

TITLE: *North American Dinosaurs* (**informational**; this is a series of books, each one about a different dinosaur)

AUTHOR: Various

PUBLISHER, COPYRIGHT DATE: Rourke Publishing, c2007

ANNOTATION: Included in the series are Allosaurus, Troodon, Hadrosaurus, Ankylosaurus, Triceratops, and Tyrannosaurus rex.

DVD

TITLE: *Bizarre Dinosaurs* (2009); 50 minutes (**informational**)

DISTRIBUTOR: PBS

ANNOTATION: This documentary introduces not-so-well-known dinosaurs with amazing appendages: Mamenchisaurus, Chasmosaurus, Parasaurolophus.

Websites

TITLE; AGENCY: *The Dinosauria*; University of California Museum of Paleontology

URL: http://www.ucmp.berkeley.edu/diapsids/dinosaur.html

ANNOTATION: Get the answers to common questions about dinosaurs. Also, follow the links to a slide show of photographs about the mounting of a T. rex exhibit.

TITLE; AGENCY: *Zoom Dinosaurs*; Enchanted Learning

URL: http://www.enchantedlearning.com/subjects/dinosaurs

ANNOTATION: This site is all about dinosaurs: "It is designed for students of all ages and levels of comprehension. . . . [with a] structure that allows readers to start at a basic level on each topic, and then to progress to much more advanced information as desired, simply by clicking on links."

Dinosaurs Matrix

Instructions to Students for Completing the Matrix:

1. Questions and answers are recorded on front and back.

2. Sources used are recorded in the first column, and the last box is used to write a summary when research is complete.

Name of dinosaur	How did it <u>look</u>? Size, height, weight, body covering, scales, and so on	What did it <u>eat</u>? Food, diet	How did it <u>move</u>? Walk, run, swim, fly

Resources:

Figure 6.6. Dinosaurs Matrix

From *Pop-Up Books: A Guide for Teachers and Librarians* by Nancy Bluemel and Rhonda Taylor. Santa Barbara, CA: Libraries Unlimited. Copyright © 2012.

Sample of matrix completed:

Stegosaurus	How did it <u>look</u>? Size, height, weight, body covering, scales, and so on	What did it <u>eat</u>? Food, diet	How did it <u>move</u>? Walk, run, swim, fly
Enchanted Learning	26–30 feet 6,800 pounds,	Plants, ferns, mosses, cycads	Walked on four legs
	17 plates on back, tail w/spikes, beak	horsetails, conifers	
	Stegosaurus was 26 to 30 feet long and weighed 6,800 pounds. It had a beak and 17 plates on its back. It also had spikes on its tail.	It ate plants. These included ferns, mosses, cycads, horsetails, and conifers.	Stegosaurus walked on four legs

From *Pop-Up Books: A Guide for Teachers and Librarians* by Nancy Bluemel and Rhonda Taylor. Santa Barbara, CA: Libraries Unlimited. Copyright © 2012.

THEME: Fables Today

TITLE: *Pop-Up Aesop*

PAPER ENGINEER: Arty Projects Studio

AUTHOR: John Harris

ILLUSTRATOR: Calef Brown

PUBLISHER, COPYRIGHT DATE: Getty Publications, c2005

ANNOTATION:

The first fable in this book is about the familiar tortoise and the hare; the other four are perhaps less familiar. The book is designed to encourage younger readers to create their own fables; a spinner in the back of the book allows them to select characters to add to their own fables. The pop-ups are sophisticated in movement, reminding one of puppets.

MAJOR CURRICULUM AREAS:

Language Arts
Literature (Diversity, Fables)

ACTIVITY OVERVIEW:

In this introductory activity to the fable, children can update the literary form of a fable to reflect their own interests.

DESCRIPTION OF ACTIVITY:

1. Share the concept of a fable with the children (see the website in the Additional Resources section). Then, share the fables in the book. Ask the children about any other Aesop fables that they might know and how they first learned them.
2. Then, ask the children about any fables they know that aren't from Aesop, being sure to point out that all cultures have fables. The teacher and librarian collaborate in identifying and introducing fables from other cultures to share with the children.
3. Have the children brainstorm a list of moral lessons that they still remember, passed along to them from others, such as parents, neighbors, teachers, and so on.
4. Have the each of the children select one moral lesson from their lists. Then, help the children brainstorm who might be characters (similar to Aesop and the fable) that could appear in a fable about their moral lessons. Assist each student in writing a short fable of her or his own.

5. For younger children, each one can illustrate her or his fable with the art technique of choice, including making a pop-up (see Figure 6.9 in "THEME: Time to Rhyme"). Then the child uses the illustration to help in the telling of her or his fable to the class. For older children, have them work in groups to devise a short skit illustrating their fables for presentation to the other children. At the end of each skit, the writer should remember to sum up in one sentence what the moral of the fable is.

ADDITIONAL RESOURCES:

Other Pop-Up Books

TITLE: *The Boy Who Cried Wolf*

PAPER ENGINEER: Carla Dijs

PUBLISHER, COPYRIGHT DATE: Little Simon, c1997

ANNOTATION: This familiar tale of the shepherd boy who cried wolf is charmingly rendered in a small book with simple but artful pop-ups. It is part of a series of four titles; the others are: *The Tortoise and the Hare*, *The Little Red Hen*, and *The Lion and the Mouse*.

Books without Interactivity

TITLE: *The Lion & The Mouse* (**fiction**)

ILLUSTRATOR: Jerry Pinkney

PUBLISHER, COPYRIGHT DATE: Little, Brown, c2009

ANNOTATION: In this wordless version of the well-known fable, placed in the African Serengeti, a small mouse saves the mighty lion.

TITLE: *The Tortoise and the Hare* (**fiction**)

AUTHORS: Aesop and Janet Stevens (adaptation)

ILLUSTRATOR: Janet Stevens

PUBLISHER, COPYRIGHT DATE: Holiday House, c1984

ANNOTATION: Dialog and colorfully attired characters bring the Aesop fable to life.

DVD

TITLE: *The Tortoise and the Hare* (an episode of the PBS *Reading Rainbow* television series); 30 minutes (**fiction, informational**)

DISTRIBUTOR: GPN Educational Media

ANNOTATION: In addition to the book being read, in this episode there are testimonials from kids who've faced difficulties, profiles of athletes, and demonstrations by students of the Japan International Karate Center.

Website

TITLE; AGENCY: *Aesop's Fables: Online Collection*; John R. Long (**informational for teacher**)

URL: http://www.aesopfables.com/

ANNOTATION: This online collection of fables can be accessed as text and as audio, supplemented with resources such as information about Aesop and charts of the morals of the fables.

THEME: Healthy Living: Nutrition and Exercise

TITLE: *I Will Not Ever Never Eat a Tomato Pop-Up!*

PAPER ENGINEER: Corinna Fletcher

AUTHOR: Lauren Child

ILLUSTRATOR: Lauren Child

PUBLISHER, COPYRIGHT DATE: Candlewick Press, c2000, 2007

AWARD ALERT: The original book was awarded the Kate Greenaway Medal (established by The [British] Library Association) in 2001.

ANNOTATION:

Part of the Charlie and Lola and series, this pop-up book reflects a common reaction of children: "I will not ever never." This is especially true when they are confronted with unfamiliar or popularly rejected foods, but this book demonstrates that it's all in how you see things.

MAJOR CURRICULUM AREAS:

Health
Math (Counting, Shapes, Measurement)
Physical Education

ACTIVITY OVERVIEW:

Helping children to understand how nutritious eating and exercise will fit into their lives helps to prepare them for lifelong health. This amusing pop-up book can be used to help them to consider what might be healthier choices.

DESCRIPTION OF ACTIVITY:

PART 1

1. Share the pop-up book with children, in which food dislikes change. Then, ask them what foods they already like. Help them to create a list of foods that represent the class's choices of foods that the students like to eat. Discuss with children the differences that there are among individual food preferences.
2. Introduce the concept of MyPlate to the children. The website in the Additional Resources for this activity has tips and resources and print resources, such as a coloring sheet. Have the children cut out shapes to match the foods that they have identified as being of geometric shapes. On each shape, write what food it is representing. Then, have each child identify where her or his shape goes on MyPlate—for example, does a donut go in the vegetable group?
3. Use a large chart of the MyPlate. Have children attach their shapes of food in the correct groups on the illustration. Help the children to see what groups of foods the class is consuming most often. Follow with a discussion of what foods MyPlate says that children should eat to stay healthy. Discuss with the children what is meant by healthy.
4. Return to the list generated by the children regarding their preferred food choices. Discuss which of those foods are healthier than others.

PART 2

1. Explain to children that a healthy lifestyle requires both good nutrition and exercise. Ask the children what physical activities (not necessarily formal games or exercises) that they do each day. Share with them a capture of daily activities that they don't necessarily consider to be exercise, such as walking to school or doing household chores (see website in Additional Resources of this section).
2. Discuss with the children ideas about how they might increase their activity level by five extra minutes each day (for older children) or by one additional activity (for younger children). Ask children to follow through for one week. After that time, talk with the children about their experiences.

ADDITIONAL RESOURCES:

Other Pop-Up Books

TITLE: *Ballet Magic: A Pop-Up Book*

AUTHOR: Emma Rose

ILLUSTRATOR: Jan Palmer

PUBLISHER, COPYRIGHT DATE: Cartwheel Books, c1996

ANNOTATION: This book shows a variety of ballet steps, with the practice leading to a performance on stage. The dancers are older children.

TITLE: *Just Like Mr Croc*

AUTHOR: Jo Lodge

PUBLISHER, COPYRIGHT DATE: Backpack Books, c2006

ANNOTATION: Similar to "Simon Says," Mr. Croc, in pop-ups, engages in physical activities. Bold primary colors and the simple illustrations are striking.

TITLE: *Sam's Pizza*

PAPER ENGINEER: David Pelham

AUTHOR: David Pelham

ILLUSTRATORS: David Pelham and Mick Brownfield

PUBLISHER, COPYRIGHT DATE: Dutton Children's Books, c1996

ANNOTATION: This clever pop-up book is a pizza pie in a pizza box. Each layer of the pizza is a page in the book, revealing the storyline about Sam's creation of a very icky pizza for his unsuspecting sister, Samantha. Flaps on each layer reveal the real ingredient!

Other Books with Interactivity

TITLE: *Freddie Works Out: A Pull-the-Tab Book*

PAPER ENGINEER: Ruth Tilden

PUBLISHER, COPYRIGHT DATE: Hyperion Books for Children, c1995

ANNOTATION: This small book highlights physical fitness for younger kids. And, who could resist joining in exercises with a green frog in red shorts and a white t-shirt!

TITLE: *Waddle!*

AUTHOR: Rufus Butler Seder

PUBLISHER, COPYRIGHT DATE: Workman Publishing, c2009

ANNOTATION: As each page is turned, the Scanimation technique (similar to a hologram with motion) gives the illusion that the animals are leaping, prancing, and so on. And, each page asks a question, such as "Can you hop like a frog?"

Books without Interactivity

TITLE: *The Berenstain Bears and Too Much Junk Food* (**fiction**)

AUTHORS: Stan Berenstain and Jan Berenstain

ILLUSTRATORS: Stan Berenstain and Jan Berenstain

PUBLISHER, COPYRIGHT DATE: Random House, c1985

ANNOTATION: Too much junk food is not good for the Berenstain Bear family, and Mama and Dr. Grizzly help everyone to change diets and to exercise.

TITLE: *Eating Green* (**informational**)

AUTHOR: Sunita Apte

PUBLISHER, COPYRIGHT DATE: Bearport, c2010

ANNOTATION: Covers what it means to "eat green," buying organic food, grass-fed animals, the journey from producer to market, and so on.

TITLE: *Gregory, the Terrible Eater* (**fiction**)

AUTHOR: Mitchell Sharmat

ILLUSTRATORS: Jose Aruego and Ariane Dewey

PUBLISHER, COPYRIGHT DATE: Scholastic, c1980

ANNOTATION: Gregory doesn't eat standard fare for goats: he is a "terrible" eater who prefers fruits, veggies, and the like.

TITLE: *Wallie Exercises* (**fiction**)

AUTHOR: Steve Ettinger

ILLUSTRATOR: Pete Proctor

PUBLISHER, COPYRIGHT DATE: Active Spud Press, 2011

ANNOTATION: Wallie the dog is definitely not active. With help, he learns to exercise.

DVD

TITLE: *Gregory, the Terrible Eater* (episode of the PBS *Reading Rainbow* television series); 30 minutes (**fiction, informational**)

DISTRIBUTOR: GPN Educational Media

ANNOTATION: Gregory the goat will not eat shoes and tin cans; he wants only fruits, vegetables, eggs, and orange juice. In addition to the book being read, in this episode LeVar Burton visits a restaurant where workers dress as goats, the kitchen of the San Diego Zoo, zoo animals eating, and a New York hotel where children cook a gourmet meal.

Websites

TITLE; AGENCY: *Kids Eat Right*; American Dietetic Association and American Dietetic Association Foundation (**informational for teacher**)

URL: http://www.eatright.org/kids

ANNOTATION: The site provides information about shopping smart, cooking healthy, and eating right to help kids "grow healthy."

TITLE; AGENCY: *Mornings on PBS Kids: Exercise: Family Activities to Do Together*; PBS

ULR: http://www.pbs.org/parents/preschool/exercise.html

ANNOTATION: Hints on how to incorporate exercise into children's daily routines and has links to books to share with children.

TITLE; AGENCY: *Choose MyPlate.gov*; United States Department of Agriculture.

URL: http://www.choosemyplate.gov/index.html

ANNOTATION: The site explains the food groups in the MyPlate concept of healthy eating. It includes tips and resources and print materials, such as a coloring sheet and graphics.

THEME: Noah's Ark

TITLE: *The Ark: A Pop-Up*

PAPER ENGINEER: Matthew Reinhart

AUTHOR: Matthew Reinhart

ILLUSTRATOR: Matthew Reinhart

PUBLICATION, COPYRIGHT DATE: Little Simon, c2005

ANNOTATION:

This retelling of the Bible story of Noah's ark is captured by complex pop-ups of paper collage illustrations.

MAJOR CURRICULUM AREAS FOR ACTIVITY:

Math (Counting, Measurement)
Science (Nature: Animals, Weather)

ACTIVITY OVERVIEW:

Use the pop-up book to introduce children to the story of Noah's Ark and its meaning, to counting, and to basic natural science about animals and weather (rain and rainbows).

DESCRIPTION OF ACTIVITY:

1. After sharing the pop-up book with the children, ask them: What is the story of Noah's Ark saying to us?
2. As the pop-up book is shared with the children, have them count all the animals in the book. How many are in the book?
3. Assist the children in graphing how many of the book's animals fly or crawl or walk.
4. Ask the children: What would you have to bring along on the ark for the animals to eat? Assist children in researching the diets of various animals on the ark, in print or digital resources.
5. Use Jan Brett's home page website (see the Additional Resources for this section) to download printouts of Noah, the ark, the animals, and trees to create a coloring mural about Noah's ark. Have the children color the images before they are pasted to the mural.

EXTENSIONS

1. Show the children how to fold a simple origami animal (see the Additional Resources for this section and the websites that have illustrated instructions) and then have the children fold their own animals.
2. Ask the children why there is a rainbow in the story of Noah's Ark. Then use the website in the Additional Resources for this section for instructions on helping the children to conduct experiments with creating rainbows and to gain understanding about the science behind them.
3. Add a rain gauge to an outside window of the classroom. Have the children graph the rain over a set period of time. Discuss with them how many inches of rain it might take to "flood."

ADDITIONAL RESOURCES:

Other Pop-Up Books

TITLE: *The Animals Went in Two by Two: A Noah's Ark Pop-Up Book*

PAPER ENGINEERS: Helen Balmer and Martin Taylor

ILLUSTRATORS: Jan Pieńkowski and David Walser (assistant illustrator)

PUBLISHER, COPYRIGHT DATE: Candlewick Press, 2003

ANNOTATION: A counting-themed rendition that combines humor with paper engineering.

Books without Interactivity

TITLE: *First Animal Encyclopedia* (**informational**)

AUTHOR: Penelope Arlon

ILLUSTRATOR:

PUBLISHER, COPYRIGHT DATE: DK Publishing, c2004

ANNOTATION: Photographs bring to life this introductory coverage of the animals of the world.

TITLE: *Naamah and the Ark at Night* (**fiction**)

AUTHOR: Susan Campbell Bartoletti

ILLUSTRATOR: Holly Meade

PUBLISHER, COPYRIGHT DATE: Candlewick Press, c2011

ANNOTATION: Noah's wife Naamah sings nightly to the animals and her family during their forty days in the Ark.

TITLE: *On Noah's Ark* (**fiction**)

AUTHOR: Jan Brett

ILLUSTRATOR: Jan Brett

PUBLISHER, COPYRIGHT DATE: Putnam, c2003

ANNOTATION: Brett's distinctive art style lends a new freshness to this timeless story, as seen through the eyes of Noah's granddaughter.

Websites

TITLE; AGENCY: Jan Brett's website; Jan Brett

URL: http://www.janbrett.com/newsnotes/on_noahs_ark_newsnotes_page_1.htm

ANNOTATION: Visit the illustrated web pages to find Jan Brett's explanation of how the book *On Noah's Ark* came to be conceived and created—the feel of the pages is similar to a graphic novel.

TITLE; AGENCY: *Names of Males, Females, Babies, and Groups of Animals*; Enchanted Learning

URL: http://www.enchantedlearning.com/subjects/animals/Animalbabies.shtml

ANNOTATION: Click on the chart's alphabetical links of animal names to find information about animals, including a line drawing of them and a description of their diets.

TITLE; AGENCY: *On Noah's Ark Coloring Mural*; Jan Brett's website

URL: http://janbrett.com/mural/on_noahs_ark_coloring_mural.htm

ANNOTATION: This page has links to the images of Noah, the ark, the animals, and trees, that can be used for creating a mural. They are the same images that can be downloaded to create individual coloring pages: http://janbrett.com/activities_pages_artwork.htm.

TITLE; AGENCY: *Origami KinderCrafts*; Enchanted Learning

URL: http://www.enchantedlearning.com/crafts/origami

ANNOTATION: This page has simple illustrations and steps for creating an origami jumping frog.

TITLE; AGENCY: *Simple Origami Lamb*; DLTK's Growing Together

URL: http://www.dltk-kids.com/animals/simple_origami_lamb.htm

ANNNOTATION: This web page, including a printable version, provides easy-to-follow steps and line-drawing steps for folding a simple origami lamb (the head).

TITLE; AGENCY: *Rainbow Experiments*; First-School.WS Preschool Activities and Crafts

URL: http://www.first-school.ws/activities/science/rainbow-experiment.htm

ANNOTATION: This web page provides a preschool lesson plan to help children create a rainbow indoors (in a jar of water) and outdoors (with a garden hose).

THEME: Reading and Library Use

TITLE: *The Monster Who Loved Books*

PAPER ENGINEER: Keith Faulkner

ILLUSTRATOR: Jonathan Lambert

PUBLISHER, COPYRIGHT DATE: Orchard Books, c2002

ANNOTATION:

A visit to Storyland teaches a book-eating monster about the joys of reading.

MAJOR CURRICULUM AREAS:

Language arts (Library Use, Reading)
Literature

ACTIVITY OVERVIEW:

At the beginning of the school year, teachers and school library media specialists will enjoy using this book to introduce children to the joys of reading books and using the library to explore their own interests.

DESCRIPTON OF ACTIVITY:

1. After reading *The Monster Who Loved Books* to the children, provide them with some basic instructions on how to handle books so that they can be enjoyed repeatedly. Then ask the children how they would handle pop-up books differently than other books.
2. Discuss with children what types of interests that Bradley, the little boy in *The Monster Who Loved Books*, had in the story. Ask children what they like to do when they play. Examples often given by children include responses such as playing ballgames, playing with their dogs, playing with dolls, and so on. From a group of library books that you have pre-selected for typical responses, pass out books at random to the children. Allow time for them to look at the books. Then, have them share what they like or don't like about their selections. Engage children in a discussion about whether they would like to read another book similar to the one that they have.
3. If doing this lesson at home or in the classroom, make a visit to the library. Take the children to the Easy section and let each child select a book that interests her or him. Assist students in the process of checking the books out of the library, explaining why each step is required.
4. Discuss with the children what they enjoyed about their library visit. Share their observations with the librarian.

ADDITIONAL RESOURCES:

Other Pop-Up Books

TITLE: *We're Bored!*

AUTHOR: Pamela Hall

ILLUSTRATOR: Nicola Slater

PUBLISHER/COPYRIGHT DATE: Piggy Toes Press, c2005

ANNOTATION: A twin boy and girl who are bored discover the wonder of books.

Other Books with Interactivity

TITLE: *Little Bo Peep's Library Book*

AUTHOR: Cressida Cowell

ILLUSTRATOR: Cressida Cowell

PUBLISHER, COPYRIGHT DATE: Orchard Books, c1999

ANNOTATION: Little Bo Peep goes in search of her sheep and looks for hints in Mother Goose's library. Pull tabs are actually the spines of miniature books that are the stories of various Mother Goose characters.

Books without Interactivity

TITLE: *D.W.'s Library Card* (**fiction**)

AUTHOR: Marc Brown

ILLUSTRATOR: Marc Brown

PUBLISHER, COPYRIGHT DATE: Little Brown Books for Young Readers, c2003

ANNOTATION: Arthur the Aardvark's little sister, D.W., is eager to have a library card. It takes Arthur to help her understand how to take care of library books while still enjoying them.

TITLE: *I Took My Frog to the Library* (**fiction**)

AUTHOR: Eric A. Kimmel

ILLUSTRATOR: Blanche Sims

PUBLISHER, COPYRIGHT DATE: Puffin, c1992

ANNOTATION: Bridgett takes her animal friends (chicken, python, elephant, etc.) to the library, with predictable consequences.

TITLE: *The Librarian from Black Lagoon* (**fiction**)

AUTHOR: Mike Thaler

ILLUSTRATOR: Jared Lee

PUBLISHER, COPYRIGHT DATE: Cartwheel Books, c2008

ANNOTATION: Rumors about the school librarian (termed the "laminator") lead Hubie to dread his visit to the library.

TITLE: *Tomás and the Library Lady* (**fiction**)

AUTHOR: Pat Mora

ILLUSTRATOR: Raul Colon

PUBLISHER, COPYRIGHT DATE: Dragonfly Books, c2000 (also available in Spanish)

ANNOTATION: A librarian brought books into the life of Tomás Rivera, a child in a migrant worker family, who would eventually become a university chancellor.

DVD

TITLE: *Elmo and the Bookaneers: Pirates Who Love to Read* (2009); 41 minutes (**fiction**)

DISTRIBUTOR: PBS Kids (http://shop.pbskids.org/)

ANNOTATION: The Bookaneers come to Sesame Street in search of book treasures, because they love to read. Can Elmo learn something from them?

Website

TITLE; AGENCY: *The Library*; Enchanted Learning (**informational for teachers**)

URL: http://www.enchantedlearning.com/library

ANNOTATION: Worksheets, information, and activities about the library (for grades 5–6).

THEME: Singing as We Go Along

TITLE 1: *Wheels on the Bus*

PAPER ENGINEER: Rodger Smith

AUTHOR: Paul O. Zelinsky (adaptation)

ILLUSTRATOR: Paul O. Zelinsky

> **AWARD ALERT:** Zelinksy is a 1998 Caldecott Award Medalist and had Honor books in 1995, 1987, and 1985.

PUBLISHER, COPYRIGHT DATE: Orchard Books, c1990

ANNOTATION:

The wheels on the bus go 'round and 'round, and the movable parts of this now-classic interactive book accompany the rhythm.

TITLE 2: *The Whistle on the Train: A Rollicking Railroad Pop-Up Book!*

PAPER ENGINEER: Gene Vosough

AUTHOR: Margaret McNamara

ILLUSTRATOR: Richard Egielski

PUBLISHER, COPYRIGHT DATE: Hyperion Books, c2008

ANNOTATION:

This version of the popular song "Wheels on the Bus" uses a train as the moving vehicle with original verses for the familiar tune. The pop-ups move to accompany the lyrics that are the text.

MAJOR CURRICULM AREAS FOR THE ACTIVITY:

Music
Social Studies

ACTIVITY OVERVIEW:

Song is an important part of children's everyday lives, whether at scout gatherings, on family outings, on camping trips, or at school, and rounds are one of the most popular forms of group singing.

DESCRIPTION OF ACTIVITY:

1. Share the interactive book *Wheels on the Bus*. Then, have the children sing the song.
2. Share the pop-up book *The Whistle on the Train*. Then, have the children sing the song to the same tune as the "Wheels on the Bus." Discuss with the children the fact that the tune is the same but the words are different (compare and contrast).
3. Discuss with the children what songs they already know and like. Ask them about the occasions on which they sing these songs: camping trips, sitting in the back seat on car travels, and so on.
4. Have the children, as a group, sing some of the more familiar songs that they identified.
5. Help the children to make up their own words to one of these familiar tunes, to be sung if they were going to a special place or occasion, such as visiting the zoo, a cookout, church, and so on.
6. Record the children singing their original songs and let them listen to their singing. Make a copy of the songs for them to share at home.

EXTENSION

Have groups of children sing their original songs while accompanied by other children playing recorders or other musical instruments.

ADDITIONAL RESOURCES:

Other Pop-Up Books

TITLE: *Jingle Bells: A Pop-Up Holiday Song Book*

PAPER ENGINEER: Michael Caputo

ILLUSTRATOR: Eren Blanquet Unten

PUBLISHER, COPYRIGHT DATE: Price Stern Sloan, c2009

ANNOTATION: The pop-ups leap from the pages, illustrating this familiar seasonal song.

TITLE: *On Top of Spaghetti: A Silly Song Book*

PAPER ENGINEER: Cintya Roman

DESIGNER: Treesha Runnells

ILLUSTRATOR: Gene Barretta

PUBLISHER, COPYRIGHT DATE: Piggy Toes Press, c2004

ANNOTATION: The humorous illustration and flaps and pop-ups follow the progress of the stray meatball, out of the restaurant and out into the world.

TITLE: *Pop Goes the Weasel: A Silly Song Book*

AUTHOR: Annie Auerbach

ILLUSTRATOR: Christopher Gaisey

DESIGNER: Melanie Random

PUBLISHER, COPYRIGHT DATE: Piggy Toes Press, c2005

ANNOTATION: A boy sings of his pet weasel, whose white fur encounters paint cans and a lot of other things as he races through the house.

TITLE: *Row Your Boat*

AUTHOR: Anthony Lishak

ILLUSTRATOR: Graham Percy

PUBLISHER, COPYRIGHT DATE: DK Publishing, c1999

ANNOTATION: This pop-up and push-tab book uses mice characters to illustrate the familiar "Row Your Boat" refrain. A nice touch is the framing that appears around each scene as the pages are turned.

TITLE: *We're Going on a Bear Hunt: A Celebratory Pop-Up Edition*

AWARD ALERT: The original book was recognized as a 1990 Horn Book Honor title.

AUTHOR: Michael Rosen (adaptation)

ILLUSTRATOR: Helen Oxenbury

PUBLISHER, COPYRIGHT DATE: Little Simon, c2007

ANNOTATION: Three children and their father have an adventure hunting a bear; pop-ups, tabs, flaps, and sounds add to the charm of the original book's words and illustrations.

Other Books with Interactivity

TITLE: *Knick Knack Paddywhack*

PAPER ENGINEER: Andrew Baron

AUTHOR: Paul Zelinksy

ILLUSTRATOR: Paul O. Zelinksy

PUBLISHER, COPYRIGHT DATE: Dutton, c2002

ANNOTATION: Wheels, flaps, and pull tabs provide the motion to match the lyrics of the familiar song.

AWARD ALERT: Andrew Baron received the 2004 Meggendorfer Prize, recognizing the paper engineering in this pop-up book. The prize is given biennially by The Movable Book Society.

TITLE: *Anthony Browne presents the Animal Fair: A Spectacular Pop-Up*

AUTHOR: Anthony Browne

PUBLISHER, COPYRIGHT DATE: Walker, 2002

ANNOTATION: Follow a pop-up book rendition of the song "I Went to the Animal Fair."

TITLE: *Old MacDonald Had a Farm* (**fiction**)

AUTHOR: Salina Yoon

ILLUSTRATOR: Salina Yoon

PUBLISHER, COPYRIGHT DATE: Price Stern Sloan, 2008

ANNOTATATION: The song "Old MacDonald Had a Farm" is pictured with the various animals and is brought to new life with these pop-ups.

TITLE: *Take Me Out to the Ballgame*

PAPER ENGINEER: Gene Vosough

AUTHOR: Jack Norworth

ILLUSTRATOR: John Stadler

PUBLISHER, COPYRIGHT DATE: Little Simon, 2005

ANNOTATION: This pop-up version of "Take Me Out to the Ballgame" follows the action and words of the song, but with characters cast as animals.

Books without Interactivity

TITLE: *Amelia Bedelia Goes Camping* (**fiction**)

AUTHOR: Peggy Parish

ILLUSTRATOR: Lynn Sweat

PUBLISHER, COPYRIGHT DATE: Greenwillow Books, c2006

ANNOTATION: Another in the series of books about a beloved character. When housekeeper Amelia Bedelia goes on a camping trip with her employers, she interprets all instructions literally, with typically funny results.

DVD

TITLE: *Hot Potatoes: The Best of the Wiggles* (2010); 123 minutes (**fiction**)

DISTRIBUTOR: Warner

ANNOTATION: Thirty-five of their most popular songs are performed by the children's entertainment group the Wiggles. Included is "Twinkle, Twinkle, Little Star."

Website

TITLE; AGENCY: *NIEH Kids' Page: Young and Young at Heart!*; National Institute of Environmental Health Sciences

URL: http://kids.niehs.nih.gov/musicchild.htm

ANNOTATION: Click on the alphabetized titles of the list of familiar children's songs to see the lyrics and/or to hear the music to the song.

THEME: Symbols of America

TITLE: *America the Beautiful*

PAPER ENGINEER: Robert Sabuda

AUTHOR: Robert Sabuda

ILLUSTRATOR: Robert Sabuda

PUBLISHER, COPYRIGHT DATE: Little Simon, c2004

ANNOTATION:

The beloved patriotic song "America the Beautiful" is translated into a pop-ups that are almost all entirely done in white, placed against solid-color backgrounds. The pop-ups capture important and diverse American structures and locations: the Golden Gate Bridge, the Great Plains, Mount Rushmore, Mesa Verde, the Mississippi River, the U.S. Capitol, and the Statue of Liberty.

MAJOR CURRICULUM AREAS:

Fine Arts (Art)
Language Arts
Social Studies

ACTIVITY OVERVIEW:

Symbols are an important part of identity. The topic of symbols of America provides a way to help students become familiar with the facts of American history and consider the meaning of these symbols in their lives.

DESCRIPTION OF ACTIVITY:

1. Introduce students to the concept of "symbol." Then share with them the pop-up book, asking them to identify the symbols that they see in it.
2. In groups, have the students use discussion to generate lists of well-known symbols of America. Compile a collective list of the symbols to share with the class and decide which ones the class will research. Each student will be responsible for one symbol, which will be researched using library print and digital resources.
3. Using the information that is located, each student will create a fan book, which will contain facts and illustrations done by the student (digital clip art

can be used as templates or the art can be original) (see Figure 6.7 at the end of this theme). The fan books will be kept on display in the classroom for a set period of time determined by the teacher. While on display, the students will examine and learn the information, for which they will then be responsible in the game (see steps 4 and 5) to be played.

4. Students will play a modified version of the television game show (also available as a DVD game) of *Who Wants to be a Millionaire?*

5. The students will assume the various roles from the TV show, including a team of three collaborating contestants, a master of ceremonies who asks the questions, the audience, a scorekeeper, and a panel of friends (see Figure 6.8 at the end of this theme). The roles will rotate so that everyone has a chance to participate in various ways. The fan books will be used for the questions. Provide a template for the question format to the master of ceremonies. Teams generate points. The team with the highest number of points is designated the "American millionaire."

EXTENSIONS

1. Students research other symbols that represent America but which did not get on the original list (generated during the brainstorming) from which students selected topics.

2. Students draw their own symbols of America, to be used for a postage stamp or coin (point out the U.S. quarters that have symbols of individual states, and postage stamps and their symbols).

3. Students brainstorm what are "typical" American foods. Students research, in the library's print and digital resources, the origins of these "American" foods. Then, they share experiences with foods that are of their own communities or families. Discuss with students the idea that American identity encompasses.

ADDITIONAL RESOURCES:

Other Pop-Up Books

TITLE: *"America the Beautiful": The Famous Song by Katharine Lee Bates*

PAPER ENGINEER: Carrie Jordan

AUTHOR: Calvert Gamwell

ILLUSTRATOR: Carrie Jordan

PUBLISHER, COPYRIGHT DATE: Carah Kids, c2003

ANNOTATION: The words to the first (and most well-known) verse of the song are illustrated with double-page pop-ups that are done in watercolor.

TITLE: *Pop-Up Book about the Pledge of Allegiance Illustrated with Eight of America's Most Well-known National Monuments*

PAPER ENGINEER: Carrie Jordan

AUTHOR: Calvert Gamwell

ILLUSTRATOR: Carrie Jordan

PUBLISHER, COPYRIGHT DATE: Carah Kids, c2002

ANNOTATION: Each double-page spread of pop-ups illustrates not only the pledge of allegiance but these national monuments: the U.S. Capitol building, Iwo Jima Memorial, Mount Rushmore, the Liberty Bell and Independence Hall, the Lincoln Memorial, the Washington Monument, the Vietnam Veterans Memorial, and the Statue of Liberty. Each memorial is accompanied by a short description.

TITLE: *"The Star-spangled Banner": America's National Anthem by Francis Scott Key*

PAPER ENGINEER: Carrie Jordan

DESIGNER: Carrie Jordan

AUTHOR: Calvert Gamwell

ILLUSTRATOR: Carrie Jordan

PUBLISHER, COPYRIGHT DATE: Carah Kids, c2002

ANNOTATION: The words to the national anthem are the text that illustrates double-page spreads of recognizable American landmarks, activities, and events, from baseball games to the White House.

Books without Interactivity

TITLE: *How to Bake an American Pie* (**informational**)

AUTHOR: Karma Wilson

ILLUSTRATOR: Raul Colon

PUBLISHER, COPYRIGHT DATE: Margaret K. McElderry, c2007

ANNOTATION: The American Pie is created through the verses of "America the Beautiful," interspersed with values such as justice, freedom, forgiveness, and so on.

TITLE: *Oh Say Can You See? America's Symbols, Landmarks, and Inspiring Words* (**informational**)

AUTHOR: Sheila Keenan

ILLUSTRATOR: Ann Boyajian

PUBLISHER, COPYRIGHT DATE: Scholastic, c2004

ANNOTATION: American icons, such the Bill of Rights, the bald eagle, the White House, the flag, and so on, are introduced with facts and color drawings.

TITLE: *The Postal Service Guide to U.S. Stamps* (**informational**)

PUBLISHER: The U.S. Postal Service (http://www.usps.com), 2011 is the 38th edition

DVD

TITLE: *My America: A Poetry Atlas of the United States* (episode of the PBS *Reading Rainbow* PBS television series); 30 minutes (**fiction, informational**)

DISTRIBUTOR: GPN Educational Media

ANNOTATION: There is a poem for each region of America the Beautiful, and this episode highlights reading about Hawaii, New England, and Tennessee. In addition to the book being read, in this episode kids from around the country share information about their home states.

Website

TITLE; AGENCY: *H.I.P Pocket Change: Coins and Medals*; United States Treasury, United States Mint.

URL: http://www.usmint.gov/kids/coinsMedals

ANNOTATION: This is the site to visit for definitive information about the issuance of, and history behind the symbols of, the Presidential dollar coins, the Westward Journey nickel series, the Native American dollar coins, the state quarter coins, and so on.

TITLE; AGENCY: *Who Wants to Be a Millionaire?* (online game) DisneyABC Domestic Television

URL: http://millionairetv.com/game/index.html

ANNOTATION: This web addition to the television show allows viewers to play the game online (no prizes!).

Fan Book

One **8 ½ × 11-inch piece of sturdier paper (white or color)** can be cut into four fan ribs (2 ¾ inches wide by 8 ½ inches tall).
One 28 × 22-inch piece of paper can be cut into 21 ribs.

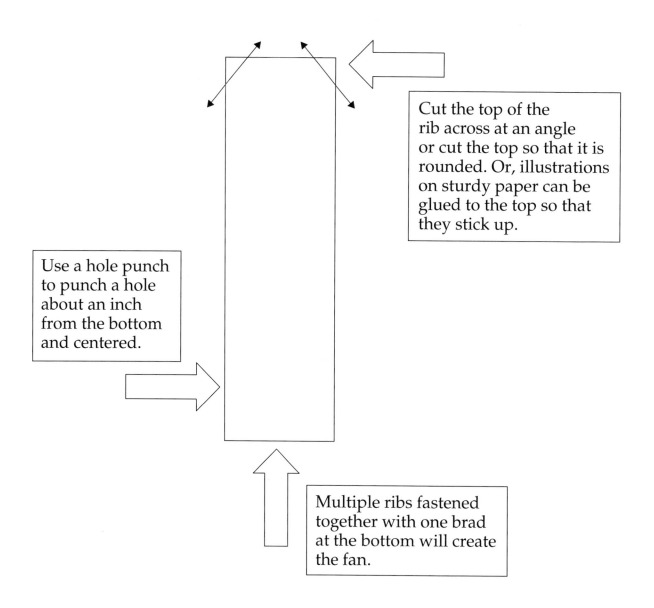

Cut the top of the rib across at an angle or cut the top so that it is rounded. Or, illustrations on sturdy paper can be glued to the top so that they stick up.

Use a hole punch to punch a hole about an inch from the bottom and centered.

Multiple ribs fastened together with one brad at the bottom will create the fan.

Figure 6.7. Fan Book

Making "Who Wants to be a Millionaire?"– Type Questions

Instructions for students:

The question should be one sentence.
The question should have four possible answers (A, B, C, D).
The answers should be parallel in structure (such as they are all nouns or all names, etc.).

Sample Question

QUESTION:

What is the name of the official home of the President of the United States?

    A. The Capitol Building
    B. Graceland
    C. Monticello
    D. The White House

Figure 6.8. Making "Who Wants to be a Millionaire?"–Type Questions

From *Pop-Up Books: A Guide for Teachers and Librarians* by Nancy Bluemel and Rhonda Taylor. Santa Barbara, CA: Libraries Unlimited. Copyright © 2012.

THEME: Time to Rhyme

TITLE: *A Pop-Up Book of Nursery Rhymes*

PAPER ENGINEER: Matthew Reinhart

ILLUSTRATOR: Matthew Reinhart

PUBLISHER, COPYRIGHT DATE: Little Simon, c2009

ANNOTATION:

This elaborate pop-up book re-enlivens traditional Mother Goose nursery rhymes in a selection that includes favorites such as "Mary Had a Little Lamb," "Old Mother Hubbard," "I'm a Little Teapot," and so forth.

MAJOR CURRICULUM AREAS:

Fine Arts (Art)
Language Arts

ACTIVITY OVERVIEW:

Rhyme enriches our everyday lives, and this activity emphasizes that fact to children; it also provides them the opportunity to try their hands at this special type of verse.

DESCRIPTION OF ACTIVITY:

1. Share the pop-up book with the children. As it is shared, discuss with them the concept of rhyme (words that sound the same) and where it is used in the book. Help them to see that the rhyme adds to the humor of the book, as do the pop-ups.
2. Offer the children a common word (such as bee) and ask them to think of another word that sounds the same (such as see) (see the Additional Resources for a website of rhyming words).
3. The teacher and librarian collaborate to schedule a library story time in which the librarian will read aloud several books in which the story is written in rhyme. Discuss the rhymes with the children.
4. Help the children to pick a theme for a class book (such as seasonal or a special event at school).
5. Depending on the age/ability of the children, assist them in composing a two-word rhyme that can be printed for them on an eight-by five-inch color page. Older children can independently write a rhyme of their own creation and of any length (remind them to leave room for the pop-up illustration to be added). The children then illustrate the rhyme with a simple pop-up (see Figure 6.9 at the end of this theme, or use Robert Sabuda's website in the Additional Resources section).

EXTENSIONS

1. Talk about where the children might encounter rhymes in their everyday lives, in commercials on television, cheers, hip hop, jump rope, and so on.

2. Collaborate with other teachers to get a small group of older students to demonstrate jump-rope rhymes to the younger children and to share how they learned those rhymes (such as other children or siblings taught them).

3. As a class, compose a rhyme to be mounted on the Giggle Poetry website (see the Additional Resources for this section); it should be about a topic selected by the children.

ADDITIONAL RESOURCES:

Other Pop-Up Books

TITLE: *Crazy Pops: Silly Rhymes and Crazy Pop-Ups*

PAPER ENGINEER: Keith Faulkner

ILLUSTRATOR: Jonathan Lambert

PUBLISHER, COPYRIGHT DATE: Borders Press, 1998

ANNOTATION: As each double-page spread is turned, a large pop-up captures the animal being portrayed in a rhyme that describes its antics, such as the water-skiing horse, Lee.

TITLE: *The Movable Mother Goose*

PAPER ENGINEERS: Robert Sabuda and Matthew Reinhart (additional design work)

ILLUSTRATOR: Robert Sabuda

PUBLISHER, COPYRIGHT DATE: Little Simon, c1999

ANNOTATION: The addition of shiny paper to enhance the amazingly elaborate pop-ups makes the rhymes more magical.

Other Books with Interactivity

TITLE: *If You Love a Nursery Rhyme: A Treasury of Classic Nursery Rhymes*

PAPER ENGINEER: Alan Brown

DESIGNER: Laura Hambleton

ILLUSTRATOR: Susanna Lockheart

PUBLISHER, COPYRIGHT DATE: Barron's Educational Series, c2008

ANNOTATION: The action of popular nursery rhymes occurs with the transformation that slides with the turning of the pages.

TITLE: *Over the Moon! A Collection of Best-Loved Nursery Rhymes*

ILLUSTRATORS: David Melling and Richard Amari (typography)

PUBLISHER, COPYRIGHT DATE: Dutton Children's Books, c1999

ANNOTATION: Cardboard-weight nursery rhyme characters, in bright primary colors, slide across the pages to illustrate the action of the familiar rhymes.

Books without Interactivity

TITLE: *Mary Engelbreit's Mother Goose: One Hundred Best-Loved Verses* (**fiction**)

AUTHOR: Mary Engelbreit

ILLUSTRATOR: Mary Englebreit

PUBLISHER, DATE: HarperCollins, 2005

ANNOTATION: Engelbreit's distinctive illustration style enlivens a hundred familiar Mother Goose rhymes. Included is Engelbreit's description of the approaches that she took in illustrating the book.

DVD

TITLE: *Jim Henson's Mother Goose Stories* (2005); 64 minutes (**fiction**)

DISTRIBUTOR: Lionsgate

ANNOTATION: The video has six Mother Goose stories: "Humpty Dumpty," "Mother Hubbard," "Little Boy Blue," "It's Raining, It's Pouring," "Duke of York," "Tommy Tucker," "Dicky Birds & Little Girl with A Curl."

Websites

TITLE; AGENCY: *Giggle Poetry*; Meadowbrook Press

A Simple Pop-Up Card

Steps for the activity:

1. Each child will need **two 8 ½ × 11-inch pieces of paper (white or color)**. One of the pieces should be sturdy.

2. Have each child write a rhyme of her or his own creation in a notebook or on the computer.

3. Demonstrate how to make the pop-up base and card (instructions follow), using **scissors** to make the single cut needed for the base.

4. Assist the child as needed in **gluing** the base into the card.

5. Have the child add a **figure** to the pop-up base (such as an original drawing on sturdy paper, a cut-out picture glued to a sturdier paper backing, etc.). The figure should illustrate the rhyme that was written.

6. Have the child write the rhyme in the card (or print it out on the computer and then glue it into the card).

Figure 6.9. A Simple Pop-Up Card

Steps for demonstrating a simple pop-up base and card:

1. Fold one 8 ½ × 11-inch piece of paper (color or white) in half so that it becomes 5 1/2 × 8 inches in size. This will become the outside of the pop-up card. Set it aside.

2. For the inside of the card (the pop-up base), fold the second, sturdier piece of 8 ½ × 11-inch piece of paper in half to become 5 ½ × 8 ½ inches. Then, fold it in half once again, so that it is now 4 × 5 ½ inches.

3. Hold the scissors in one hand. For the twice-folded piece of paper, hold it in the other hand by the corner that is folded. The loose ends will be free. Your thumb should be parallel to the 5 ½-inch side of the paper (the longer side). Hold your thumb as close as possible to the longer side of the paper. Use the scissors to make one cut (approximately one inch in length) next to your thumb (the right side of your thumb if you're right handed) and perpendicular to the short side of the paper.

4. Carefully unfold the paper. It now has two parallel cuts in the center of it. Push the center of the parallel cuts (a rectangle) out from the paper while pushing the creases beside it backwards. You have created what looks like a little step or platform. This is the base for the pop-up.

5. Glue a cut-out figure to the pop-up base.

From *Pop-Up Books: A Guide for Teachers and Librarians* by Nancy Bluemel and Rhonda Taylor. Santa Barbara, CA: Libraries Unlimited. Copyright © 2012.

Step 3

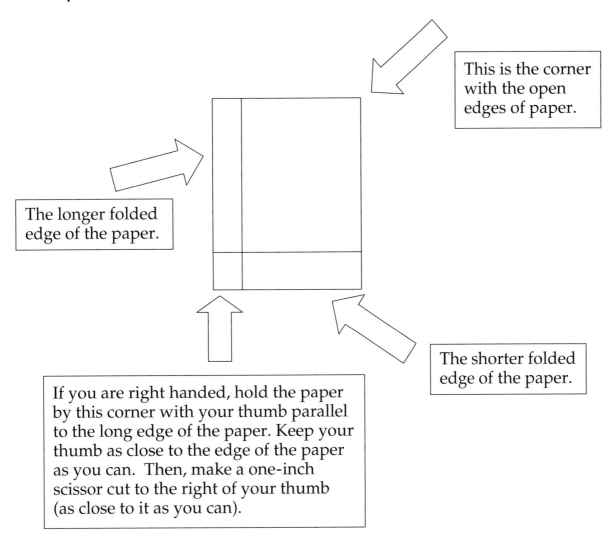

This is the corner with the open edges of paper.

The longer folded edge of the paper.

The shorter folded edge of the paper.

If you are right handed, hold the paper by this corner with your thumb parallel to the long edge of the paper. Keep your thumb as close to the edge of the paper as you can. Then, make a one-inch scissor cut to the right of your thumb (as close to it as you can).

Step 4

The first piece of paper (that was folded once) is glued to the back of the pop-up base.

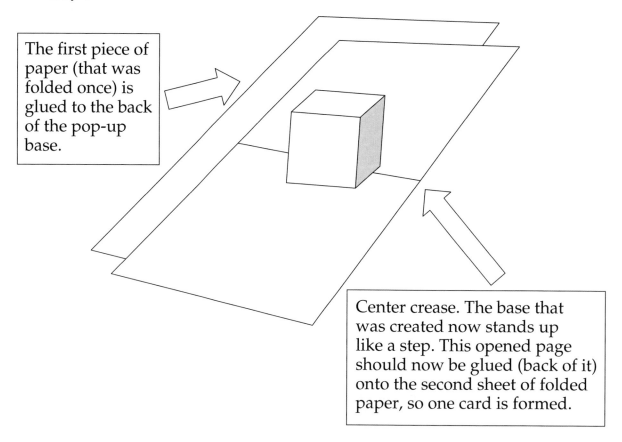

Center crease. The base that was created now stands up like a step. This opened page should now be glued (back of it) onto the second sheet of folded paper, so one card is formed.

Step 5

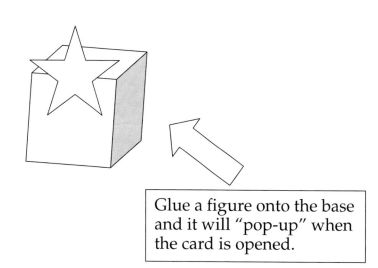

Glue a figure onto the base and it will "pop-up" when the card is opened.

URL: http://www.gigglepoetry.com

ANNOTATION: The website has categorized poems sent by children, and there are "hundreds of poems to read & rate."

TITLE; AGENCY: *Simple Pop-Ups You Can Make!*; RobertSabuda.com

URL: http://robertsabuda.com/popmake/basics/mouth/popmake_mouth-step1.asp

ANNOTATION: Robert Sabuda's website; follow the simple directions for making a mouth. It can be decorated to become any sort of creature.

TITLE; AGENCY: *Super Grover in the Nick of Rhyme*; Sesame Street

URL: http://pbskids.org/sesame/#/games

ANNOTATION: An animated Grover as a superhero must locate lost items. The viewer assists by identifying (clicking on) the correctly rhyming item.

THEME: A World in Balance: Endangered Creatures

TITLE 1: *Predators: A Pop-Up Book with Revolutionary Technology*

AUTHORS: Lucio Santoro and Meera Santoro

PUBLISHER, DATE: Little Simon, c2008

ANNOTATION:

The pop-ups are visually stunning in their intricacy, and they depict what many would consider to be very dangerous animals: sharks, polar bears, crocodiles, spiders, and so on.

TITLE 2: *Sharks*

PAPER ENGINEER: Rodger Smith

AUTHOR: Martin Kasso

ILLUSTRATOR: Matthew Jeffirs

PUBLISHER, COPYRIGHT DATE: Intervisual Books, c2008

ANNOTATION:

The book has an attention-getting pop-up of a great white shark and incorporates flaps into the detailed description of the lives of sharks. The last two pages discuss conservation of sharks.

TITLE 3: *Wild Oceans: A Pop-Up Book with Revolutionary Technology*

PAPER ENGINEER: Santoro Graphics

DESIGNER: Santoro Graphics (design concept and structural format)

AUTHORS: Lucio Santoro and Meera Santoro

ILLUSTRATOR: Santoro Graphics (artwork) and special thanks to artist Robert Hynes

PUBLISHER, COPYRIGHT DATE: Little Simon, c2010

ANNOTATION:

Stunning pop-ups with elements that "swing" freely above the page portray the creatures of the tides, the open sea, the deep, coral reefs, and frozen oceans. Reversing the book gives a different view of the two-page spreads, including some text.

TITLE 4: *Wolves*

PAPER ENGINEER: Colin Howard

AUTHOR: Robyn Hood Black

PUBLISHER, COPYRIGHT DATE: Intervisual Books, c2008

ANNOTATION:

The world of wolves is revealed in this book through a spectacular pop-up, revolving wheels, and a pull tab that illustrate the factual presentation about this animal species that has existed for a million years. The last two pages discuss the controversy about the conservation of this predator.

TITLE 5: *Birdscapes: A Pop-Up Celebration of Bird Songs in Stereo Sound*

PAPER ENGINEERS: Gene Vosough, Renee Jablow, and Andy Baron

AUTHOR: Miyoko Chu with the Cornell Lab of Ornithology

ILLUSTRATOR: Julia Hargreaves

PUBLISHER, COPYRIGHT DATE: Chronicle Books, c2008

ANNOTATION:

This incredible oversized pop-up book opens to reveal the birds' natural habitats, such as the grasslands and the cypress swamps, and their bird populations. As each two-page spread opens, the reader hears the sounds of the birds in that environment.

MAJOR CURRICULUM AREAS:

Language Arts
Math
Science (Nature: Animals)

ACTIVITY OVERVIEW:

This activity provides the opportunity for students to consider the place of wild creatures (both familiar ones and those with "bad reps") in a world shared with humans.

DESCRIPTION OF ACTIVITY:

1. Have groups of students examine and read one of the selections of pop-up books about potentially endangered creatures.
2. Allow the students brainstorming time to think of creatures about which they would be interested in knowing more. Assist the class in devising questions that they will all find out about their creatures. Make sure that the students include the topic of challenges faced by that creature in continuing its existence. One point for discussion should be why it is important to know about and to protect wild creatures.
3. Students will research their creatures, using online and print library resources.
4. Assist students in thinking of how they might present their information, both its organization and in the use of data in charts, graphs, and so on. Each student should have a chart or graph of information to help with her or his presentation of information.
5. Each student will give a presentation (this could be oral or digital) about her or his creature, including the challenges to its continued existence.
6. In groups, the students will brainstorm what they, individually and/or collectively, might do to assist in the stewardship of endangered creatures.

EXTENSIONS

1. Invite an authoritative individual in the community to give a presentation about stewardship of wildlife and what students can do to assist.
2. As a class, decide on a creative fundraiser for a one-time donation to assist in the stewardship of wild animals, such as adopting an animal in a protected environment.

ADDITIONAL RESOURCES:

Other Pop-Up Books

TITLE: *The Butterfly*

PAPER ENGINEER: James Diaz

DESIGNER: Lynette Ruschak

AUTHOR: Maria M. Mudd

ILLUSTRATOR: Wendy Smith-Griswold

PUBLISHER, COPYRIGHT DATE: Piggy Toes Press, c1992

ANNOTATION: The center pop-up is a "larger-than-life" monarch butterfly. Side flaps of information provide small pop-ups. The text includes information on all aspects of the lives of butterflies.

TITLE: *In the Air and Everywhere: The Scientific American Pop-Up Book of Birds*

AUTHOR: Jody Marshall

ILLUSTRATOR: Elizabeth McClelland

PUBLISHER, COPYRIGHT DATE: Scientific American Books for Young Readers, c1994

ANNOTATION: This book's organization places birds within their natural habitats of shore and sea, desert, open spaces, and so forth. Each double-page pop-up spread is a full scene of many birds that are colorfully and realistically illustrated. Oversized pull-out tabs reveal cards with identification keys to the birds in each scene.

TITLE: *Nature's Creatures of the Dark: A Pop-Up Exploration*

AUTHOR: David Taylor

PUBLISHER, COPYRIGHT DATE: Backpack Books, c2004

ANNOTATION: Each of the double-page pop-ups in this book elaborately illustrates a creature that lives in darkness, including owls, glowworms, and viper fish. The text provides a variety of facts about each creature and also provides an actual photograph. The book emphasizes the threats to the continued existence of these creatures.

TITLE: *Sounds of the Wild: Ocean*

PAPER ENGINEER: Richard Hawke

DESIGNERS: Jonathan Lambert and Caroline Reeves

AUTHORS: A. J. Wood and Valerie Davies

ILLUSTRATOR: Maurice Pledger

PUBLISHER, COPYRIGHT DATE: Silver Dolphin Books, c2007

ANNOTATION: Panoramic, double-page pop-ups capture the variety of wildlife in various areas of the marine world, both above (such as birds) and in it (such as sharks). The book also includes ocean sounds. It concludes with a statement about the necessity to learn how to protect the oceans and these creatures.

Books without Interactivity

TITLE: *Bald Eagles: A Chemical Nightmare* (**informational**)

AUTHOR: Meish Goldish

PUBLISHER, COPYRIGHT DATE: Bearport Publishing, 2008

ANNOTATION: Introduces the challenges and the successes in fostering the continued existence of the living symbol of the United States: the bald eagle.

TITLE: *Endangered Animals* (**informational**)

AUTHORS: Ben Hoare and Tom Jackson

PUBLISHER, COPYRIGHT DATE: DK Publishing, c2010

ANNOTATION: Covers a wide range of topics related to the survival of wild animals, including pollution, farming practices, invasive species, and so on.

TITLE: *Gone Wild: An Endangered Animal Alphabet* (**informational**)

AUTHOR: David McLimans

PUBLISHER, COPYRIGHT DATE: Walker Books for Young Readers, c2006

ANNOTATION: This 2007 ALA Caldecott Honor Book transforms letters of the alphabet into beautifully rendered drawings of endangered animals, many of which are unfamiliar to most people. Includes basic facts about the animals.

DVD

TITLE: *Bugs! A Rainforest Adventure* (2007); 40 minutes (**informational**)

DISTRIBUTOR: Image Entertainment

ANNOTATION: Filmed in Borneo, this film was a documentary for IMAX theaters. It shows bugs many times their size, so that there is a real sense of them as important living creatures.

Website

TITLE; AGENCY: *National Geographic Kids. Animals & Pets*; National Geographic Society

URL: http://kids.nationalgeographic.com/Animals

ANNOTATION: Visit this website often to see photographs and slide shows with sound and to read about animals from around the world.

TITLE; AGENCY: Wildlife Conservation Society Home website; Wildlife Conservation Society

URL: http://www.wcs.org

ANNOTATION: On this website, learn about "saving wildlife," "saving wild places," and "conservation challenges." It has wonderful photographs.

7

Using Pop-Ups in Activities and Programs Continued (Middle Grades)

MIDDLE (GRADES 6, 7, 8)

THEME: *Ancient Egypt: The Past Meets the Present*

TITLE: *The Ancient Egypt Pop-Up Book*

PAPER ENGINEER: David Hawcock

AUTHOR: James Putnam

PUBLISHER, COPYRIGHT DATE: Universe, c2003

ANNOTATION:

The book is rich with elaborate pop-ups, flaps, fold-outs, and photographs of artifacts from the British Museum.

MAJOR CURRICULUM AREAS:

Language Arts
Social Studies (Diversity, History, Geography)

ACTIVITY OVERVIEW:

Learning about history is a gateway to understanding the present, and studying other cultures is a way to be reflective about one's own.

DESCRIPTION OF ACTIVITY:

1. Share the pop-up book and point out its highlights: the Nile and agricultural life, the erection of pyramids, arts and crafts, foods, and so on.

2. Teacher and librarian will have collaborated to identify topics about historical and contemporary Egypt that can be easily researched with print and digital library resources. The teacher will provide topics on pyramid-shaped papers, from which the student will draw for a topic selection.

3. Students research both the historic fact and the current connections (such as the continuing importance of the Nile River).

4. The class will collectively make two friezes (murals) on butcher paper, using graphic illustration and a printed explanation/description on cards. One of the friezes will have historic information and the other will have contemporary information. Each student creates both a historic and a modern frame based on her or his topic, providing both of her or his illustrations (done in her or his choice of medium and technique) with explanations.

5. Display the students' friezes in the school hallway.

EXTENSION

Expand the study to examine other contemporary cultures with existing historical structures, such as tombs and temples, in locations such as Crete, Mexico, China, Greece, and Italy.

ADDITIONAL RESOURCES:

Other Pop-Up Books

TITLE: *The Ancient Egypt Pack: A Three-Dimensional Celebration of Egyptian Mythology, Culture, Life and the Afterlife*

PAPER ENGINEER: Christos Kondeatis

AUTHOR: Sara Maitland

ILLUSTRATOR: Christos Kondeatis

PUBLISHER, COPYRIGHT DATE: Bullfich Press, 1996

ANNOTATION: This book provides abundant illustration, interactivity, and information.

TITLE: *Secret Treasures*

PAPER ENGINEER: Tor Lokvig

AUTHOR: Catherine Herbert Howell

ILLUSTRATOR: John Buxton

PUBLISHER, COPYRIGHT DATE: National Geographic Society, c1992, 1997

ANNOTATION: Treasures of Tut's tomb, Tikal, Mesa Verde, Pompeii, and Xi'an are included.

TITLE: *Tutankhamen's Tomb: Uncover the Secrets and Treasures of Ancient Egypt*

AUTHOR: Jen Green

PUBLISHER, COPYRIGHT DATE: Barron's Educational Series, c2006

ANNOTATION: Uses a variety of interactive mechanisms, including pop-ups, as well as photographs, to guide the reader through this Pharaoh's tomb and Egyptian burial practices.

Other Books with Interactivity:

TITLE: *Discovering Ancient Egypt: A Magic Skeleton Book*

DESIGNER: Nicola Sokell

AUTHOR: James Harrison

ILLUSTRATOR: Jan Smith (story) and Peter Bull (cross sections)

PUBLISHER, COPYRIGHT DATE: Sterling Publishing, c2004

ANNOTATION: A school class takes a tour of Egypt. The "magic skeleton" technique has pull tabs that transform the clear overlays into color illustrations.

Books without Interactivity

TITLE: *Egypt in Spectacular Cross-Section* (**informational**)

AUTHOR: Stewart Ross

ILLUSTRATOR: Stephen Biesty

PUBLISHER, COPYRIGHT DATE: Oxford University Press, c2007

ANNOTATION: Set around 1200 BCE, a family's trip on the Nile to attend a wedding highlights important Egyptian structures, including Ramses's palace, Amun-Ra's temple, a pyramid, and the like. Incorporates Biesty's characteristic use of cross-sections.

TITLE: *Technology in the Time of Ancient Egypt* (**informational**)

AUTHOR: Judith Crosher

PUBLISHER, COPYRIGHT DATE: Raintree Steck-Vaughn, c1998

ANNOTATION: Photographs and drawings illustrate the technology used by Egyptians in building, producing cloth, warfare, travel, writing, and so on.

TITLE: *Tutankhamen's Gift* (**informational**)

AUTHOR: Robert Sabuda

ILLUSTRATOR: Robert Sabuda

PUBLISHER, COPYRIGHT: Aladdin Paperbacks, c1994

ANNOTATION: This biographical coverage of the young Tutankhamen is used to teach about ancient Egyptian customs, accomplishments, and lifestyles.

TITLE: *You Are in Ancient Egypt* (**informational**)

AUTHOR: Ivan Minnis

PUBLISHER, COPYRIGHT DATE: Raintree, c2005

ANNOTATION: This title is part of the "You Are There Series!" and uses a young person's view to highlight art, food, technology, law, religion, and so on, in Ramses II's Egypt.

Websites

TITLE; AGENCY: *National Geographic Kids. People & Places*; National Geographic Society

URL: http://kids.nationalgeographic.com/Places/

ANNOTATION: Visit people and places of the world on this website, including Egypt.

THEME: Art Everyday: Its Techniques and Creators

TITLE 1: *Brooklyn Pops Up*

PAPER ENGINEERS: Various (this is a collection)

AUTHOR: Pamela Thomas

ILLUSTRATORS: Various (this is a collection)

PUBLISHER, COPYRIGHT DATE: Little Simon, c2000

ANNOTATION:

This remarkable book collaboration was developed "to coincide with the exhibi-tion 'Brooklyn Pops Up: The History and Art of the Movable Book.'" Each of the pop-up spreads celebrating a Brooklyn landmark has been created by an acclaimed paper engineering individual or team.

TITLE 2: *Popigami: When Everyday Paper Pops!: Where Pop-Up Meets Origami*

PAPER ENGINEER: James Diaz

ILLUSTRATOR: Francesca Diaz

PUBLISHER, COPYRIGHT DATE: Intervisual Books, c2007

ANNOTATION: In this unique book, everyday, throw-away paper objects become origami that leaps from the pages.

MAJOR CURRICULUM AREAS:

Careers Fine Arts (Art)

ACTIVITY OVERVIEW:

Art surrounds us in our daily lives. How different would our lives be if not for the richness of design that transforms ordinary structures and objects into things that please us!

DESCRIPTION OF ACTIVITY:

1. Share the *Brooklyn* pop-up book. Emphasize that in the book, art in a city is found in such things as museums, brownstone buildings, and carousels. Dis-cuss with the students how different artists and paper engineers have used their own individual styles to create the illustrations and the pop-ups in this book.
2. Share the *Popigami* book. Discuss with the students how everyday objects, such as packing peanuts, newspaper, and paper coffee cups have been trans-formed into origami and into art.

PART 1—Art Around Us

1. Brainstorm with the students where they see art in their daily lives.
2. Have the students make their own individual lists of ordinary objects that: (1) might be used as subjects of art, or (2) might be used to create art. Have them label each object on their lists as being either or both of these options.

PART 2—Who Creates the Art in Our Lives? They Do and We Do!

1. Have students use library print and digital resources to research famous artists (chosen by the teacher) who have used everyday scenes, people, and/or activities in their art (paintings, sculptures, collages, textiles, etc.). Have each student devise her or his own story that this art might be telling or explaining.
2. Have students share their examples of the artist's work (such as in a book or on the Internet) and their original stories with the class.
3. Using their self-generated lists of objects that might be used as subjects or mediums for art, have the students select several to create their own pop-up pages (standard size to be determined by the teacher) using buildings or other identifiers (such as industries or bridges, etc.) in their community. These might also be thematically centered on a forthcoming community observation, such as a festival.
4. The teacher and librarian and the literature teacher(s) collaborate to arrange an exhibit of the pop-up pages, with attribution of the student's name and class. Each of the literature class students will view the exhibit, and will provide three-by-five card reactions (such as a comment, a verse, or an illustration), signed with their names, that explain why they like one to three of the pages. These reaction cards are displayed with the art.

PART 3—Art and Careers

1. The teacher and librarian will collaborate to generate a list of careers in which art is necessary: illustrators, paper engineers, graphic artists, architects, various types of designers, sculptors, animators, and so on.
2. Depending on the number of students, assign two to three students to investigate each career, using the library's print and digital resources.
3. Have each team of students share information with each other and decide who will present which pieces of information. Have students form a morning news team that will collaboratively share information with the audience of other students in a conversational, did-you-know, breaking-news format. The session can be recorded on video.

EXTENSIONS

1. Divide the class into groups. Have each student share her or his pop-up page and talk about the ideas that spurred its creation. Have the other students take notes

about what the artist says. Then, the group members will give their notes to the artist, who will use those to make a short recording explaining the art of the pop-up page. Use a digital camera to take pictures of the pop-up pages and mount them with the students' oral descriptions on the school website (collaborate with the Webmaster).

2. Students use their initial lists of everyday objects and their original stories to first plan and then to create art objects using techniques and mediums of their choice and that tell their own stories.

ADDITIONAL RESOURCES:

Other Pop-Up Books

TITLE: *The Kids' Art Pack*

PAPER ENGINEERS: Mark Hiner and Ron van der Meer

DESIGNERS: Mark Hiner and Ron van der Meer

AUTHOR: Frank Whitford

ILLUSTRATOR: Paul Compton (main illustrations) and Corina Fletcher (additional illustrations)

PUBLISHER, COPYRIGHT DATE: Dorling Kindersley, c1997

ANNOTATION: This book is indeed a "pack" with an abundance of pop-ups, flaps, facsimiles, and a guide book to help kids understand "how art is made."

Books without Interactivity

TITLE: *Art is . . .* (**informational**)

AUTHOR: Bob Raczka

PUBLISHER, COPYRIGHT DATE: The Millbrook Press, 2003

ANNOTATION: Selected artwork representing different time periods and mediums helps the reader to expand her or his definition of what art is.

TITLE: *Art Auction Mystery: Find the Fakes, Save the Sale!* (**informational**)

AUTHOR: Anna Nilsen

PUBLISHER, COPYRIGHT DATE: Kingfisher, c2005

ANNOTATION: An art auctioneer is tipped off to the possibility that half of the paintings to be sold are fakes. The reader must use information on identifying forgery techniques and other clues to identify the fake paintings and to calculate how much was paid for them.

TITLE: *What the Painter Sees: Portraits, Still Lifes, Landscapes, Trick Painting, Animals, Water, and Light* (**informational**)

AUTHOR: Sheila Keenan (adapter)

PUBLISHER, COPYRIGHT DATE: Scholastic, c1994

ANNOTATION: This book allows the reader to see what the painter saw in various works chosen from a range of time periods.

DVD

TITLE: *Between the Folds* (2010); 60 minutes (**informational**)

DISTRIBUTOR: PBS

ANNOTATION: This *Independent Lens* documentary is about origami and its creators, who come from different backgrounds, draws clear connections between origami, art, and math and science. It is supported with a website (http://www.pbs.org/indepen dentlens/between-the-folds/history.html), which includes a video interview with the director/producer.

Websites

TITLE; AGENCY: *Make Beliefs Comix*; Bill Zimmerman

URL: http://www.makebeliefscomix.com/Comix/

ANNOTATION: Students can write their own comics in the templated panels, in English, Spanish, French, German, Italian, Latin, and Portuguese. The site includes teacher resources and printables.

TITLE; AGENCY: *Exploring Career Information from the Bureau of Labor Statistics*; U.S. Bureau of Labor Statistics

URL: http://www.bls.gov/k12

ANNOTATION: This interactive website for students allows them to find information about careers selected by their interest areas.

TITLE; AGENCY: *Origami-instructions.com*; Origami-instructions.com

URL: http://www.origami-instructions.com

ANNOTATION: Photographs of step-by-step instructions assist viewers in creating origami projects, which are arranged thematically (such as origami animals, origami flowers, etc.).

THEME: The Cinderella Story

TITLE: *Cinderella: A Pop-Up Fairy Tale*

PAPER ENGINEER: Matthew Reinhart

AUTHOR: Matthew Reinhart (adaptation)

PUBLISHER, COPYRIGHT DATE: Little Simon, c2005

ANNOTATION:

This book is a retelling of the classic story of Cinderella, who is treated badly by her stepmother and stepsisters. With the help of her fairy godmother, she finds true love with a prince. The spectacular pop-ups liberally use foil, patterned papers, and ribbons. The large pop-ups that cover two pages are accompanied by smaller ones hidden beneath miniature book pages.

MAJOR CURRICULUM AREAS:

Language Arts
Literature (Diversity, Folk and Fairy Tales)
Social Studies

ACTIVITY OVERVIEW:

This activity covers a wide range of grades since the lavishly detailed pop-ups will hold the interest of younger readers already familiar with the story, while the higher reading level of the storyline can be enjoyed by older readers exploring traditional tales. This version of Cinderella can also be comfortably used with students with a wide range of abilities. In literature, this pop-up book can be compared to other retellings of the Cinderella story, both those in print and in popular media, including movies. In the social studies area, the book is an excellent introduction to a unit focusing on traditional tales from various cultures or to a unit focusing on countries of the world.

DESCRIPTION OF ACTIVITY:

1. Introduce students to characterization, plot, and setting elements in fiction. Then, share Reinhart's *Cinderella* and a second pop-up variation of the Cinderella story, such as *Rexerella: A Jurassic Classic Pop-Up* book (see the Additional Resources), with the students. After sharing the two books with the students,

brainstorm with them about the differences between the two stories, which can then be used to fill out a class matrix (see Figure 7.1 at the end of this theme) of literary approaches (vocabulary, characterizations, plot, and setting as well as illustrations and pop-up presentation) compared and contrasted in the two Cinderella stories.

2. The teacher and librarian collaborate in selecting a popular non-pop-up version of the Cinderella story, which is shared with the students. Using students working in groups, have each group read one retelling of the story from another country or culture, either a pop-up or non-pop-up version (some examples of multicultural retellings are included in Additional Resources below). Have each group fill out a blank copy of the class matrix, comparing and contrasting the differences and similarities between the popular version shared with the class and the multicultural version that the group read. After completing its matrix, each group gives a synopsis of the book that the members read and reports to the class about their findings.

3. Ask students to poll their classmates about what types of facts (such as food, climate, daily activities, local animals and plants, etc.) regarding the story's locale would be of interest to them. Assist students in graphically illustrating the opinions of the class. Using the school library media center and/or public library's print and web sources, have students research the country or culture from which their retelling of Cinderella came. When research is complete, students can point out the locale of their story on a map or globe and share their findings with their classmates.

4. Using the computer's word-processing and graphics tools, have each student write her/his own version of Cinderella set in the community in which he lives. Students should modify the characters to reflect that environment. Publish the students' stories in a class collection or on a class wiki.

EXTENSIONS

1. Students write the Cinderella story from the perspective of one of the other characters in the tale, such as the Prince or the Fairy Godmother, and so on, and then students illustrate their own original stories.

2. Students view a movie version of Cinderella, selected by the teacher and/or librarian, and compare and contrast that version with the versions that they have read, including addressing the effectiveness of illustration and motion.

ADDITIONAL RESOURCES:

Other Pop-Up Books

TITLE: *Cinderella: A Pop-Up Book*

PAPER ENGINEER: Nick Denchfield

AUTHOR: Phillida Gili

ILLUSTRATOR: Phillida Gili

PUBLISHER, COPYRIGHT DATE: Bloomsbury Publishing, c2006

ANNOTATION: Soft shades of blue, pink, green, and white, combined with illustrations reminiscent of the 18th century, lend a classic and somewhat dreamy air to this retelling of the story. Tabs, flaps, and pop-ups provide the motion, and a facsimile invitation to the ball is included.

TITLE: *Rexerella: A Jurassic Classic Pop-Up*

PAPER ENGINEER: Jonathan Lambert

AUTHOR: Keith Faulkner

ILLUSTRATOR: Graham Kennedy

PUBLISHER, COPYRIGHT DATE: Little Simon, c2001

ANNOTATION: Anyone can be Cinderella—even a dinosaur!

Other Books with Interactivity

TITLE: *Cinderella: A Pop-Up Book*

PAPER ENGINEER: Alan Brown

DESIGNER: Laura Hambleton

AUTHOR: Saviour Pirotta

ILLUSTRATOR: Susanna Lockheart

PUBLISHER, COPYRIGHT DATE: Barron's Educational Series, 2008

ANNOTATION: There are two fairy tales in this book (the first one is Cinderella), and it is memorable for its ovals of wonderful slide scenes that transform seamlessly when a flap is lifted.

Books without Interactivity

TITLE: *Cendrillon: A Caribbean Cinderella* (**fiction**)

AUTHOR: Robert D. San Souci

ILLUSTRATOR: Brian Pinkney

PUBLISHER, COPYRIGHT DATE: Simon & Schuster, c1998

ANNOTATION: This is a version of the French Creole story of "Cendrillon", which integrates the familiar Cinderella story with West Indian culture. Includes a brief glossary of French Creole words and phrases.

TITLE: *The Egyptian Cinderella* (**fiction**)

AUTHOR: Shirley Climo

ILLUSTRATOR: Ruth Heller

PUBLISHER, COPYRIGHT DATE: HarperCollins, c1989

ANNOTATION: This variation of the Cinderella tale is the story of Rhodopis, a Greek girl enslaved in ancient Egypt. With the intervention of the god Horus, she becomes the Pharaoh's wife.

TITLE: *Mufaro's Beautiful Daughters: An African Tale* (**fiction**)

AUTHOR: John Steptoe

PUBLISHER, COPYRIGHT DATE: Lothrop, Lee & Shepard, c1987

ANNOTATION: Mufaro's two daughters journey to see the Great King, who is seeking a wife. Nyasha is not only beautiful but kindly, and Manyara is also beautiful but ill-tempered. A 1988 ALA Caldecott Honor Book. **NOTE:** This book is also available in a Spanish version.

DVD

TITLE: *Mufaro's Beautiful Daughters* (episode of the PBS Reading Rainbow television series); 30 minutes (**fiction, informational**)

DISTRIBUTOR: GPN Educational Media

ANNOTATION: Set in Africa, this is the story of Mufaro's two daughters, who are very different from the other one. In each of their travels to the city to become a potential bride for the king, their true selves are revealed. In addition to the book being read, in this episode LeVar Burton visits an African drum maker, an artist who creates African musical instruments, and an African dance troupe.

Website

TITLE; AGENCY: *International Children's Digital Library: A Library for the World's Children*; International Children's Digital Library Foundation

URL: http://en.childrenslibrary.org

ANNOTATION: Do a search for "Cinderella" to find a full-text facsimile of an 1858 publication of the Cinderella story, with illustrations.

Cinderella Matrix

ELEMENT	STORY 1	STORY 2
vocabulary		
characterizations		
plot		
setting		
illustrations		
pop-up presentation		

Figure 7.1. Cinderella Matrix

From *Pop-Up Books: A Guide for Teachers and Librarians* by Nancy Bluemel and Rhonda Taylor. Santa Barbara, CA: Libraries Unlimited. Copyright © 2012.

**THEME: Dragons Yesterday and Today—Myth and Legend,
Literature, Nature**

PART 1—Dragons in Myth and Legend, Literature

TITLE: *Dragons: A Pop-Up Book of Fantastic Adventures*

PAPER ENGINEER: Keith Moseley

DESIGNER: Liz Turner

AUTHOR: Anna McQuinn

ILLUSTRATOR: M. P. Robinson

PUBLISHER, COPYRIGHT DATE: Henry A. Abrams, c2006

ANNOTATION:

Each double-page spread is a pop-up of one of the spectacular dragons that is highlighted: the dragon of Saint George, the Four Dragons, Maud and the Wyvern, the Fire Dragon of Beowulf, and the Sea Dragon Princess.

MAJOR CURRICULUM AREA:

Fine Arts
Language Arts
Literature (Diversity, Legends, Myths)

ACTIVITY OVERVIEW:

Dragons exist in story, song, and art across time and geography. This activity combines skill building in art and language as students discover what peoples around the world have thought about these immortalized creatures.

DESCRIPTION OF ACTIVITY:

1. Introduce the concepts of myths and legends to the students, emphasizing that myths and legends reflect the cultures to which they belong. Then, share the pop-up book with the students. Point out, as the book does, that dragons represent stories from different cultures.
2. The teacher/librarian collaborates to locate stories about dragons from different cultures. Then, share these stories with the students through classroom reading time and library story times.
3. The students pick a culture for which they will illustrate a dragon. They can create their own original versions either by hand or with computer-assisted design or they can get inspiration from drawing books on the topic, such as *Drawing Dragons* (see the Additional Resources for this section) or incorporate clip art elements, either print or digital. Remind students to leave space

on the page for a background to be added later. Use the pop-up book *Step Inside Dragons* (see the Additional Resources for this section) as an example of dimension and background elements in illustrations of dragons.

4. Then, in groups, have students go to the library and find pictures, either print or digital, that illustrate the cultures represented by their dragons. These pictures will serve as inspiration for providing appropriate backgrounds for the students' dragon pictures. Have students share their completed illustrations with the class.

5. Show students how to create an origami dragon (see the Additional Resources for this section). Students can then make their own origami dragons. Discuss with students the differences in approaches and final product between the three-dimensional origami dragons and their own illustrations, which are two-dimensional but offer an illusion of being three-dimensional.

EXTENSION

Students write original stories to accompany their dragon pictures and origami figures.

ADDITIONAL RESOURCES:

Other Pop-Up Books

TITLE: *Dragons*

PAPER ENGINEER: Keith Moseley

DESIGNER: Keith Moseley

AUTHOR: Gail Peterson

ILLUSTRATOR: Greg Hildebrandt

PUBLISHER, COPYRIGHT DATE: Compass Productions, c1994

ANNOTATION: It is the double-page spread pop-ups of the dragons in this oversized book that command the attention of the reader. Included are the Wyern, the Amphitere, the Lindworm, the Dragon of St. George, and a Chinese dragon. The text provides short explanation of these various creatures.

TITLE: *Step Inside Dragons: A Magic 3-Dimensional World of Dragons*

PAPER ENGINEER: Richard Jewitt

DESIGNER: Brierley Books

AUTHOR: Gaby Goldsack

ILLUSTRATOR: Nick Harris

PUBLISHER, COPYRIGHT DATE: Sterling, c2006

ANNOTATION: Each full-page illustration is actually a three-dimensional framed picture about some aspect of dragons, such as dragon babies and dragon enemies.

Books without Interactivity

TITLE: *How to Draw Dragons* (**informational**)

AUTHORS: Jim Hansen and John Burns

PUBLISHER, COPYRIGHT DATE: Rosen, c2008

ANNOTATION: A beginner's guide to drawing dragons.

DVD

TITLE: *Popular Mechanics for Kids: Gators and Dragons and Other Wild Beasts* (2005); 92 minutes (**informational**)

DISTRIBUTOR: Koch Vision

ANNOTATION: Four episodes from the television series focus on kid learning about zoos, real-life dragons, and alligators.

Website

TITLE; AGENCY: *Origami Dragon Diagrams*; Sqidoo

URL: http://www.squidoo.com/origamidragon-instructions

ANNOTATION: This web page provides links to a variety of skill level instructions for creating origami dragons, ranging from simple to extremely complex.

PART 2—Dragons in Nature

TITLE: *Dragon World: A Pop-Up Guide to These Scaled Beasts*

PAPER ENGINEER: Keith Moseley

DESIGNERS: Sue Casebourne and Chad W. Beckerman (cover)

AUTHOR: Skip Skwarek

ILLUSTRATOR: Milivoj Ceran

PUBLISHER, COPYRIGHT DATE: Abrams Books for Young Readers, c2007

ANNOTATION:

Colorful dragons leap beyond the double-page spreads of this pop-up book. Each one represents one of the categories of dragons covered: dragons alive, European dragons, eastern dragons, flying serpents. The book also mentions the real-life Komodo dragon.

MAJOR CURRICULUM AREAS:

Fine Arts
Language Arts
Literature (Myths, Legends)
Science (Nature, Animals)

ACTIVITY OVERVIEW:

Dragons exist not only in story, but they also dwell in the world that students inhabit today. This lesson introduces students to those real dragons, while encouraging skill building in language and fine arts as they learn good research practices.

DESCRIPTION OF ACTIVITY:

1. Share Mosley's pop-up book with the students. With the students, brainstorm a list of the shared characteristics of the dragons in the pop-up book (see Figure 7.2 at the end of this theme).
2. Then, have students research the Komodo dragon in digital and print sources. Although endangered, Komodo dragons are in existence in the world today. The students will look for information that helps them to answer the question: Are Komodos truly dragons?
3. As a group or individually, the students complete the handout of the chart of the legendary dragons' characteristics and comparative information about characteristics of the Komodo dragon (see Figure 7.2 at the end of this theme). Then, discuss with students the similarities and differences (compare and contrast) that they have identified between the dragons of legend and the real Komodo dragon.

EXTENSION

Students explore the topic of sea dragons to learn about their characteristics and to determine if there are "real" sea dragons.

ADDITIONAL RESOURCES:

Books without Interactivity

TITLE: *Komodo Dragon: The World's Biggest Lizard* (**informational**)

AUTHOR: Natalie Lunis

PUBLISHER, COPYRIGHT DATE: Bearport Publishing, c2007

ANNOTATION: Photographs and lots of facts about habitat, food, physical characteristics, and so on, introduce the fascinating Komodo Dragon.

TITLE: *Endangered Komodo Dragons* (**informational**)

AUTHOR: Bobbie Kalman

PUBLISHER, COPYRIGHT DATE: Crabtree Publishing, c2004

ANNOTATION: Coverage of the dragons' behavior, life cycle, food, and so on, is included along with address of the challenges to their continued survival. Includes photographs.

TITLE: *Seahorses and Sea Dragons* (**informational**)

AUTHOR: Mary Jo Rhodes

ILLUSTRATOR: David Hall (photographer)

PUBLISHER, COPYRIGHT DATE: Children's Press, c2006

ANNOTATION: Habitat, food, life cycle, and so on, are covered in this book that is illustrated with many photographs of these fascinating creatures.

DVD

TITLE: *Creepy Creatures: A Magical Brew of Slimy, Scaly, Squirmy Creatures!* (2005); 30 minutes (**informational**)

DISTRIBUTOR: National Geographic

ANNOTATION: Besides vampire bats and the black widow spider, young viewers are introduced to the Komodo dragon.

TITLE: *Creatures of the Shallow Seas* (2010); 55 minutes (**informational**)

DISTRIBUTOR: National Geographic

ANNOTATION: This documentary includes great footage and details about sea horses as well as other residents of the North Atlantic coast marshes. In the classroom, most useful if shown as clips.

Dragon Matrix

Characteristics	Dragon 1: ___	Dragon 2: ___	Dragon 3: ___	Dragon 4: ___	Dragon 5: ___	Dragon 6: ___	Komodo Dragon

Figure 7.2. Dragon Matrix

Websites

TITLE; AGENCY: *Fishes: Seahorses*; Tennessee Aquarium

URL: http://www.tnaqua.org/OurAnimals/Fishes.aspx

ANNOTATION: Click on the pictures of the dwarf seahorse, lined seahorse, and pot-belly seashore. The links go to facts, pictures, and video.

TITLE; AGENCY: *Creature Features*; Metropolitan Museum of Art

URL: http://www.metmuseum.org/learn/for-kids/family-guides/~/media/Files/Learn/Family%20Map%20and%20Guides/Creature%20Features.ashx

ANNOTATION: This illustrated *Family Guide* to the Metropolitan Museum of Art highlights "three imaginary creatures", including a dragon from ancient Iraq. The guide includes activities for kids.

TITLE; AGENCY: *Komodo Dragon*; Honolulu Zoo

URL: http://www.honoluluzoo.org/komodo_dragon.htm

ANNOTATION: Besides learning the facts about Komodo dragons, see videos of the dragons.

TITLE; AGENCY: *Sea Dragons*; Monterey Bay Aquarium

URL: http://www.mbayaq.org/efc/efc_splash/splash_animals_seadragon.aspx

ANNOTATION: Learn fun facts about the two types of sea dragons and see color photos of them.

THEME: Exploration on Earth and Beyond

TITLE: *Moon Landing: Apollo 11 40th Anniversary Pop-Up*

PAPER ENGINEER: David Hawcock

AUTHOR: Richard Platt

ILLUSTRATORS: David Lawrence, Lee Montgomery, Anne Sharp, Nick Walton; photographs by NASA

PUBLISHER, COPYRIGHT: Candlewick, c2008

ANNOTATION:

Photographs, elaborate pop-ups, and ample information about all aspects of the Apollo mission introduce the reader to humans' first visit to the moon.

MAJOR CURRICULUM AREAS:

Social Studies (Diversity, History, Geography)

ACTIVITY OVERVIEW:

Explorations (past, present, and future), whether of ocean, over land, or in space, provide the opportunity to consider the political, economic, and practical implications of such activities.

DESCRIPTION OF ACTIVITY:

1. Share the pop-up book with the students and then discuss with them the potential issues regarding sending someone into space. Explain that going to the moon was a type of exploration.
2. Ask the students about other types of historical exploration with which they are familiar (such as the Lewis and Clark expedition).
3. Teacher and librarian have collaborated to identify historical and contemporary explorations that can be easily researched with the library's print and digital resources.
4. Have teams of four students draw a topic (which will be phrased as a debate topic). Have each team research its topic and gather information that can be use for a debate (see the website about debate in the Additional Resources). Two students will take the pro side, and two will take the con side.
5. The students present their debate about the topic.

ADDITIONAL RESOURCES:

Other Pop-Up Books

TITLE: *Explorer*

PAPER ENGINEERS: Tor Lokvig and Dennis K. Meyer

DESIGNER: Jon Z. Haber

AUTHOR: Robert Ballard

ILLUSTRATOR: James Dietz

PUBLISHER, COPYRIGHT DATE: Turner Publishing, c1992

ANNOTATION: Ballard's deep-sea explorations, including discovery of the sunken Titanic, are highlighted in this book, with motion provided by pop-ups, tabs, and a wheel.

TITLE: *Seven Great Explorations: A Pop-Up Book*

AUTHOR: *Celia King*

PUBLISHER, COPYRIGHT DATE: Chronicle Books, c1996

ANNOTATION: This small book is packed with good information and excellent pop-ups. It covers famous explorations.

TITLE: *Voyage Through Space*
PAPER ENGINEERS: Serina White and Alan Brown
AUTHOR: Joe Fullman (editor)
ILLUSTRATORS: Sebastian Quigley and Gary Slater
PUBLISHER, COPYRIGHT DATE: Barron's Educational Services, c2007
ANNOTATION: Pop-up, flaps, and wheels of a book capture the history of space discovery, including missions to the moon and the space stations. Illustrations include digital artwork and photographs.

TITLE: *The Voyage of Columbus: In His Own Words: A Pop-Up Book*
PAPER ENGINEER: Rodger Smith
AUTHOR: Stacie Strong
ILLUSTRATOR: Michael Welply
PUBLISHER, COPYRIGHT DATE: Sears, Roebuck and Co., c1991
ANNOTATION: This pop-up includes "excerpts taken from The Journal of Christopher Columbus."

Books without Interactivity

TITLE: *Space* (**informational**)
AUTHOR: Mike Goldmith
PUBLISHER, COPYRIGHT DATE: Kingfisher, c2005

TITLE: *Space Travel* (**informational**)
AUTHOR: Ian Graham
PUBLISHER, COPYRIGHT DATE: Dorling Kindersley, c2004
ANNOTATION: This book is one of the publishers' Google E.guides, providing a pathfinder to links on a dedicated website (see further down in this Additional Resources section).

DVD

TITLE: *Blast Off! A Kid's Introduction to the Space Program* (2010); 30 minutes (**informational**)

DISTRIBUTOR: Kenbow Communications

ANNOTATION: Major Impact, a future historian, is the guide to the history of the space program. This Parent's Choice Award video is recommended for ages three through eleven.

Websites

TITLE; AGENCY: *e. encyclopedia Science*; Dorling Kindersley

URL: http://www.science.dke-encyc.com/search.asp?keyword=space+station&searchImage.x=9&searchImage.y=9

ANNOTATION: This site is to be used in conjunction with the book *Space Travel* (see above in this Additional Resources). It is rich with links to other sites with details, photos, and videos about space travel.

TITLE; AGENCY: *Teaching Debate in the Elementary Classroom*; Ruth Sundra (**informational for teacher**)

URL: http://www.kyrene.org/schools/brisas/sunda/debate/teaching_debate.htm

ANNOTATION: The sophisticated site has guidance, handouts, rubrics, and resources for teaching debate, provided by a gifted resource teacher.

THEME: Geometry and Art

TITLE: *One Red Dot: A Pop-Up Book for Children of All Ages*

PAPER ENGINEER: David A. Carter

AUTHOR: David A. Carter

ILLUSTRATOR: David A. Carter

PUBLISHER, COPYRIGHT DATE: Little Simon, c2004

ANNOTATION:

Look for the one red dot hidden in ten stunning 3-D pop-up sculptures!

AWARD ALERT: David Carter received the Meggendorfer Prize, recognizing the paper engineering of this pop-up book. The prize is given biennially by The Movable Book Society.

MAJOR CURRICULUM AREAS:

Careers Fine Arts (Mobiles, Modern Art)
Math (Geometry)

ACTIVITY OVERVIEW:

Carter's elaborate pop-ups are easily used to introduce geometric concepts and to inspire 3-D construction. Also, their shapes are reminiscent of forms in modern art.

DESCRIPTION OF ACTIVITY:

1. Ask students to do research on modern art and identify artists whose works remind them of the pop-ups in the *One Red Dot* book. Discuss the similarities and differences between the pop-ups and the artists' work.
2. Share the pop-up book with students and have them select one of the pop-ups to analyze for geometric concepts such as isometric, oblique, and perspective, symmetry, tessellations, and so on.
3. Introduce students to the concept of mobiles, drawing on Alexander Calder's work (see Additional Resources for a website that provides reproductions of his work). Have students create a rubric for what would constitute a well-done mobile. Have students design and construct mobiles that use only geometric shapes and that fit the rubric for quality.
4. Have students research and identify careers in which understanding geometry are required. For a career of the student's choice, have each student compose a blog posting that explains what education and experiences (including familiarity with software such as computer-aided design products) is required for success in that particular career.

ADDITIONAL RESOURCES:

Other Pop-Up Books

TITLE: *Blue 2: A Pop-Up Book for Children of All Ages*

PAPER ENGINEER: David A. Carter

AUTHOR: David A. Carter

ILLUSTRATOR: David A. Carter

PUBLISHER, COPYRIGHT: Little Simon, c2006

ANNOTATION: Dimension, illusion, and complex paper engineering lead a reader through the search for the "blue 2."

TITLE: *White Noise: A Pop-Up Book for Children of All Ages*

PAPER ENGINEER: David A. Carter

AUTHOR: David A. Carter

ILLUSTRATOR: David A. Carter

PUBLISHER, COPYRIGHT: Little Simon, 2009

ANNOTATION: This is the final book in Carter's series of color-focused pop-up books. As with the other books, it is characterized by elaborate, sculptural pop-ups.

TITLE: *Yellow Square: A Pop-Up Book for Children of All Ages*

PAPER ENGINEER: David A. Carter

AUTHOR: David A. Carter

ILLUSTRATOR: David A. Carter

PUBLISHER, COPYRIGHT: Little Simon, c2008

ANNOTATION: This book is simple in its text but sophisticated in concept and pop-up construction. Readers track a yellow square through the book's pages.

Books without Interactivity

TITLE: *Alexander Calder and His Magical Mobiles* (**informational**)

AUTHOR: Jean Lipman

PUBLISHER, COPYRIGHT DATE: Hudson Hills Press, c2008

ANNOTATION: Readers can learn about Calder's life, career, and his ideas about his works while viewing illustrations of many of his mobiles.

Website

TITLE; AGENCY: Calder website; Calder Foundation (**informational**)

URL: http://calder.org

ANNOTATION: Visit this website for information about Calder's life and works. Includes many photographs.

TITLE; AGENCY: *Careers in Math*; Coolmath.com

URL: http://www.coolmath.com/careers.htm

ANNOTATION: This page provides links to websites focused on various careers that require a background in math.

TITLE; AGENCY: *Geometry in Action*; David Epstein, University of California Irvine (**informational for teacher**)

URL: http://www.ics.uci.edu/~eppstein/geom.html

ANNOTATION: A collection of links to real-life applications of geometry in various fields, including architecture, medicine, and robotics.

THEME: Ghostbusting: Researching the Supernatural in Literature

TITLE: *Dracula*

PAPER ENGINEER: David Hawcock

AUTHORS: Bram Stoker and Claire Bampton

ILLUSTRATOR: Anthony Williams

PUBLISHER, COPYRIGHT DATE: Universe Publishing, c2009

ANNOTATION:

This graphic novel of the nineteenth-century novel has spectacular double-page pop-ups.

MAJOR CURRICULUM AREAS:

Literature
Math (Timeline)

ACTIVITY OVERVIEW:

From Shakespeare's play about the ill-fated Macbeth, to Charles Dickens's ever-popular *A Christmas Carol*, to J.K. Rowling's Harry Potter series, to Stephenie Meyer's *Twilight* series, literature has made ample use of the supernatural, whether ghosts, vampires, unicorns, and so on. This activity is designed to encourage students to learn about these literary traditions.

DESCRIPTION OF ACTIVITY:

1. Share the pop-up book with the students and discuss with them the role of the supernatural being (Dracula) in the plot of the story. Discuss his portrayal in this graphic novel, both as illustration and as character.
2. Discuss with the students what other supernatural figures they have encountered in literature that they read (including graphic novels). Make a list of these.
3. Have groups of students select a type of supernatural figure (ghost, vampire, etc.), and using brainstorming and research in library's print and digital resources, locate literature that they can read or reread (each student should

have at least one story). Have the students select a format of graphic organizer (see the Additional Resources) to use to analyze the role of the supernatural character in each of the student's readings.

4. Have each group discuss the graphic organizers that they have created. Have them come to conclusions or formulate ideas about patterns that they are seeing, which they can share with the class.

5. Have the class create a timeline, using bibliographic information about dates of publication, of the collective appearance of supernatural figures in the literature that they have read. Talk about the patterns that they see.

ADDITIONAL RESOURCES:

Other Pop-Up Books

TITLE: *A Christmas Carol*

PAPER ENGINEER: Bruce Foster

AUTHOR: Charles Dickens

ILLUSTRATOR: Chuck Fischer (paintings)

PUBLISHER, COPYRIGHT DATE: Little Brown, 2010

ANNOTATION: Lavish pop-ups bring this classic story to life, and the original story and biography of Dickens are captured in accompanying booklets.

TITLE: *Seven Mythical Creatures*

PAPER ENGINEER: Celia King

PUBLISHER, COPYRIGHT DATE: Chronicle Books, c1994

ANNOTATION: This hand-sized book introduces the Mermaid, Phoenix, Unicorn, Sphinx, Gorgon Medusa, and Pegasus as double-page pop-ups accompanied by page-length explanations of their origins.

Books without Interactivity

TITLE: *Dracula's Dark World* (**informational**)

AUTHOR: Michael Burgan

PUBLISHER, COPYRIGHT DATE: Bearport Publishing, c2011

ANNOTATION: The Middle Ages' Prince Vlad Dracula inspired the legendary Count Dracula—this book tells his story.

TITLE: *Witchcraft in Salem* (**informational**)

AUTHOR: Steven L. Stern

PUBLISHER, COPYRIGHT DATE: Bearport Publishing, c2011

ANNOTATION: Coverage of the historic Salem witchcraft accusations and trials, including address of the question: "Why did it happen?"

Website

TITLE; AGENCY: *Classroom Resources: Graphic Organizers*; Houghton Mifflin Harcourt

URL: http://www.eduplace.com/graphicorganizer

ANNOTATION: This web page has links to almost forty graphic organizers (the site gives teachers permission to copy and distribute for classroom use).

THEME: Inventions in Our Lives

TITLE: *Amazing Pop-Up House of Inventions*

PAPER ENGINEER: Robert Crowther

PUBLISHER, COPYRIGHT DATE: Candlewick Press, c2000

ANNOTATION:

Each two-page spread is a pop-up of one very detailed room of a house, and each item in the room is labeled with information about who invented it and when. There is a chronology chart in the back of the book.

MAJOR CURRICULUM AREAS:

Language Arts
Science Math
Social Studies

ACTIVITY OVERVIEW:

The featured pop-up book highlights objects students see everyday in their homes. It is a good springboard to encourage them to look closely at other familiar items and consider how their lives would be different without them.

DESCRIPTION OF ACTIVITY:

1. Introduce the concept of inventions: What is an invention? Share the pop-up book.
2. Have students brainstorm to think of the one invention that each of them would not want to live without. Make a list of the inventions that the students chose. This list will become the ballot for step 6 in this activity.
3. Students go to the library to research digital and print resources about their individual inventions, and they complete the fact-gathering handout (see Figure 7.3 at the end of this theme).
4. Students take home their fact-gathering handout to use in composing a persuasive essay that addresses the topic: Why is this invention one that we don't want to live without?
5. Students share their arguments for their inventions with the class. Their presentations have to fit a time limit.
6. The class votes, by ballot, for the top five inventions that they would not want to live without.
7. Have a group of students count the votes and tally them in a chart for the class to see. Have the students, individually, convert the counts into percentages. Then, fill in the percentages next to the counts. Discuss with the students what the advantages and disadvantages are for having the data presented as numbers (counts) as opposed to percentages.
8. Have students visit websites that list inventions that changed the world (see the Additional Resources). Ask them what arguments are offered in defense of those selections. Have students compare those lists with their own lists and discuss: What are the differences and similarities?

EXTENSION

Divide the students into teams to debate a class selection of the top ten inventions before letting the class vote on the top five inventions.

ADDITIONAL RESOURCES:

Other Books with Pop-Ups

TITLE: *Gutenberg's Gift: A Book Lover's Pop-Up Book*

PAPER ENGINEER: Bruce Foster

AUTHOR: Nancy Willard

ILLUSTRATOR: Bryan Leister

PUBLISHER, COPYRIGHT DATE: Harcourt Brace, c1995

ANNOTATION: Gutenberg and his printing press changed the world, and the pop-ups, pull-tabs, and illustrations taken from oil paintings capture the flavor of the time period as well as the accomplishments.

TITLE: *Book*

AUTHOR: Karen Brookfield

PUBLISHER: DK for Kids, c1993, c2000

ANNOTATION: Packed full visually and textually, this book focuses on the history of writing, printing, and the book. It has an international coverage.

Books without Interactivity

TITLE: *Amazing Inventions* (**informational**)

AUTHOR: Ian Stevens

PUBLISHER, COPYRIGHT DATE: Bearport, c2006

ANNOTATION: This title is part of a "Top 10" series. The "amazing inventions" included in this book are ranked from 1 to 10.

TITLE: *Black Stars: African American Women Scientists and Inventors* (**informational**)

AUTHORS: Otha Richard Sullivan and Jim Haskins (editor)

PUBLISHER, COPYRIGHT DATE: John Wiley, c2002

ANNOTATION: Profiles 25 African American women, from historic to contemporary, notable for accomplishments as scientists and inventors.

TITLE: *Girls Think of Everything: Stories of Ingenious Inventions by Women* (**informational**)

AUTHOR: Catherine Thimmesh

ILLUSTRATOR: Melissa Sweet

PUBLISHER, COPYRIGHT DATE: Houghton Mifflin, c2000

ANNOTATION: Highlights women and girls who invented things ranging from chocolate chip cookies to paper bags to computer compilers to space bumpers.

DVD

TITLE: *Bill Nye the Science Guy: Inventions* (1996); 26 minutes (**informational**)

DISTRIBUTOR: Walt Disney

ANNOTATION: In this episode from the popular television series, Bill Nye investigates how inventions come to be.

Websites

TITLE; AGENCY: *Guide to Writing a Basic Essay*; Kathy Livingston

URL: http://www.dsusa.org/index.html

ANNOTATION: This is an easy-to-follow, interactive website that guides a student through writing an essay. Also includes a Spanish version.

TITLE; AGENCY: "Top 10 'inventions' that changed the world"; *The Telegraph*

URL: http://www.telegraph.co.uk/science/4981964/Top-10-inventions-that-changed-the-world.html

ANNOTATION: An article from the British newspaper *The Telegraph* about the British Science Association panel list of the "10 inventions that changed the world."

TITLE; AGENCY: *Zoom Inventors and Inventions*; Enchanted Learning

URL: http://www.enchantedlearning.com/inventors/transportation.shtmdebate

ANNOTATION: Facts about a variety of inventions through history, arranged by time periods and also by topics (such as transportation, clothing, food, etc.). Includes some links.

Inventions Worksheet

Everyone has an invention that they couldn't live without. What is your favorite invention?

Collect the following information in a fact-gathering mission, and then use it as part of the argument that you present to your classmates. You want to convince them that your choice is the best one.

Example of completed worksheet:

1. **What:** Mass production of automobiles, which began with the invention of the assembly line.
2. **Who:** Henry Ford
3. **When:** 1913
4. **Where:** Highland Park, Michigan
5. **Impact of the invention:** It was the beginning of the Automobile Age. Automobiles became affordable for the ordinary person. They prompted the building of the national highway system in the U.S., as well as the growth of suburbs.
6. **Most recent developments of the invention:** hybrids; electric cars

---

The Invention I Can't Live Without

1. What:

2. Who:

3. When:

4. Where:

5. Impact of the invention:

6. Most recent developments of the invention:

Figure 7.3. Inventions Worksheet

From *Pop-Up Books: A Guide for Teachers and Librarians* by Nancy Bluemel and Rhonda Taylor. Santa Barbara, CA: Libraries Unlimited. Copyright © 2012.

THEME: Knights and Castles

TITLE: *Castle: Medieval Days and Knights*

PAPER ENGINEER: Kyle Olmon

ILLUSTRATOR: Tracy Sabin

PUBLISHER, COPYRIGHT DATE: Orchard Books, c2006

ANNOTATION:

Explore the daily activities in a medieval castle setting, both interior and exterior. The book is illustrated by intricate double-page pop-ups, supported by many smaller pop-ups beneath side flaps.

MAJOR CURRICULUM AREAS:

History (including Diversity)
Language Arts
Literature

ACTIVITY OVERVIEW:

Knights and castles are always appealing for boys. The study of world history will be enhanced with the substantial text and elaborate pop-ups of Olmon's book of "medieval days and knights."

DESCRIPTION OF ACTIVITY:

1. Before sharing the pop-up book with students, have a discussion with them about "castles" and "knights," asking them what they think of when they hear these two words. Ask students where they got their ideas: from a book or a movie or a television series or a video game or travel experiences, and so on. Then, share the pop-up book with the students.

2. Using library resources, including online ones, have students prepare short reports to share, focusing on such questions as: Who were the knights in medieval times in Western Europe? How did one get to be a knight? What happened in the daily lives of knights? Were there famous knights who are still remembered today? In what countries in Western Europe were knights located? Could women be knights? What happened in the daily lives of people other than knights?

3. Using library resources, including online ones, have students investigate the concept of "castle." For instance, what is the difference between a palace and a castle? Do other countries and cultures use the word "castle" or are there other terms for this idea? Have students investigate, using library resources, knights and castles in other cultures, including castles in the United States (for instance, see the Barbara Knox book about Hearst Castle in Additional Resources).

4. Have each student write a short story, using the information that he or she has learned as background. The story should include knights and castles, but it may be any genre (such as a mystery or science fiction or the text for a graphic novel).

EXTENSIONS

1. Students investigate coats of arms and their purpose (to identify knights garbed in their armor). Students design their own individual coats of arms, based on their interests, using either drawing, collage, or computer graphics. They can transfer the coats of arms to posters or t-shirts.

2. Knights had codes of conduct. Do the students know if their school has a code of conduct? If so, what is it? Have students create their own individual codes of conduct.

3. Students make and decorate their own pop-up castles, following the directions on the website in Additional Resources.

ADDITIONAL RESOURCES:

Other Pop-Up Books

TITLE: *Castles: A 3-Dimensional Exploration*

PAPER ENGINEER: David Hawcock

AUTHORS: Gillian Osband and Robert Andrew

ILLUSTRATOR: Robert Andrew

PUBLISHER, COPYRIGHT DATE: Orchard Books, c1991

ANNOTATION: Oversized pop-ups cover life in a castle and famous castles.

TITLE: *A Genuine and Most Authentic Knight: A Noble Guide for Young Squires*

DESIGNER: Andy Mansfield

AUTHOR: Sir Geoffrey de Lance (Dugald Steer)

ILLUSTRATORS: Milivoj Ceran, Neil Chapman, and Alastair Graham

PUBLISHER, COPYRIGHT DATE: Candlewick Press, c2006

ANNOTATION: Explanations of the life of a knight are enhanced with ample illustration and flaps, tabs, and pop-ups.

TITLE: *A Knight's City*

PAPER ENGINEER: Keith Williams

DESIGNER: Simon Morse

AUTHOR: Philip Steele

ILLUSTRATORS: Alan Lathwell, Andrew Wheatcroft (Virgil Pomfrit), Nick Harris (Virgil Pomfrit), Francis Phillipps (Linden Artists), Roger Hutchines, and Phil Park (Shannon Associates)

PUBLISHER, COPYRIGHT DATE: Little Simon, c2008

ANNOTATION: The focus of this book is on the life within medieval cities. Double-page spreads of buildings with the city are quite impressive.

TITLE: *Knights: A 3-Dimensional Exploration*

PAPER ENGINEER: David Hawcock

AUTHOR: John Howe

PUBLISHER, COPYRIGHT DATE: Orchard Books, c1995

ANNOTATION: Each two-page spread of a pop-up covers a topic in the history of the lives of medieval European knights: suits of armor, the first knights, myths and courtly love, the Crusades, and famous knights.

TITLE: *Pendragon Castle: A Panorama Pop-Up Book*

PAPER ENGINEER: Keith Moseley

DESIGNER: Keith Moseley

AUTHOR: Peter Seymour

ILLUSTRATOR: Keith Moseley

PUBLISHER, COPYRIGHT DATE: Holt, Rinehart and Winston, c1982

ANNOTATION: This eight-and-a-half-inch tall book folds out into a diorama of Pendragon Castle, with a view of all of its activities.

Books without Interactivity

TITLE: *How Castles Were Built* (**informational**)

AUTHOR: Peter Hicks.

ILLUSTRATOR: Peter Dennis

PUBLISHER, COPYRIGHT DATE: PowerKIDS Press, c2008

ANNOTATION: Explains and illustrates different types of castles, arranged chronologically. Includes instructions for building a castle from everyday objects.

TITLE: *Hearst Castle: An American Palace* (**informational**)

AUTHOR: Barbara Knox

PUBLISHER, COPYRIGHT DATE: Bearport Publishing Co., c2006

ANNOTATION: Coverage of the building of the American Hearst Castle, including its fascinating history and owner (William Randolph Hearst).

TITLE: *Knight* (**informational**)

AUTHOR: Christopher Garrett

PUBLISHER: Dorling Kindersley, 2007

ANNOTATION: This book also includes a DVD of clip art and a poster.

TITLE: *Stephen Biesty's Cross-Sections Castle* (**informational**)

AUTHOR: Stephen Biesty

PUBLISHER, COPYRIGHT DATE: DK Children, c1994

ANNOTATIONS: All aspects of a 14th-century castle, ranging from its construction to entertainment at the castle, are revealed in cross-sections.

DVD

TITLE: *Castle* (2006); 60 minutes (**informational**)

DISTRIBUTOR: PBS

ANNOTATION: This tour of a 13th century Welsh castle is hosted by David McCaulay. The film is an award-winning documentary (not targeted to juvenile audiences). It includes details of daily life.

Website

TITLE; AGENCY: *Robert Sabuda Official Web Site: Simple Pop-Ups You Can Make! Pop-Up Castle*; Robert Sabuda

URL: http://robertsabuda.com/popmakesimple.asp

ANNOTATION: Step-by-step directions, with templates and a photograph of the final product, are provided for making one's own pop-up castle.

THEME: Literature Bridges to Math

CONTRIBUTOR TO ACTIVITY: Lora Krantz (see Appendix for information on this contributor)

TITLE: *Alice's Adventures in Wonderland*

PAPER ENGINEER: Robert Sabuda

AUTHOR: Lewis Carroll

ILLUSTRATOR: Robert Sabuda

PUBLISHER, COPYRIGHT DATE: Little Simon, c2003

ANNOTATION:

This lavish pop-up version of Alice is true to the Tenniel style of illustration from the classic and also to Carroll's original story, and the pop-ups themselves are beyond impressive.

MAJOR CURRICULUM AREAS:

Literature
Math

ACTIVITY OVERVIEW:

Introducing students to the math connections in other subjects, such as literature, broadens its appeal to a wider range of students; it helps students to see math in the "everyday." and to see math and other subjects as integrated. *Alice's Adventures in Wonderland,* long used for its math connections, offers new appeal in pop-up versions that highlight popular scenes from the book and provides a springboard for students to analyze other literature for bridges to math.

DESCRIPTION OF ACTIVITY:

1. Share the pop-up version of *Alice's Adventures in Wonderland.* Use the opportunity to highlight math concepts and potential math problems from the story and the book format that are relevant for the proficiency level of the students. For instance, there are Alice's varying heights and her relationship to other objects (such as the rabbit's house and the mushrooms) and the book's pop-up arch of playing cards (what size arch could one make from real-sized cards?).
2. Ask the students to make a short list of their favorite books. In small groups, have students brainstorm what they remember that might potentially relate to math in those books. Then, have a discussion with the whole class about what math problems might be found in literature.

3. Have students select a book, either one from home or one selected from a library, that they have previously read, and have them design a math problem related to that book's content.

4. Students will share their math problems with the class.

EXTENSION

1. Show clips from various movie versions of *Alice in Wonderland* and have the students discuss how literature translated to media might change how they would construct their math problems.

2. Share the *Elements of Pop-Up* book with students (see the Additional Resources). Discuss how and why each piece works as it does. Have print outs of Figure 7.4 (see the end of this theme) on green paper and provide cardstock for a card. Ask the students to predict what the project will become. Instruct them to cut out the pieces carefully, cutting only the black lines. Students then take the four longest pieces and construct the base by putting them together (demonstrate). Continue adding the longest pieces that are left, layer after layer. Eventually they will see a tree, which must stay together and not fall apart when the card is opened and closed. If it disassembles, the pieces were not placed properly. When this happens, help the students to analyze why the project needs to be adjusted. At the end of the project, discuss with students the processes of managing a project to a successful completion, including adjustments.

ADDITIONAL RESOURCES:

Other Pop-Up Books

TITLE: *Alice in Pop-Up Wonderland*

PAPER ENGINEER: James R. Diaz

DESIGNER: J. Otto Seibold

AUTHOR: Lewis Carroll

ILLUSTRATOR: J. Otto Seibold

PUBLISHER, COPYRIGHT DATE: Scholastic, c2003

ANNOTATION: The text is characteristic Seibold (looks hand-written in a busy variety of colors and styles) and the pop-ups do justice to the amusing illustrations in this "fractured" version of Alice—a style that is also typical of Seibold's work.

TITLE: *The Elements of Pop-Up: A Pop-Up Book for Aspiring Paper Engineering*

PAPER ENGINEERS: David A. Carter and James Diaz

PUBLISHER, COPYRIGHT DATE: Little Simon, c1999

ANNOTATION: This book is every would-be paper engineer's dream come true. It is both a pop-up book and a guide to creating all of the structures that bring paper engineering to life.

TITLE: *Lewis Carroll's Alice's Adventures in Wonderland*

DESIGNER: Carlton Books Limited

AUTHOR: Lewis Carroll (retold by Harriet Castor)

ILLUSTRATOR: Zdenko Basic

PUBLISHER, COPYRIGHT DATE: Barron's Educational Services, 2009

ANNOTATION: Flaps, tabs, and one concluding two-page-spread pop-up of playing cards lead the reader through Alice's adventures. This version of Alice renders her strikingly doll-like, with large eyes and an almost-poseable body. The text has clever asides, such as "Advice for Surviving a Mad Tea Party." Twelve hidden keys in the text provide letters in a clue to how to get to Wonderland.

TITLE: *Peter Pan: A Pop-Up Adaptation of J. M. Barrie's Original Tale by Robert Sabuda*

PAPER ENGINEER: Robert Sabuda

AUTHOR: J. M. Barrie

ILLUSTRATOR: Robert Sabuda

PUBLISHER, COPYRIGHT DATE: Little Simon, c2008

ANNOTATION: Elaborate pop-ups, characteristic of Sabuda's work, bring to life the adventures of the forever boy, Peter Pan. Be prepared for the stunning Jolly Roger ship on the last pages.

TITLE: *Peter Pan: A Classic Story Pop-Up Book With Sounds*

PAPER ENGINEER: Andy Mansfield

AUTHOR: J. M. Barrie (retold by Libby Hamilton)

ILLUSTRATOR: Paul Hess

PUBLISHER, COPYRIGHT DATE: Silver Dolphin Books, c2009

ANNOTATION: The story of Peter Pan flies from each two-page spread, accompanied by sound, including that familiar ticking of the watch in the crocodile.

Books without Interactivity

TITLE: *Alice's Adventures in Wonderland; Through the Looking Glass: The Definitive Illustrated Editions* (**fiction**)

AUTHOR: Lewis Carroll

ILLUSTRATOR: John Tenniel

PUBLISHER, COPYRIGHT DATE: Morrow, afterword, c1992

ANNOTATION: First published in 1866, this version displays the original artwork by John Tenniel Sr.

TITLE: *The Annotated Alice: The Definitive Edition* (**informational for teacher**)

AUTHORS: Lewis Carroll and Martin Gardner (introductions and notes)

ILLUSTRATOR: John Tenniel

PUBLISHER, COPYRIGHT DATE: W.W. Norton, c1960, 1988, 1990, 2000

ANNOTATION: The copious annotations in the book's margins explain the references, allusions, and math puzzles found in the classic *Alice*.

TITLE: *The Annotated Peter Pan: The Centennial Edition* (**informational for teacher**)

AUTHORS: J.M. Barrie and Maria Tatar (introduction and notes)

PUBLISHER, COPYRIGHT DATE: W.W. Norton & Co., c2011

ANNOTATION: Understanding this classic text is facilitated not only with the explanatory annotations but with color illustrations and photographs.

TITLE: *Peter Pan: 100th Anniversary Edition* (**fiction**)

AUTHOR: J.M. Barrie

ILLUSTRATOR: Michael Hague

PUBLISHER, COPYRIGHT DATE: Henry Holt, c1997 (illustrations)

ANNOTATION: Rediscover the adventures of Peter Pan in its original writing.

DVD

TITLE: *Disney's Alice in Wonderland* (2010); 108 minutes (**fiction**)

DISTRIBUTOR: Walt Disney

ANNOTATION: This contemporary sequel to *Alice in Wonderland* revisits the original story and Wonderland, as seen by an adult Alice.

TITLE: *Walt Disney's Alice in Wonderland: The Masterpiece Edition* (1951); 75 minutes (**fiction**)

DISTIBUTOR: Walt Disney

ANNOTATION: The 1951 animated version has remained popular for half a century.

Websites

TITLE; AGENCY. *Maths Dictionary for Kids*; Jenny Eather

URL: http://www.amathsdictionaryforkids.com/

ANNOTATION: Click on the alphabetical math term (600-plus of them) to see an illustrated explanation. Definitions may be printed.

TITLE; AGENCY: International Children's Digital Library: A Library for the World's Children; International Children's Digital Library Foundation

URL: http://en.childrenslibrary.org

ANNOTATION: Do a simple search to find several facsimiles (full-text and illustrated) of *Alice's Adventures in Wonderland* that can be read online.

TITLE; AGENCY: *Chart of Children's Literature Featured in the Math Solutions Publications Series Math, Literature, and Nonfiction, Listed with Grade Levels and Topics*; Math Solutions (**informational for teacher**)

URL: http://mathsolutions.com/documents/lessons_chart-2.pdf

ANNOTATION: This web page is a chart of children's literature (fiction) and nonfiction (informational books) listed with grade levels and math topics found in those books.

Tree Pop-Up by Lora Krantz

For this template, follow the instructions in the **Extensions** of this activity.

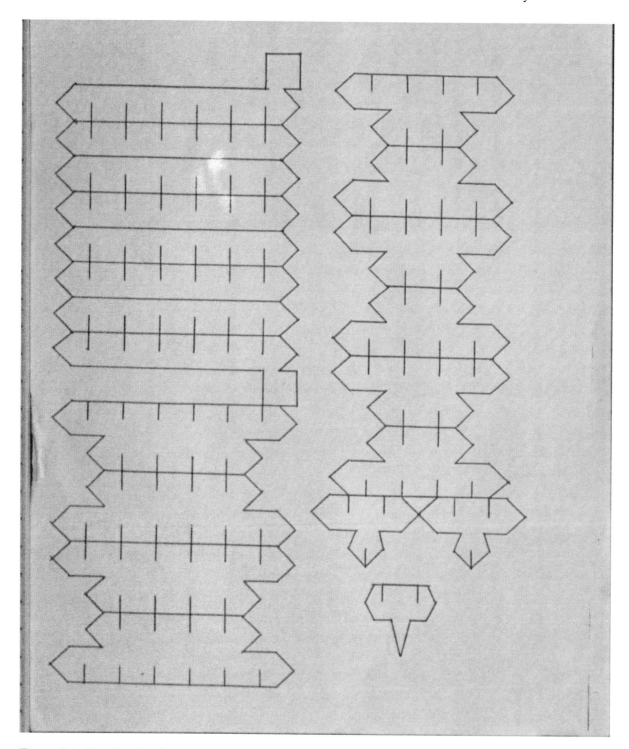

Figure 7.4. Tree Pop-Up by Lora Krantz

From *Pop-Up Books: A Guide for Teachers and Librarians* by Nancy Bluemel and Rhonda Taylor. Santa Barbara, CA: Libraries Unlimited. Copyright © 2012.

THEME: Poetry Trails

TITLE: *Trail: Paper Poetry*

PAPER ENGINEER: David Pelham

PUBLISHER, COPYRIGHT DATE: Little Simon, c2007

ANNOTATION:

This book is a unique blending of wheels of movable poetry and stark-white, very complex pop-ups.

MAJOR CURRICULUM AREAS:

Fine Arts
Literature (Poetry)
Math

ACTIVITY OVERVIEW:

Trail inspires middle through high school students to delve into poetry and to investigate multiple art forms as they explore their own creativity. It can also be used by teachers to capture the students' interest for introduction to classic poets.

DESCRIPTION OF ACTIVITY:

1. Share the pop-up book with the students, taking time to emphasize the complex and unusual pop-ups. Point out the poetry that is written on a wheel. The book is both movable art and movable poetry. Ask the students if they were creating books similar to this one, would they start with the artwork or with the poetry and why?
2. Have students look at Robert Sabuda's *Winter in White* (see Additional Resources), which is also done in all white, but it has a much more simplistic approach to poetry and pop-ups. Guide the students in comparing and contrasting how each of the two very different approaches in language and visual presentation affects the reader and why.
3. Make available to students several resources on creating their own pop-ups (using Chapter 8 of this book to identify resources). Using these sources, have students identify what they would use in a pop-up book, based on their own preferences and abilities.
4. Brainstorm with the students what steps they would have to follow if they were going to plan their own pop-up books. Then students can use those steps to plan their own pop-up books, starting with either the art or the poem (depending on how they answered the question in Step 1 of this activity). Following their plans, each student should create a book that has both pop-ups and poetry. After completion of their books, students should self-evaluate what they would have done differently to modify their creations.

EXTENSIONS

1. Have the students' books placed on display in the library.

2. Have the students share their creations with a lower grade level class.

3. Have the students use a poetry pop-up book by Nick Bantock (such as *Kubla Khan* in the Additional Resources) or another paper engineer and compare it to the all-white works by Pelham and by Sabuda.

4. Have students use the book *The Place My Words are Looking For* (see the Additional Resources), or another resource in which poets or artists share their own "thoughts, inspirations, anecdotes, and memories," or a resource selected from Chapter 8, as an inspiration for considering their personal connections with their own creations and the approaches that they take to them.

5. Students use a set of "create your own poetry" refrigerator magnets (available from http://www.magneticpoetry.com), or a set made by them, or online magnets (also available at http://www.magneticpoetry.com), to write a poem. Then, thinking again about *Trail*, they consider the challenges of using paper as a medium. They should consider the boundaries of using one set of magnets, including those online, for creating poetry and art.

ADDITIONAL RESOURCES:

Other Pop-Up Books

TITLE: *The Elements of Pop-Up: A Pop-Up Book for Aspiring Paper Engineering*

PAPER ENGINEERS: David A. Carter and James Diaz

PUBLISHER, COPYRIGHT DATE: Little Simon, c1999

ANNOTATION: This book is every would-be paper engineer's dream come true. It is both a pop-up book and a guide to creating all of the structures that bring paper engineering to life.

TITLE: *The Imagination Cycle*

PAPER ENGINEER: Bruce Foster

AUTHOR: Ginny Ruffner

ILLUSTRATOR: Ginny Ruffner

PUBLISHER, COPYRIGHT DATE: Museum of Northwest Art, c2008

ANNOTATION: This remarkable book was produced in conjunction with an exhibit of works by Ginny Ruffner, a multimedia artist. It is a paperback book in a case, and it follows the wandering path of the "imagination," and then the book turns to reverse back on itself.

TITLE: *Kubla Khan: A Pop-Up Version of Coleridge's Classic*

PAPER ENGINEERS: Nick Bantock and Dennis K. Meyer

DESIGNERS: Barbara Hodgson and Nick Bantock

AUTHOR: Samuel Taylor Coleridge

ILLUSTRATOR: Nick Bantock

PUBLISHER, COPYRIGHT DATE: Viking Penguin, c1994

ANNOTATION: This rendering of Coleridge's poem uses pop-up and dark colors to capture the flavor of dream-like Xanadu.

TITLE: *Winter in White: A Mini Pop-Up Treat*

PAPER ENGINEER: Robert Sabuda

PUBLISHER, COPYRIGHT DATE: Little Simon, c2007

ANNOTATION: This "mini pop-up treat" is a short poem that is illustrated with white pop-ups of wintery symbols (such as snowflakes) against soft color backgrounds.

Books without Interactivity

TITLE: *Authors & Artists for Young Adults* (this is a reference book set of 70-plus volumes; also available online as a database) (**informational**)

PUBLISHER, COPYRIGHT DATE: Gale, multiple volumes (volume 1 is 1988, volume 88 is 2012)

TITLE: *A Kick in the Head: An Everyday Guide to Poetic Forms* (**informational**)

AUTHOR: Paul B. Janeczko

ILLUSTRATOR Chris Raschka

PUBLISHER, COPYRIGHT DATE: Candlewick, c2009

ANNOTATION: This accessible guide to poetic forms combines definitions, examples, and drawings.

TITLE: *The Place My Words Are Looking For: What Poets Say About and Through Their Work* (**informational**)

AUTHOR: Selected by Paul B. Janeczka

PUBLISHER, COPYRIGHT DATE: Simon & Schuster, c1990

ANNOTATION: Thirty-nine poets share their own ideas and reflections about their craft; includes examples of their poetry.

TITLE: *The Poet Slave of Cuba: A Biography of Juan Francisco Manzano* (informational)

AUTHOR: Margarita Engle

ILLUSTRATOR: Sean Qualls

PUBLISHER, COPYRIGHT DATE: Henry Holt, c2006.

ANNOTTION: Juan Francisco Manzano was born in 1797. His mistreatment as a slave in Cuba is in stark contrast to his identity as a talented poet. The book is in verse.

TITLE: *Poetry and Pop-Ups: An Art-Enhanced Approach to Writing Poetry* (**informational for teacher**)

AUTHOR: Mary A. Lombardo

PUBLISHER, COPYRIGHT DATE: Linworth, c2003

ANNOTATION: Pop-ups are the art technique used to reinforce student skills in poetry writing. Includes classroom activities, teacher tips, and worksheets.

TITLE: *Talking with Artists,* volumes 1–3 (**informational**)

AUTHOR: Pat Cummings (compiler and editor)

PUBLISHERS, COPYRIGHT DATES: volume 1: Macmillan, c1992; volume 2: Simon & Schuster, c1995; volume 3: Simon & Schuster, c1999

ANNOTATION: Conversations with 14 illustrators familiar to young people (such as Chris Van Allsburg and Lois Ehlert) will have great appeal for their fans and for those who hope to join their ranks.

THEME: The Renaissance: Many Talents

TITLE 1: *Shakespeare's Globe: An Interactive Pop-Up Theatre*

AUTHOR: Toby Forward

ILLUSTRATOR: Juan Wijngaard

PUBLISHER, COPYRIGHT DATE: Candlewick Press, c2005

ANNOTATION:

This book pops out into the Globe Theater. It is accompanied by short scene scripts and a first-person view of the history of and playgoer experiences in the Globe.

TITLE 2: *Galileo's Universe*

PAPER ENGINEER: Bruce Foster

DESIGNERS: Rita Marshall and Bea Jackson

AUTHOR: J. Patrick Lewis

ILLUSTRATOR: Tom Curry

PUBLISHER, COPYRIGHT DATE: Creative Editions, c2005

ANNOTATION:

Poems and pop-ups illustrate the life and contributions of Galileo.

TITLE 3: *Journal of Inventions: Leonardo da Vinci*

PAPER ENGINEER: David Hawcock

ILLUSTRATOR: David Lawrence (pop-up illustrations)

AUTHOR: Jaspre Bark

PUBLISHER, COPYRIGHT DATE: Silver Dolphin Books, Advantage Publishers Group, c2008

ANNOTATION:

Pop-up and flaps bring life to da Vinci's sketches, against backdrops of writings from his journals. The entire book is rendered in soft shades of coloring reminiscent of old manuscripts.

MAJOR CURRICULUM AREAS:

Careers
Fine Arts
Science (Invention)
Social Studies (Renaissance)

ACTIVITY OVERVIEW:

The Renaissance was characterized by individuals who combined creative abilities and genius in multiple areas, such as science and art, and this activity helps students to understand the interrelatedness of many areas of interest and talent.

DESCRIPTION OF ACTIVITY:

1. While sharing the pop-up book about Galileo, ask the students how Galileo's endeavors were influenced by questions that he wanted to investigate. Discuss with the students what questions that they are noticing in the book.

2. Share the other two pop-up books (about Shakespeare and da Vinci) and discuss with students the meaning of the word Renaissance, which refers to a time of questioning, and why that is a good name for this time period. Have teams of students, after reviewing basic search strategies with them, identify major activities of the Renaissance, in assigned areas such as art, inventions, architecture, and so on.

3. Have each student generate a question that she or he would have about the Renaissance, [such as, what else did da Vinci and other notables invent; are there inventions from the Renaissance that we still use; were there famous artists at that time, who supported the arts (including theater) and artists during that time; were there women of the period who are famous for their achievements; was the Renaissance in other places than Italy, etc.]. Have the students do a short, simple research project in the library, using print and digital resources to find the answers to their questions.

4. After reviewing the major interests of Renaissance individuals of accomplishment, discuss with students the fact that most contemporary careers also require skills in several areas—for example, a career in graphic art requires both knowledge of art and computer software. Have students identify their current interests. Have students research, using online searching, careers that would incorporate their interests. Have students fill out the worksheet of information that they need to know about a career choice (see Figure 7.5 at the end of this theme).

EXTENSION

Leonardo da Vinci wrote his notes in mirror-image. Students can investigate codes (such as in the Janeczko book in Additional Resources), try using some of them, and then experiment with creating their own.

ADDITIONAL RESOURCES:

Other Pop-Up Books

TITLE: *All the World's a Stage*

DESIGNER: Vandy Ritter (book)

AUTHOR: Michael Bender

PUBLISHER, COPYRIGHT DATE: Chronicle Books, c1999

ANNOTATION: This pop-up biography of Shakespeare is divided by periods of his life, such as "The Lost Years." The back of the book has a chronology and a glossary.

TITLE: *The Kids' Art Pack*

PAPER ENGINEERS: Mark Hiner and Ron van der Meer

AUTHORS: Ron van der Meer and Frank Whitford

ILLUSTRATORS: Paul Crompton and Corina Fletcher (additional illustrations)

PUBLISHER, COPYRIGHT DATE: Dorling Kindersley, c1997

ANNOTATION: This interactive book is indeed packed with interactive elements (pop-ups, flaps, 3-D structures) that explain art principles.

TITLE: *Leonardo da Vinci: The Artist, Inventor, Scientist in Three-Dimensional Movable Pictures*

PAPER ENGINEER: John Strejan

AUTHORS: Alice Provensen and Martin Provensen

AWARD ALERT: The illustration team comprises 1984 Caldecott Award–winning artists, and they had a Caldecott Honor Book in 1982.

ILLUSTRATORS: Alice Provensen and Martin Provensen

PUBLISHER, COPYRIGHT DATE: Viking Press, c1984

ANNOTATION: This unique book provides historical context for wonderful pop-ups taken from da Vinci's art and inventions.

TITLE: *Waiting for Filippo: The Life of Renaissance Architect Filippo Brunelleschi*

AUTHOR: Michael Bender

PUBLISHER, COPYRIGHT DATE: Chronicle Books, c1995

ANNOTATION: The life and achievements of the 13th-and 14th-century Florentine architect with pop-ups of his architectural creations.

Other Books with Interactivity

TITLE: *The Da Vinci Kit: Mysteries of the Renaissance Decoded*

PAPER ENGINEER: Alan Brown

AUTHOR: Andrew Langley

PUBLISHER, COPYRIGHT DATE: Running Press, c2001

ANNOTATION: This nonfiction interactive book is shaped as a box and includes facsimiles and replicas.

Books without Interactivity

TITLE: *Da Vinci and His Times* (**informational**)

AUTHOR: Andrew Langley

PUBLISHER, COPYRIGHT DATE: Dorling Kindersley, c2006

ANNOTATION: Covers many aspects of the Renaissance world of Da Vinci, ranging from inventions to art.

TITLE: *Leonardo's Horse* (**informational**)

AUTHOR: Jean Fritz

PUBLISHER, COPYRIGHT DATE: G.P. Putnam's Sons, c2001

ANNOTATION: Da Vinci created a model in clay of a horse, but it was destroyed before being cast into a bronze statue. This book covers Da Vinci's life, the saga of the horse, and a 20th-century American's creation of the bronze horse statue.

TITLE: *Leonardo da Vinci: A Nonfiction Companion to Monday with a Mad Genius* (**informational**)

AUTHORS: Mary Pope Osborne and Natalie Pope Boyce

ILLUSTRATOR: Sal Murdocca

PUBLISHER, COPYRIGHT DATE: Random House, c2009

ANNOTATION: Two student researchers find the facts about Leonardo da Vinci. This is a companion book to *Monday with a Mad Genius*.

TITLE: *Life in the Renaissance: The Court* (**informational**)

AUTHOR: Kathryn Hinds

PUBLISHER, COPYRIGHT DATE: Benchmark Books, Marshall Cavendish, c2004

ANNOTATION: Covers a variety of aspects of court life during the Renaissance, including the place of women, childhood, and the types of courts.

TITLE: *Monday with a Mad Genius* (**fiction**)

AUTHOR: Mary Pope Osborne

ILLUSTRATOR: Sal Murdocca

PUBLISHER, COPYRIGHT DATE: Random House, c2007

ANNOTATION: Two students travel to Renaissance Italy and encounter Leonardo da Vinci. Part of the Magic Tree House series.

TITLE: *Top Secret: A Handbook of Codes, Ciphers, and Secret Writing* (**informational)**

AUTHOR: Paul B. Janeczko

ILLUSTRATOR: Jenna LaReau

PUBLISHER, COPYRIGHT DATE: Candlewick, c2006

ANNOTATION: Explains the history of secret codes and reveals many codes and ciphers. Offers guidance on such techniques as creating invisible ink.

Websites

TITLE; AGENCY: *Leonardo and the Horse*; da Vinci Science Center (merger of the Discovery Center of Science and Technology and Leonardo da Vinci's Horse)

URL: www.leonardoshorse.org

ANNOTATION: View slides of the bronze horse sculpture created from da Vinci's drawings, and read about the project.

TITLE; AGENCY: *The Renaissance Connection*; Allentown Art Museum

URL: http://www.renaissanceconnection.org

ANNOTATION: "An interactive educational Web Site" about the Renaissance.

Career Worksheet

The famous individuals of the Renaissance had to possess many talents in order to become the inventors and creators of art and architecture that still have an impact on our society.

Leonardo da Vinci, a name still recognized hundreds of years later, was skilled in math, science, and the arts.

Can you become a modern day Renaissance man or woman? What skills do you need to achieve your goal? **As you research, complete this worksheet:**

1. When you have time to do whatever you want, what interests you?

2. What career could you choose that would enable you to put your interests to work?

3. What would your major responsibilities or tasks be in your chosen career?

4. What skills or special knowledge are needed to prepare you for it?

5. How do you acquire the skills that you need (e.g., on-the-job training, college, etc.)?

6. Does this job require you to live in a special geographic location? If so, where?

7. What is the salary range for this career?

8. Now that you know more about it, would you still select this career?

Figure 7.5. Career Worksheet

THEME: Stories on Stage

TITLE: *Beauty and the Beast: A Pop-Up Book of the Classic Fairy Tale*

PAPER ENGINEER: Robert Sabuda

AUTHOR: Robert Sauda

ILLUSTRATOR: Robert Sabuda

PUBLISHER, COPYRIGHT DATE: Little Simon, c201J

ANNOTATION:

Elaborate pop-ups rise from two-page spreads, literally serving as backdrops to the action of the familiar story. Flaps uncover small pop-ups, and tunnels can be lifted from the sides of the page, for peeking at the bereft beast in his lonely castle.

MAJOR CURRICULUM AREAS:

Fine Arts (Reader's Theater)
Language Arts (Folk and Fairy Tales, Literary Form, Writing)

ACTIVITY OVERVIEW:

Familiar folk and fairy tales provide the plots and characters for students to write their own scripts and plan their own reader's theater productions.

DESCRIPTION OF ACTIVITY:

1. Ask about the experiences that the students have had with versions (including movie and television) of *Beauty and the Beast*. If they don't know about the stage version of the Disney movie, tell them about that (see the Additional Resources). Ask them to identify the main characters and then ask them to share the plot of the story.
2. Share the book with the students, asking them to view the pop-up pages as stage sets, against which the characters and the action are set.
3. Students should use library resources to locate their own familiar or unfamiliar fairy or traditional story. Then, share some "fractured fairy tales" with the students. Then, they will rewrite the story to be their own original plot in a one-page version.
4. Share the components of a play script with the students. They will translate their original stories into a script.
5. The students use whatever medium that they want, including pop-ups, to illustrate a couple of sets for their original stories. They present those to the class along with reading their scripts.

EXTENSIONS

1. The class selects several scripts to work on as small groups so that they can present the plays to younger students as a reader's theater production. Emphasize to them that the audience must be considered when devising the script.

2. Students write original scripts in poetry, using nursery rhymes of their choice.

ADDITIONAL RESOURCES:

Other Pop-Up Books

TITLE: *Beauty and the Beast and Other Fantastic Fairy Tales*

AUTHOR: Ron Van der Meer

ILLUSTRATOR: Fran Thatcher

PUBLISHER, COPYRIGHT DATE: Random House, c1994

ANNOTATION: Four fairy tales pop up as two-page spreads reminiscent of stage sets. Each is accompanied by a miniature book that tells the story. Included are Snow White and the Seven Dwarfs, the Pied Piper of Hamelin, Beauty and the Beast, and Pinocchio.

TITLE: *The Diary of Hansel and Gretel*

PAPER ENGINEER: Kees Moerbeek

AUTHOR: Kees Moerbeek

ILLUSTRATOR: Kees Moerbeek

PUBLISHER, COPYRIGHT DATE: Little Simon, c2002

ANNOTATION: The Grimms' fairy tale is translated into a handwritten and sketched diary of the adventures of Hansel and Gretel. There is a pop-up gingerbread house.

TITLE: *Every Page a Stage: Nursery Tales: 5 Interactive Pop-Up Stories to Perform*

PAPER ENGINEER: Nghiem Ta

DESIGNER: Nghiem Ta

CONCEPT: Keith Finch

AUTHOR: Dug Steer

ILLUSTRATOR: Steve Lavis

PUBLISHER, COPYRIGHT DATE: Backpack Books, c2004

ANNOTATION: The Three Little Pigs, Hansel and Gretel, Puss in Boots, Goldilocks and the Three Bears, and Little Red Riding Hood are the five fairy tales that are each illustrated with a 3-D stage capture that uses tabs to move the characters across the scenes. Each story is told in a one-page poem.

TITLE: *Peek-a-Boo! Pop-Up Fairy Tales*

PAPER ENGINEER: Keith Faulkner

ILLUSTRATOR: Jonathan Lambert

PUBLISHER, COPYRIGHT DATE: Starlight Editions, c1991

ANNOTATION: Each of five fairy tales is played out in a pop-up room, which the reader can view through windows.

TITLE: *Pop-Up Storybook Theater: Goldilocks and the Three Bears*

PAPER ENGINEERS: Bruce Foster and Ed Galm

AUTHOR: Teddy Slater

ILLUSTRATOR: Lane Yerkes

PUBLISHER, COPYRIGHT DATE: Ottenheimer, c1995

ANNOTATION: Goldilocks can be presented on stage with this book.

TITLE: *Pop-Up Theater Proudly Presents Cinderella*

PAPER ENGINEER: Richard Fowler

DESIGNER: Richard Fowler (settings and costumes)

AUTHORS: Charles Perrault and David Wood (adapter)

ILLUSTRATOR: Richard Fowler

PUBLISHER, COPYRIGHT: Kingfisher, c1994

ANNOTATION: This book opens to become a pop-up, 3-D stage with movable backdrops and is accompanied by a script for a play about Cinderella; the props that are the characters, and so on.

TITLE: *Princess Polly and the Pea: A Royal Tactile and Princely Pop-Up*

PAPER ENGINEER: Matt Powers

DESIGNER: Laurie Young

AUTHOR: Laurie Young

ILLUSTRATOR: Johanna Hantel

PUBLISHER, DATE: Piggy Toes Press, c2007

ANNOTATION: The queen's test of a "real" princess is helped out by a sympathetic prince, king, jester, and cook. Touchable textures enhance the story, as does the ending of a two-page spread of a pop-up of the wedding.

TITLE: *The Sleeping Beauty Ballet Theatre*

DESIGNER: David Hawcock (theater based on his original design)

AUTHORS: Viola Ann Seddon

ILLUSTRATOR: Jean Mahoney

PUBLISHER, DATE: Candlewick Press, c2007

ANNOTATION: The stage folds down, the dancers emerge from a drawer, the CD provides the music, and the paperback book tells the story, explains the ballet's history, and offers a recipe for pavlova.

TITLE: *Snow White: A Three-Dimensional Fairy-Tale Theater*

AUTHOR: Jane Ray

PUBLISHER, COPYRIGHT DATE: Candlewick Press, 2009

ANNOTATION: There are six double-page scenes that pop out into 3-D stage settings, framed by red curtains that are actually flaps. Open the side curtains, and the text of the story explains the story plot.

TITLE: *The Three Little Wolves and the Big Bad Pig*

AWARD ALERT: The original book was highly commended for the Kate Greenaway Medal (established by The [British] Library Association).

PAPER ENGINEER: Keith Finch

AUTHOR: Eugene Trivizas

ILLUSTRATOR: Helen Oxenbury

PUBLISHER, COPYRIGHT DATE: Egmont Books, c2003

ANNOTATION: The big, bad pig is the villain in this retelling of the classic story. Flaps, wheels, and pop-ups move the action along.

TITLE: *The True Story of Goldilocks*

AUTHORS: Agnese Baruzzi and Sandro Natalini

ILLUSTRATORS: Agnese Baruzzi and Sandro Natalini

PUBLISHER, COPYRIGHT DATE: Templar Company, c2009

ANNOTATION: In this retelling of a familiar fairy tale, the reader learns the backstory behind that tale, when Goldilocks and the three bears had a much better relationship! At the end of the book, the bears' house pops up.

Other Books with Interactivity

TITLE: *Fairytale Mix-Up*

DESIGNER: Melanie Random

AUTHOR: Jane Smith

ILLUSTRATOR: Jackie Raynor

PUBLISHER, COPYRIGHT DATE: Piggy Toes Press, c2005

ANNOTATION: Flaps transform fairy-tale characters into an almost infinite variety of other characters.

TITLE: *Mimi's Scary Theater*

PAPER ENGINEER: David Hawcock

AUTHOR: Elzbieta

ILLUSTRATOR: Elzbieta

PUBLISHER, COPYRIGHT DATE: Hyperion Books for Children, c1993

ANNOTATION: This book is "a play in nine scenes for seven characters and an egg," and the book opens to become the stage. Tabs and flaps create the action for each set, which also include the script for that scene.

TITLE: *The True Story of Little Red Riding Hood*

AUTHORS: Agnese Baruzzi and SandroNatalini

ILLUSTRATORS: Agnese Baruzzi and SandroNatalini

PUBLISHER, COPYRIGHT DATE: Templar Company, c2007

ANNOTATION: It seems that once upon a time, the wolf was actually reformed with the help of Little Red Riding Hood. Unfortunately jealousy took over . . . but then, you *do* know the rest of the story.

Books without Interactivity

TITLE: *Good Masters! Sweet Ladies! Voices from a Medieval Village*

AUTHOR: Laura Amy Schlitz

ILLUSTRATOR: Robert Byrd

PUBLISHER, COPYRIGHT DATE: Candlewick Press, c2007

ANNOTATION: The folk in a medieval village include the lord's nephew, the black-smith's daughter, the doctor's son, and the like. The monologues (designed for student presentation) in this book bring each one to life.

TITLE: *The Stinky Cheese Man and Other Fairly Stupid Tales* (**fiction**)

AUTHOR: Jon Scieszka

ILLUSTRATOR: Lane Smith

PUBLISHER, COPYRIGHT DATE: Viking, c1992

ANNOTATION: The book has 10 "fractured" fairy tales, such as "The Really Ugly Duckling" and "Tortoise and the Hair."

DVD

TITLE: *The Best of Fractured Fairy Tales, Vol. 1* (1961, 1999); 15 episodes, approximately 6 minutes each (**fiction**)

DISTRIBUTOR: Classic Media

ANNOTATION: Fifteen episodes from the Mr. Peabody and Sherman segments on the 1960s television animated series *Rocky and Bullwinkle and Friends*, "fracture" classic fairy tales, including Snow White, Cinderella, The Brave Little Tailor, and so on.

TITLE: *Tangled* (2011); 100 minutes (**fiction**)

DISTRIBUTOR: Walt Disney

ANNOTATION: In this animated retelling of the Rapunzel tale, she is not the typical princess.

Website

TITLE; AGENCY: *The Beauty and the Beast* online tour web page; NETworks Presentations, Inc.

URL: http://www.beautyandthebeastontour.com

ANNOTATION: See video clips from the stage production on this site.

TITLE; AGENCY: *Reader's Theatre Scripts and Plays: Free Printables, Themes, Lessons & More for Your K–3 Classroom*; Teaching Heart

URL: http://www.teachingheart.net/readerstheater.htm

ANNOTATION: Access free scripts for reader's theater, as well as tips and guidance on this type of performance. Also very useful is "a downloadable set of twenty practice sheets to use in team scripting exercises" (requires Adobe Acrobat).

THEME: **The Wizard of Oz,** *Fantasy Literature, Social Science*

TITLE: *The Wonderful Wizard of Oz: A Commemorative Pop-Up By L. Frank Baum*

PAPER ENGINEERS: Robert Sabuda

AUTHOR: L. Frank Baum

ILLUSTRATORS: Robert Sabuda (art) and Matthew Reinhart (additional design work)

PUBLISHER, COPYRIGHT DATE: Little Simon, c2000

ANNOTATION:

Double-page spreads of pop-ups and multiple small flaps with pop-ups are reminiscent of the original artwork from the book.

AWARD ALERT: Robert Sabuda received the 2002 Meggendorfer Prize, recognizing the paper engineering in this pop-up book. It is given biennially by The Movable Book Society.

MAJOR CURRICULUM AREAS:

Language arts
Literature (Fantasy)
Social Studies

ACTIVITY OVERVIEW:

Fantasy literature is not only a portal for students to understand the role of fantasy in literature but also to explore aspects of community.

DESCRIPTION OF ACTIVITY:

1. Introduce the topic of fantasy in literature to the students. Then, while sharing the pop-up book *The Wonderful Wizard of Oz*, discuss with the students what elements of fantasy are present and how the pop-ups capture those elements.
2. The original *The Wonderful Wizard of Oz* was set on the Kansas prairie, which was home to the author, L. Frank Baum. Within his setting he used people, places, and events that were familiar to him, such as a scarecrow, a farm, and a cyclone. Brainstorm the following question with the students: If they were writing a fantasy about their locale, what settings, characters, and events would they use? Then, have each of the students write a short fantasy that incorporates elements distinctive to the locale of the community.
3. Read the cyclone scene from the original book. Then, share with the students the cyclone scene, with its motion, from the pop-up book. Follow with a showing of a clip of the cyclone scene from the original *The Wizard of Oz*, starring Judy Garland movie (1939). After the viewing, ask the students how each version conveys the image of the cyclone to the reader or viewer.
4. Lead the students in brainstorming how they want to have their fantasy stories translated into other media. For instance, would they choose to have the original story become a pop-up book, a short story in a book, a graphic novel, a videogame, a movie script, and so on?

EXTENSION

Students convert their fantasy stories into three-dimensional media (including digital) of their choice.

ADDITIONAL RESOURCES:

Other Pop-Up Books

TITLE: *The Wizard of Oz*

PAPER ENGINEER: Rodger Smith

AUTHORS: Jay Scarfone and William Stillman

PUBLISHER, COPYRIGHT DATE: Intervisual Books, c2000

ANNOTATION: The classic Judy Garland, MGM film is resurrected in pop-ups and sound.

Other Books with Interactivity

TITLE: *If You Love a Magical Tale: The Wizard of Oz and Aladdin*

PAPER ENGINEER: Alan Brown

DESIGNER: Laura Hambleton

AUTHOR: Saviour Pirotta (adaptation)

PUBLISHER, COPYRIGHT DATE: Barron's, c2010

ANNOTATION: Lift the full-page flaps and transformations change the scene in the middle. The book is rendered in many colors, but they are soft, almost pastel.

Books without Interactivity

TITLE: *The Annotated Wizard of Oz: Centennial Edition* (**informational for teacher**)

AUTHORS: L. Frank Baum and Michael Patrick Hearn (editor; introduction and notes)

ILLUSTRATOR: W.W. Denslow

PUBLISHER, COPYRIGHT DATE: W.W. Norton, c1973, 2000

ANNOTATION: The facsimile edition of the *Wizard* is greatly enhanced with detailed annotations, including biographical information about the creator of this American classic and its original illustrator (Denslow).

TITLE: *The Road to Oz: Twists, Turns, Bumps, and Triumphs in the Life of L. Frank Baum* (**informational**)

AUTHOR: Kathleen Krull

ILLUSTRATOR: Kevin Hawkes

PUBLISHER, COPYRIGHT DATE: Knopf Books for Young Readers, c2008

ANNOTATION: This illustrated biography of the author of *The Wonderful Wizard of Oz* introduces him to younger readers.

TITLE: *The Wonderful Wizard of Oz, 100th Anniversary Edition* (**fiction, informational**)

AUTHOR: L. Frank Baum

ILLUSTRATOR: W.W. Denslow

PUBLISHER, COPYRIGHT DATE: HarperCollins, c1987

ANNOTATION: It's always a rewarding experience to return to the original version of a beloved classic.

TITLE: *The Wonderful Wizard of Oz* (graphic novel) (**fiction**)

AUTHOR: L. Frank Baum

ILLUSTRATORS: Eric Young and Skottie Young

PUBLISHER, COPYRIGHT DATE: Marvel, c2010

ANNOTATION: The transformation of the 100-year-old story into a graphic novel gives it a contemporary life.

Website

TITLE; AGENCY: *The Wonderful Wizard of Oz by L. Frank Baum*; Project Gutenberg

URL: http://www.gutenberg.org/ebooks/55

ANNOTATION: Read the book online or download it to Kindle or other devices, as part of this collaborative digital library project of copyright-free books.

8

Using Pop-Ups in Activities and Programs Continued (Secondary Grades, Program for Teachers or Librarians, Program for Public Library Story Times)

SECONDARY (GRADES 9, 10, 11, 12)

THEME: Ancient and Modern Civilizations: Cultural Collections and Ethics

TITLE: *The Pompeii Pop-Up*

PAPER ENGINEER: David Hawcock

AUTHOR: Peter Riley

PUBLISHER, COPYRIGHT DATE: Universe, c2007

ANNOTATION:

This impressive pop-up book covers not only many details about the city of Pompeii, which was lost to a volcano, but also information about the archaeological history of its uncovering.

MAJOR CURRICULUM AREAS:

Language Arts
Social Studies (Archaeology, Diversity, Ethics, Geography, History)

ACTIVITY OVERVIEW:

Issues of ownership, destruction, and appropriation of cultural resources, and the place of cultural resources in the lives of communities and the larger world provide the opportunity for students to combine research with critical thinking skills.

DESCRIPTION OF ACTIVITY:

1. Share the pop-up book with the students. Ask them who they think "owns" the archaeological treasures that are shown. Have a discussion with them about the ideas that they have regarding "discovery" and "ownership."
2. Provide teams of students with topics about current and historic issues related to art, archeology, cultural treasures, ethics, ownership of cultural artifacts, and so on. This list is a collaboration of the librarian and teacher. Such a list might include:

   Afghanistan's Bamiyan Statues
   Kennewick Man
   Gustav Klimpt's Gold Portrait
   NAGPRA (Native American Graves and Repatriation Act)
   Archaeological Institute of America Code of Ethics
   Archaeological Resources Protection Act of 1979

3. Have each team of students do enough research to collect a list of the "issues" that are raised about this topic.
4. Teams of students will contribute their list to a collective list of issues generated by the class.
5. Individual students will choose an issue, do more research with library resources, and then write a position paper that discusses the sides of the issue and then supports a position. Alternatively the students could use a class blog to present their positions and discuss them.

ADDITIONAL RESOURCES:

Other Pop-Up Books

TITLE: *Masks*

DESIGNERS AND PAPER ENGINEERS: Heather Simmons and Olivier Charbonnel

AUTHOR: Metropolitan Museum of Art

PUBLISHER, COPYRIGHT DATE: DK Publishing, c1997

ANNOTATION: Masks from cultures around the world, from the collections of the Metropolitan Museum of Art, are the eight two-page spreads pop-ups in this book. Each mask is accompanied by a history, including its importance within the society from which it came.

TITLE: *The Search for Tutankhamun*

PAPER ENGINEER: Julie Thompson and David Miller (tomb paper engineering)

AUTHOR: Niki Horn

ILLUSTRATOR: Andrew Hopgood (main illustrations) and Lee Krutop (additional illustrations)

PUBLISHER, COPYRIGHT DATE: Five Mile Press, c2007

ANNOTATION: This coverage of Tutankhamun's tomb and reign focuses on the archaeological endeavors that uncovered it. It is richly illustrated with photographs.

Books without Interactivity

TITLE: *Exploring the Life, Myth, and Art of Native Americans* (informational)

AUTHOR: Larry J. Zimmerman

PUBLISHER, COPYRIGHT DATE: Rosen, c2010

ANNOTATION: Covers a wide range of topics about Native American lifeways, values, and history, including daily living, spiritual practices, and art.

TITLE: *Rome: The Greatest Empire of the Ancient World* (**informational**)

AUTHOR: Nick McCarty

PUBLISHER, COPYRIGHT DATE: Rosen, 2008

ANNOTATION: Topical chapters cover a range of Roman life and history, including the building of the empire, Caesar, Augustus, slavery, and so forth.

DVDs

TITLE: *Secrets of the Dead: China's Terracotta Warriors* (2011); 60 minutes (**informational**)

DISTRIBUTOR: PBS

ANNOTATION: This is an episode from the popular PBS series.

TITLE: *When Rome Ruled* (2011); 270 minutes on 3 discs (**informational**)

DISTRIBUTOR: National Geographic

ANNOTATION: This six-part documentary includes coverage of Pompeii, gladiators, Caesar, and the role of Rome in its time. It includes interviews with scholars.

Websites

TITLE; AGENCY: *National NAGPRA; NAGPRA Training;* U.S. Department of the Interior, National Park Service

URL: http://www.nps.gov/history/nagpra/TRAINING/INDEX.htm

ANNOTATION: The National Graves and Repatriation Act is 1990 federal legislation that requires the return of "human remains, funerary objects, sacred objects, or objects of cultural patrimony" to American Indian communities. This website is dedicated to information about the legislation and its implementation, and targets resources for Native American tribes, museums, government agencies, the public, and the press.

TITLE; AGENCY: *Pompeii: Its Discovery and Preservation;* BBC

URL: http://www.bbc.co.uk/history/ancient/romans/pompeii_rediscovery_01.shtml

ANNOTATION: This BBC web space on Pompeii provides historical background and photographs of the current excavations and artifacts and restoration.

THEME: Going the Distance with Sports

TITLE: *Tour de France*

AUTHOR: Pamela Pease

PUBLISHER, COPYRIGHT DATE: Paintbox Press, c2009

ANNOTATION:

Photographs, a clear overlay, flaps, a tab, and pop-ups provide a three-dimensional view of the "World's Greatest Bike Race." There is a glossary on the last page.

MAJOR CURRICULUM AREAS:

Health and Physical Education (Disability, Sports)
Language Arts (Research Skills and Writing)
Science

ACTIVITY OVERVIEW:

The popularity of sports provides the connection to introduce students to the reason for and effective use of primary and secondary sources in research as well as helps them to broaden their understanding of who is able to engage in sports and what constitutes a sport.

DESCRIPTION OF ACTIVITY:

1. Have students generate a list of potential sources that the writer and illustrator might have used to provide facts that they cited in this pop-up book. Discuss with students the distinctions between primary and secondary sources, using questions that focus on how decisions about their selection might have impacted the writer and illustrator.
2. What other sports would the students like to see used to create a similar pop-up book? What kinds of information would a writer or illustrator need to create that book?
3. Have each student pick a sport they're interested in, either as a participant or fan, and pick one aspect of it to research as if they were responsible for giving that information to the writer and illustrator of a pop-up book about that sport. Part of the assignment is also interviewing an individual who would have insight into that sport. Review with the students the protocols for interviewing (see website in Additional Resources). Have students prepare a report form about their planning for the interview (see Figure 8.1 at the end of this theme).
4. Have each student continue researching the sport of their choice to find out how individuals with physical challenges can participate in that sport. How is technology being used to assist them? Have them add this information to their report.
5. Discuss with students the options that they will have for presentation of their reports to the class (digital, in-person, print, etc.).

ADDITIONAL RESOURCES:

Other Pop-Up Books

TITLE: *Citi Field: The Mets' New World-Class Ballpark: A Ballpark Pop-Up Book*

DESINGER: David Hawcock

AUTHOR: MLB Publishing

PUBLISHER, COPYRIGHT: Universe Publishing, c2009

ANNOTATION: In this oversized book, the two-page pop-up spread of Citi Field is the grand finale for this coverage of the records and history of the famous ballpark. The sixteen-inch-tall book is liberally illustrated with photographs.

TITLE: *An Enduring Passion: The Legends and Lore of Golf*

DESIGNER: Jeff Wincapaw

AUTHOR: Jaime Diaz

PUBLISHER, COPYRIGHT: Crown Publishers, c2002

ANNOTATION: This extensive coverage of golf covers notable players, courses, championships, and so on. This interactive book is enhanced with "removable documents and photographs."

TITLE: *Golf: A Three-Dimensional Exploration of the Game*

AUTHOR: John Garrity

PUBLISHER, COPYRIGHT DATE: Viking Penguin Books, c1996

ANNOTATION: This book highlights the world's most famous golf courses, incorporating many facts about their history, construction, and description and also about golf players and the game.

TITLE: *NASCAR Pop-Up: A Guide to the Sport*

PAPER ENGINEER: Sally Blakemore

DESIGNERS: Sally Blakemore, Paul R. Blakemore (audio design and engineering), and Arty Projects Studio (book packaging)

AUTHOR: Sally Blakemore

ILLUSTRATOR: Doug Chezem

PUBLISHER, COPYRIGHT DATE: Gibbs Smith, 2009

ANNOTATION: Pop-ups, pull tabs, and flaps provide the motion for this coverage of stock car racing, which includes details about topics from the history of the sport to the driver's safety apparel to what it takes to qualify and to win.

TITLE: *Wow! The Pop-Up Book of Sports*

PAPER ENGINEER: Bruce Foster

DESIGNER: Beth Bugler

AUTHORS: Sarah Braunstein and Jennifer Altavilla

PUBLISHER, COPYRIGHT DATE: Time, c2009

ANNOTATION: This oversize *Sports Illustrated Kids* book is overflowing with pop-ups created from photographs and information about "some of the greatest athletes of all time."

Other Books with Interactivity

TITLE: *America's Pastime: Historical Treasures from the Baseball Hall of Fame*

AUTHOR: Gabriel Schechter

PUBLISHER, COPYRIGHT DATE: Barnes and Noble, c2006

ANNOTATION: The boxed case contains a paperback book, with historic photographs and background information, and a collection of facsimile memorabilia (from the Baseball Hall of Fame) about important events in baseball history.

Books without Interactivity

TITLE: *The Biggest Nascar Races* (**informational**)

AUTHOR: Holly Cefrey

PUBLISHER, COPYRIGHT DATE: Rosen Central, c2008

ANNOTATION: The book focuses on the Nextel Cup, the Busch series, the Craftsman Truck series, and international, regional, and event NASCAR races.

TITLE: *Danica Patrick* (**informational**)

AUTHOR: Barbara Sheen

PUBLISHER, COPYRIGHT DATE: Lucent Books, c2009

ANNOTATION: A biography of Danica Patrick, the very successful woman auto racing competitor who has also been a model and has appeared in commercials.

TITLE: *Race Across Alaska: First Woman to Win the Iditarod Tells Her Story* (**informational**)

AUTHORS: Libby Riddles and Tim Jones

PUBLISHER, COPYRIGHT DATE: Stackpole Books, c1988

ANNOTATION: An autobiography of Libby Riddles, who became the first woman to win the Alaskan Iditarod dogsled race, which goes from Anchorage to Nome.

TITLE: *Super Surfers* (**informational**)

AUTHOR: Michael Sandler

PUBLISHER, COPYRIGHT DATE: Bearport, c2010

ANNOTATION: Lots of details and photographs capture the world of the super surfers.

TITLE: *Run! 26.2 Stories of Blisters and Bliss* (**informational**)

AUTHOR: Dean Karnazes

PUBLISHER, COPYRIGHT DATE: Rodale Books, c2011

ANNOTATION: Karnazes tells the story of his supermarathon racing in places all around the world.

DVD

TITLE: *Extreme* (2008); 45 minutes (**informational**)

DISTRIBUTOR: National Geographic

ANNOTATION: Profiles champion athletes who tackle snowboarding mountains, climbing frozen waterfalls, windsurfing gale winds, and so forth.

Websites

TITLE; AGENCY: Disabled Sports USA Home website; Disabled Sports USA

URL: http://www.dsusa.org/index.html

ANNOTATION: This website for the organization Disabled Sports USA explains its mission and activities. It also provides information about sports equipment resources to assist individuals with disabilities.

TITLE; AGENCY: *Oral Interview Training for the Hmong Oral History Project*; Wisconsin Historical Society (**informational for teacher**)

Sports Interview Form

You are a journalist who has been invited by a famous paper engineer to provide him or her with factual information that will be used to create a pop-up on the sport that you select.

You can also use the information that you gather to write an article for your publication, but you must narrow the topic down to only one aspect of the sport for the paper engineer's book.

As a fan, you know what your favorite sport is, but you believe that you need the help of someone involved in the sports world, such as an athlete, a coach, a trainer, and so on, to be your expert advisor.

Here are some things to consider in planning your interview. **Complete these questions:**

ANSWER BEFORE THE INTERVIEW

1. Which sport will you pick and why?

2. Who will you interview?

3. Why did you select this person?

4. What questions will you ask? LIST THEM.

5. Who are your readers?

Figure 8.1. Sports Interview Form

6. What are your readers most interested in learning about? Is it the history of the sport, famous athletes, team or individual records, training, equipment, diet, and so on?

ANSWER AFTER THE INTERVIEW

7. When the interview is concluded, reflect on what you have learned. Did you learn anything that surprised you and that will be new to your readers? What was it?

8. How will you present your interview information to the pop-up engineer? In a narrative form? In an interview form? Why would you choose this form?

9. What one aspect of the sport will you recommend to the paper engineer as the topic of the pop-up book?

URL: http://www.wisconsinhistory.org/teachers/lessons/secondary/interview. asp

ANNOTATION: This page provides a secondary lesson plan for student oral interviews, incorporating appropriate protocols.

TITLE; AGENCY: Special Olympics Home website; Special Olympics

URL: http://www.specialolympics.org

ANNOTATION: This is the site for the authoritative introduction to the Special Olympics, and it has wonderful photographs of events and contestants.

THEME: Illusion and Dimension in Art

TITLE: *ABC3D*

PAPER ENGINEER: Marion Bataille

DESIGNERS: Marion Bataille (book design) and Michael Yuen (cover design)

PUBLISHER, COPYRIGHT DATE: Roaring Book Press, c2008

ANNOTATION:

Each letter of the alphabet covers a two-page spread, and the presentation transforms them into modern works of sculpture.

AWARD ALERT: Marion Bataille received the 2010 Meggendorfer Prize, recognizing the paper engineering in this pop-up book. The prize is given biennially by The Movable Book Society.

MAJOR CURRICULUM AREAS:

Fine Arts
Language Arts
Math

ACTIVITY OVERVIEW:

This activity introduces students to concepts of illusion and dimension in art and provides them the opportunity to explore those techniques as part of their own art portfolios.

DESCRIPTION OF ACTIVITY:

1. Share the pop-up book with the students and have them analyze the use of illusion and dimension in it. Introduce and discuss with them the types of art techniques used (such as trompe l'oeil, flick cartoons, etc.) to create illusion and dimension.
2. Teacher and librarian collaborate to identify a list of artists who have used techniques to create illusion and dimension. Each student will be given one artist to research in the library's print and digital resources. The students will then show examples of their artists' works (from book or online sources, etc.) in short oral presentations and talk about the artists in a docent-type presentation. Discuss with students what is usually provided in these sorts of presentations (see Figure 8.2 at the end of this theme).
3. Each student will pick a technique of optical illusion or dimension to use in creating her or his own art piece.
4. Each student will share his or her own art piece and will discuss it as if it were a piece in a portfolio being shared for art-school admission.

EXTENSION

Students will research available art schools or departments to find out what their requirements are for admission, especially regarding portfolios.

ADDITIONAL RESOURCES:

Other Pop-Up Books

TITLE: *The Art Pack: A Unique, Three-Dimensional Tour Through the Creation of Art*

AUTHORS: Christopher Frayling, Helen Frayling, and Ron van der Meer

PUBLISHER, COPYRIGHT DATE: Tango, 1998

ANNOTATION: This book is truly a unique "pack," dense with interactive components, including pop-ups, and information, that introduce almost every aspect of art.

TITLE: *The Creation: A Pop-Up Book*

PAPER ENGINEERS: Bruce Reifel and Jose R. Seminario

AUTHOR: Brian Wildsmith

ILLUSTRATOR: Brian Wildsmith

PUBLISHER, COPYRIGHT DATE: The Millbrook Press, c1995

ANNOTATION: Illustrations and pop-ups, without words, capture the Judeo-Christian creation story. The author's explanatory notes for the two-page spreads are provided at the end, which include his ideas about using art to illustrate God. It is a great example to use in discussing abstration, illusion, the use of color, and dimension.

TITLE: *The Pop-Up Book of M.C. Escher*

AUTHORS: M.C. Escher and Michael Solomon Sachs

PUBLISHER, COPYRIGHT DATE: Pomegranate, c1992

ANNOTATION: The illusory quality of Escher's most famous works are brought to stunning life in the pop-ups.

Books without Interactivity

TITLE: *The Invention of Hugo Cabret: A Novel in Words and Pictures*

AUTHOR: Brian Selznick

ILLUSTRATOR: Brian Selznick

PUBLISHER, COPYRIGHT DATE: Scholastic Press, 2007

ANNOTATION: This more than 500-page book tells, in a unique presentation on the book's pages in "words and pictures," the story of orphaned Hugo in early 20th-century Paris. He's on a quest to fix a broken automaton; a mechanical man.

TITLE: *Look Again!* (**informational**)

AUTHOR: Linda C. Falke

ILLUSTRATOR: Metropolitan Museum of Art Photograph Studio (photography; except as noted)

PUBLISHER, COPYRIGHT: The Metropolitan Museum of Art, c2009

ANNOTATION: This 64-page book offers a peek at one element in a painting; turn the page and see the whole work. Look again—things are not always what they seem at first glance!

TITLE: *Optical Illusions in Art; Or—Discover How Paintings Aren't Always What They Seem to Be* (**informational**)

AUTHOR: Alexander Sturgis

ILLUSTRATOR: Steve Bretel

PUBLISHER, COPYRIGHT: Sterling Publishing, c1994

ANNOTATION: This book uses famous paintings to illustrate the techniques of illusion, such as perspective, mirror images, and so on.

Websites

TITLE; AGENCY: *Brian Selznick*; Scholastic Press

URL: http://www2.scholastic.com/browse/contributor.jsp?id=3180

ANNOTATION: See online, short video clips of interviews with Brian Selznick about his creation of the book *The Invention of Hugo Cabret* (see Additional Resources), including the art.

TITLE; AGENCY: *M.C. Escher: The Official Website*; M.C. Escher Foundation and The M.C. Escher Company B. V.

URL: http://www.mcescher.com

ANNOTATION: From the website: "On this website is information about the use of M.C. Escher's work, a short biography, news, bibliography, links and some fund stuff like a Virtual Ride through some of his works."

TITLE; AGENCY: *Illusion: Old or Young?*; University of Illinois at Chicago Department of Ophthalmology and Visual Sciences

URL: http://www.uic.edu/com/eye/LearningAboutVision/EyeSite/OpticalIllustions/OldYoung.shtml

ANNOTATION: On this website see the famous drawing that is either a young or old woman, depending on how you look at it.

TITLE; AGENCY: *Incredible Art Department*; Ken Rohrer

URL: http://www.princetonol.com/groups/iad/jobs/artjobs.html

ANNOTATION: Begun by an elementary school art teacher in 1994, the site offers information about different types of art jobs, such as animation and cartooning, and provides links for locating job ads for those positions.

Docent Guidelines

A **docent** is a person who leads guided tours through a museum or art gallery.

For the oral presentation that you will give on a selected artist, act as if you are a docent and your classmates are participating in your tour.

Have examples of your artist's work on display and proceed as if you are in a gallery.

Docents must be knowledgeable of both the artwork and the artist. Their goal is to help the viewer experience the art. The most enjoyable tours are those in which the docent includes some interesting anecdotes. A lot of advance preparation is necessary to become a good docent. Here are some tips to help you get started.

1. **Be prepared**. Know your subject matter. You may want to have a few key points on 3x5 index cards, which are unobtrusive but can be referred to if necessary.

2. **Introduce yourself.** Welcome your tour group to the museum, and smile! Give your name and tell them that you will be their docent for this exhibit.

3. **State what will be viewed on the tour**. For example: Impressionist paintings, Renaissance tapestries, a special traveling exhibit from the Metropolitan Museum of Art, and so on.

4. **Give some information about the artist.** A brief biography should include
   • the time period in which she or he worked
   • the country in which she or he worked
   • major accomplishments
   • if possible, some interesting bit of trivia about an actual event, humorous, sad, or inspiring, that took place in the artist's life

5. If the work that you are viewing is titled, **state the title and briefly describe the subject matter**. For example: woman with pitcher, field of sunflowers, and so on.

6. **Tell the tour participants what medium was used** to create this work of art. For example: oil paints, watercolors, collage, and so forth.

Figure 8.2. Docent Guidelines

From *Pop-Up Books: A Guide for Teachers and Librarians* by Nancy Bluemel and Rhonda Taylor. Santa Barbara, CA: Libraries Unlimited. Copyright © 2012.

7. **As each work is discussed, point out the use of the elements of art:** composition, line, color, shape, form, and texture.

8. Throughout the tour and at the conclusion, **be prepared to answer questions from the participating group members**. At the end, be sure to ask them if they have questions. Conclude by thanking them for visiting the gallery.

TITLE; AGENCY: *M.C. Escher: The Official Website*; M.C. Escher Foundation and The M.C. Escher Company B. V.

URL: http://www.mcescher.com

ANNOTATION: From the website: "On this website is information about the use of M.C. Escher's work, a short biography, news, bibliography, links and some fund stuff like a Virtual Ride through some of his works."

THEME: Modern Robin Hoods and Pirates

TITLE: *20,000 Leagues Under the Sea: A Pop-Up Book*

DESIGNERS: Neo9 Design and Sam Ita

AUTHORS: Jules Verne and Sam Ita

PUBLISHER, COPYRIGHT DATE: Sterling, c2008

ANNOTATION:

Jules Verne's tale of adventure beneath the ocean is brought to new life with double-page pop-ups illustrating this graphic novel.

MAJOR CURRICULUM AREAS:

Language Arts
Literature
Social Studies

ACTIVITY OVERVIEW:

Who is perceived as a being a "Robin Hood" and who is perceived as a "pirate" depends on whose perspective is being tapped. This activity provides students the opportunity to combine research skills with critical thinking approaches to events past and present.

DESCRIPTION OF ACTIVITY:

1. Share the pop-up graphic novel with the students. Discuss with them whether Captain Nemo is a hero or villain, a pirate or a "Robin Hood," and why they think these are their impressions.
2. Teacher and librarian collaborate to identify topics that can be researched with the library's print and digital resources about historical pirates, contemporary pirates (such as in Somalia), privateering in American history, and so on.
3. The students will do an initial literature review to determine what topics about pirates in history are of interest to them (such as women pirates). Students will then, in brainstorming, generate their own lists of questions

that they would like their research to answer. Then, after doing the research, students will write a position paper (providing supporting evidence/facts), taking a stance on the question: Were/are these individuals heroes (Robin Hoods) or pirates (villains)?

EXTENSIONS

1. Students will design and share a digital presentation that presents their "sides," based on their position papers.

2. Students will view one of the *Pirates of the Caribbean* movies (starring Johnny Depp). They will then compose an essay explaining whether Captain Sparrow is a hero or a villain and how the movie shapes that identity. Ideas from the essay may be shared on a class blog or wiki.

3. After examining the *Pirates of the Caribbean* interactive book (see the Additional Resources), students will discuss how product spin-offs, such as this book, contribute to reinforcement of the messages, including characterizations, of movies and other media.

ADDITIONAL RESOURCES:

Other Books with Interactivity

TITLE: *Oceanology: The True Account of the Nautilus by Zoticus de Lesseps, 1863*

DESIGNER: Templar Company

ILLUSTRATORS: Wayne Anderson, Ian Andrew, Gary Blythe, and David Wyatt, with Tomislav Tomić

PUBLISHER, COPYRIGHT DATE: Candlewick, c2009

ANNOTATION: This book has a scrapbook/journal format, with flaps and facsimiles. It offers a first-person account of adventures with Captain Nemo and the Nautilus.

TITLE: *Pirates Most Wanted*

DESIGNER: Drew McGovern

AUTHOR: John Matthews

PUBLISHER, COPYRIGHT DATE: Atheneum Books for Young Readers, c2007

ANNOTATION: This book's text and illustration profile "thirteen of the most bloodthirsty pirates ever to sail the high seas." It is enhanced by a center fold-out of the captain's cabin and a fold-out miniature book of pirates who achieved record notoriety.

TITLE: *Pirates of the Caribbean*

PUBLISHER, COPYRIGHT DATE: Disney Press, 2007

ANNOTATION: Flaps, slides, and envelopes are mechanisms that lend interactivity to this book which profiles the characters of the Disney movie series.

Books without Interactivity

TITLE: *The Merry Adventures of Robin Hood* (**fiction**)

AUTHOR: Howard Pyle

PUBLISHER, COPYRIGHT DATE: Kessinger Publishing, c2010

ANNOTATION: One of the standard retellings of the Robin Hood legend.

TITLE: *Robin Hood* (**fiction**)

AUTHOR: Paul Creswick

ILLUSTRATOR: N.C. Wyeth

PUBLISHER, COPYRIGHT DATE: Dodo Press, c2003, 2009

ANNOTATION: Wyeth's illustrations make this version of Robin Hood particularly memorable.

TITLE: *20,000 Leagues Under the Sea* (**fiction**)

AUTHORS: Jules Verne and Anthony Bonner (translator)

ILLUSTRATORS: Diane Dillon and Leo Dillon

PUBLISHER, COPYRIGHT DATE: HarperCollins, c2000

ANNOTATION: The story of the remarkable Captain Nemo and his even more remarkable submarine, the *Nautilus*.

DVD

TITLE: *The True Story of Robin Hood* (2006); 50 minutes (**informational**)

DISTRIBUTOR: A&E (The History Channel)

ANNOTATION: An overview of the unanswered questions about Robin Hood, including a glimpse of the time period in which he lived.

Website

TITLE; AGENCY: *Robin Hood*; City of Nottinghamshire, England

URL: http://www.experiencenottinghamshire.com/site/robin-hood

ANNOTATION: The site offers historical information and current pictures for potential visitors to Nottinghamsire, who expect the Robin Hood experience.

THEME: Personalizing Your Research

TITLE: *The California Pop-Up Book*

PUBLISHER, COPYRIGHT DATE: Los Angeles County Museum of Art and Universe, c2000

ANNOTATION:

Pop-ups, pull-outs, and facsimiles, along with an abundance of first-person accounts of the history, events, places, and people that represent California, provide a user-friendly but information-dense introduction to the state.

MAJOR CURRICULUM AREAS:

Language Arts
Music
Science
Social Studies (History, Geography)

ACTIVITY OVERVIEW:

This activity allows students to personalize their research endeavors by focusing on local communities, landmarks, and events of interest to them. It is an introduction to how to do primary-and secondary-source research.

DESCRIPTION OF ACTIVITY:

1. Introduce the students to the concept of primary and secondary sources (see the Additional Resources). Discuss with students why this distinction is im-

portant. Then, share the pop-up book and emphasize its inclusion of primary sources.

2. Allow time for students to consider what local/state/regional person, event, place, or other topics that they are interested in researching.
3. Have each of the students devise a thesis sentence to research.
4. Introduce students to the protocols for doing interviews (see the Additional Resources), which can be done in person, online, or by telephone. For students who are doing interviews as part of research, have them practice the questions with a partner in the class prior to the interview. The interviewee should provide feedback about the process to the interviewer.
5. Allow time for students to do research, using online and print library resources, and to collect entries for initial, draft bibliographies that are submitted for review. Have them indicate which of the entries are secondary resources and which are primary resources. Discuss with the students their experiences in locating these two types of resources
6. Have the students brainstorm how their information might be disseminated (the pop-up book is one not-so-typical way to do this), such as a website, a book, an article, and so on.

EXTENSION

Student can devise a Jay Leno–style "walking" activity in which they quiz other students on what should be well-known facts about their community, state, and so forth.

ADDITIONAL RESOURCES:

Other Pop-Up Books

TITLE: *Graceland: An Interactive Pop-Up Tour*

PAPER ENGINEER: Chuck Murphy

DESIGNER: Bryn Ashburn

AUTHOR: Jason Rekulak

ILLUSTRATOR: Studio Liddell

PUBLISHER, COPYRIGHT DATE: Chronicle Books, c2006

ANNOTATION: A long-term attraction for visitors to Memphis is Graceland, Elvis's home. Pop-ups and other interactive elements, along with photographs and informative text, provide a comprehensive room-by-room tour.

TITLE: *The New York Pop-Up Book*

PAPER ENGINEER: David Hawcock

DESIGNERS: Bob Bass and Edward Sorel (cover design)

AUTHOR: Marie Salerno (editor)

PUBLISHER, COPYRIGHT DATE: Universe, 1999

ANNOTATION: Pop-ups, facsimiles, and first-person accounts by famous New Yorkers highlight the history, architecture, music, events, literature, politics, and theater of this most famous of cities.

Books without Interactivity

TITLE: *It Happened in San Antonio* (**informational**)

AUTHOR: Marilyn Bennett

PUBLISHER, COPYRIGHT DATE: TwoDot Book, Morris Book Publishing, c2006

ANNOTATION: What happened in San Antonio? A lot! This book introduces fascinating persons and incidents that add to the richness of the city's history.

TITLE: *San Antonio Then and Now* (**informational**)

AUTHOR: Paula Allen

PUBLISHER, COPYRIGHT DATE: Thunder Bay Press, c2005

ANNOTATION: Explore the historical and contemporary San Antonio with the assistance of this information-rich guide.

DVD

TITLE: *American Experience: New York Underground* (1997, 2006); 56 minutes (**informational**)

DISTRIBUTOR: PBS

ANNOTATION: This documentary is part of the PBS "American Experience" series, and it profiles the building of New York City's subway system.

Website

TITLE; AGENCY: *Basic Steps in the Research Process*; Cambridge Rindge & Latin School.

URL: http://www.crlsresearchguide.org

ANNOTATION: This interactive website walks a student through 23 steps of the research process. It also provides links to translate the site into other languages.

TITLE; AGENCY: *Oral Interview Training for the Hmong Oral History Project*; Wisconsin Historical Society (**informational for teacher**)

URL: http://www.wisconsinhistory.org/teachers/lessons/secondary/interview.asp

ANNOTATION: This page provides a secondary lesson plan for student oral interviews, incorporating appropriate protocols.

TITLE; AGENCY: *Primary and Secondary Sources*; Bowling Green State University Libraries

URL: http://libguides.bgsu.edu/content.php?pid=20573&sid=145214

ANNOTATION: This web page has a succinct explanation of the difference between primary and secondary sources, illustrated with a short chart comparing examples of the two.

THEME: Sailing across U.S. History

TITLE: *The Pop-Up Book of Ships*

PAPER ENGINEER: David Hawcock

AUTHOR: Eric Kentley

ILLUSTRATOR: Gary Walton

PUBLISHER, COPYRIGHT DATE: Universe Publishing, c2009

ANNOTATION:

Two-page pop-up spreads of intricately detailed and memorable sailing vessels from across time and from around the world offer a history of the ships themselves and of maritime highlights and their relationship to other important events.

MAJOR CURRICULM AREAS FOR THE ACTIVITY:

Fine Arts
Language Arts
Music
Social Studies (Diversity, History, Geography)

ACTIVITY OVERVIEW:

The United States has coasts on the Atlantic and Pacific oceans and the Gulf of Mexico. One state is (Hawaii) in the middle of the ocean. U.S. protectorates and territories are bound by water. U.S. history and society, from the beginnings of the nation to contemporary times, has been impacted by sailing and sailing vessels. Examples include:

Native American navigation of waterways prior to European contact;
whether Vikings explored North America before Columbus's arrival;
the voyages of Columbus and of the Pilgrims;
the transportation of Africans as enslaved people;
whaling ships;
the invention of the steam engine;
the building of the Panama canal;
Civil War submarines;
the bombing of Pearl Harbor;
the sinking of the Titanic, and so on.

DESCRIPTION OF ACTIVITY:

1. Share the pop-up book with the students. Point out the many historic happenings tied to the ships that are portrayed.
2. Students choose from a list (generated by collaboration of the teacher and librarian) of potential sailing/ship-related topics (see initial list above) important in American history.
3. Students will research these topics, focusing on their historical background and their contemporary connection (such as a memorial to Pearl Harbor, current issues about territorial limits in the ocean, etc.)
4. Students will prepare an informational product that might be used to explain their topic in a setting such as a museum, memorial, and so on. They will use media of their choice (discuss with students the various options that they have observed being used in such facilities). In the discussion of media choices, assist them in considering the needs/interests of various potential audiences, which includes factors of age, background knowledge, disability, and so forth.

ADDITIONAL RESOURCES:

Other Pop-Up Books

TITLE: *Ships: A Pop-Up Book*

PAPER ENGINEER: Robert Crowther

PUBLISHER, COPYRIGHT DATE: Candlewick Press, c2008

ANNOTATION: Some minutely detailed ships are pop-ups and others move with tabs. The text offers a history of the development of ships and highlights famous ones.

TITLE: *Titanic: The Ship of Dreams*

PAPER ENGINEERS: Keith Finch and Tony Potter

AUTHOR: Duncan Crosbie

ILLUSTRATORS: Bob Moulder, Peter Kent and Tim Hutchinson

PUBLISHER, COPYRIGHT DATE: Orchard Books, c2006

ANNOTATION: A ten-year-old child's journal, based on events that happened to actual families, is the storyline that ties together the background of this great ship's end. Photographs, replicas of artifacts, maps, and chronologies document the disaster.

TITLE: *Undersea Treasures*

PAPER ENGINEER: Tor Lokvig

AUTHOR: Emory Kristof

ILLUSTRATOR: Peter Fiore

PUBLISHER, COPYRIGHT DATE: The National Geographic Society, c 1995

ANNOTATION: Beginning with a ship that sunk more than 3,000 years ago, this book highlights famous lost ships that carried immense treasures with them to the bottom of the oceans.

Other Books with Interactivity

TITLE: *Journey of Hope: The Story of Irish Immigration to America: An Interactive History*

DESIGNERS: Trina Stahl and Holly McNeill

AUTHORS: Kerby Miller and Patricia Mulholland Miller

PUBLISHER, COPYRIGHT DATE: Chronicle Books, c2001

ANNOTATION: The long story of Irish immigration to the United States (via ship) is included as interactive elements such as letters in envelopes, fold-out pamphlets, prayer cards, and so on.

Books without Interactivity

TITLE: *At Ellis Island: A History in Many Voices* (**informational**)

AUTHOR: Louise Peacock

ILLUSTRATOR: Walter Lyon Krudop

PUBLISHER, COPYRIGHT DATE: Atheneum, c2007

ANNOTATION: A young girl in contemporary America visits Ellis Island; juxtaposed with this voice is that of another young girl who escaped Armenia a century ago. These two fictional voices are placed among quotes from real immigrants who arrived at Ellis Island.

TITLE: *Immigrant Kids* (**informational**)

AUTHOR: Russell Freedman

PUBLISHER, COPYRIGHT DATE: Dutton, c1980

ANNOTATION: The book's focus is the late 19th and early 20th century, and photographs help to describe the lives of immigrant children at play, work, home, and school.

TITLE: *War to End All Wars: World War I* (**informational**)

AUTHOR: Russell Freedman

PUBLISHER, COPYRIGHT DATE: Clarion Books, c2010

ANNOTATION: World War I was "the war to end all wars." This book covers many facets of that endeavor, including the events that led to it, the technology of warfare, sea battles, and so on.

DVD

TITLE: *Island of Hope, Island of Tears: The Story of Ellis Island* (30 minutes); 1989 (**informational**)

DISTRIBUTOR: Guggenheim Productions

ANNOTATION: This documentary was directed by Charles Guggenheim, who won multiple Academy Awards. It covers the period from 1890 to 1920.

Website

TITLE; AGENCY: *Ellis Island*; U.S. National Park Service

URL: http://www.nps.gov/elis/index.htm

ANNOTATION: The official website for Ellis Island includes history, FAQs, photos, and biographies of famous people associated with the port as an immigration processing station.

THEME: Theater Production: Researching Social History

TITLE 1: *The Nutcracker: A Pop-Up Book*

PAPER ENGINEER: Patricia Fry

AUTHOR: Patricia Fry (adapted from E.T.A. Hoffmann)

ILLUSTRATOR: Patricia Fry

PUBLISHER, COPYRIGHT DATE: HarperCollins, c2008

ANNOTATION:

The pop-ups are simultaneously complicated in design and simple in illustration.

TITLE 2: *Wicked the Musical*

PAPER ENGINEER: Kees Moerbeek

DESIGNER: Headcase Design

AUTHOR: Jami Attenberg

ILLUSTRATOR: Gregg Call

PUBLISHER, COPYRIGHT DATE: Melcher Media, 2009

ANNOTATION:

This book translates the hit Broadway musical into elaborate pop-ups, making rich use of black, green, purple, and red which captures the flavor of the sets.

MAJOR CURRICULUM AREAS:

Careers
Fine Arts
Social Studies (History)

ACTIVITY OVERVIEW:

Pop-up books of theater and musical productions offer a micro look at the many endeavors that will need to be researched in support of such a production: history of the period, costume, architecture, and so on.

DESCRIPTION OF ACTIVITY:

1. While sharing the pop-up books with students, have them observe and start to brainstorm what needed to be researched to support the productions that are portrayed (such as fashion, architecture, home furnishings, the original story or book, etc.). Have them also brainstorm what products will need to be generated from such research (playbills, sets, costumes, etc.).
2. For non-theater classes, have teams of students choose an existing literary work, such as a book or play, and do the necessary research to support the sets, costumes, and so on, so they are authentic. Remind the students that many plays and musicals are transported from one time period to another (offer them examples of such productions in recent times, such as *Midsummer Night's Dream*, etc.). Have them choose a time period and use library resources to generate information that they will need.
3. Have students produce a pop-up spread, in sketches, similar to the format of the pop-up books, for one set (scene) for their selected production and present it to the class, which will offer suggestions for enhancements and/or further research.

EXTENSION

Have students consider their own interests if they were planning to choose a career path in the fashion, theater, film, or media worlds. What options are open to them besides being an actor or model? Have students determine their own options by researching the professional roles that are available in these fields and the education, skills, and personal attributes that are required for success.

ADDITIONAL RESOURCES:

Other Pop-Up Books

TITLE: *Fashion—À La Mode: The Pop-Up History of Costumes and Dresses*

PAPER ENGINEER: David Hawcock

AUTHOR: Dorothy Twining Globus

ILLUSTRATOR: Isabelle de Borchgrave (costumes)

PUBLISHER, COPYRIGHT DATE: Universe, c2000

ANNOTATION: This fabulous pop-up book presents fashion through history and is so lavishly produced that it is a work of art in its own right. It includes essays by fashion authorities such as Hubert de Givency and Karl Lagerfeld. The text is written by the director of the museum at the Fashion Institute of Technology in New York. Art, history, clothing and textile, and drama teachers will find this unique book to be a valuable resource. For all of these content areas, it can be easily used to introduce concepts of social status and identity through clothing, jewelry, make-up, hairstyles, and body art, as reflected in historical time periods and contemporary life.

TITLE: *How Does the Show Go On? An Introduction to the Theater* **(informational)**

DESIGNER: Kasey Free

AUTHOR: Thomas Schumacher, with Jeff Kurtti

ILLUSTRATOR: Scott Tilley

PUBLISHER, COPYRIGHT DATE: Disney Editions, c2007 Using contemporary Disney productions as examples and for the realia (playbills, tickets, etc.), this profusely illustrated guide covers all aspects of theater: kinds of shows, styles of theatre, performers, backstage, props, lighting, special effects, putting on a play, etc. Schumacher is the producer of the *Lion King* musical.

TITLE: *I Wonder What's Under There?: A Brief History of Underwear*

PAPER ENGINEER: David A. Carter

AUTHOR: Deborah Nourse Lattimore

ILLUSTRATOR: Deborah Nourse Lattimore

PUBLISHER, COPYRIGHT DATE: Browndeer Press, Harcourt Brace, c1998

ANNOTATION: A unique title that highlights what has been worn underneath through history and across cultures, while providing historical facts and context. The pop-ups have lift-the-flaps on clothing to see what's under there.

TITLE: *The Nutcracker: A Pop-Up Adaptation of E.T.A. Hoffman's Original Tale*

PAPER ENGINEERS: David Carter and Rick Morrison

AUTHORS: Noelle Carter and David Carter

PUBLISHER, COPYRIGHT DATE: Little Simon, c2000

ANNOTATION: The left-hand side of each double-page spread is the description of the scene. The scene itself is on the right-hand side of the page; the pulls down to become a set such as one would see on stage.

TITLE: *Nutcracker: A Musical Pop-Up Adventure*

PAPER ENGINEER: Nick Denchfield

ILLUSTRATOR: Sue Scullard

PUBLISHER, COPYRIGHT DATE: Macmillan, c2003

ANNOTATION: The five double-page pop-up spreads in this book offer the illusion of set design, and the text provides details of the storyline.

Books without Interactivity

TITLE: *Costume through the Ages: Over 1400 Illustrations* **(informational)**

AUTHOR: Erhard Klepper

PUBLISHER, COPYRIGHT DATE: Dover, c1999

ANNOTATION: This is a collection of black and white sketches of Western costume, covering the first century to 1930.

DVD

TITLE: *Fashion in Film* (2009); 56 minutes (**informational**)

DISTRIBUTOR: Starz

ANNOTATION: This documentary links fashion with the history of Hollywood and its productions.

Website

TITLE; AGENCY: *The Drexel Digital Museum Project: Historic Costume Collection;* Drexel University

URL: http://digimuse.cis.drexel.edu/

ANNOTATION: View clothing from the collection using a searchable database (in which items can be rotated in 3D using Quick Time), the digital gallery, and a mystery garment section in which information is needed about the origins.

PROGRAM FOR TEACHERS OR LIBRARIANS

THEME: Building Bridges with Pop-Up Books

TITLE: *Snowflakes: A Pop-Up Book*

PAPER ENGINEER: Yevgeniya Yeretskaya

AUTHOR: Jennifer Preston Chushcoff

ILLUSTRATOR: Yevgeniya Yeretskaya

PUBLISHER, COPYRIGHT DATE: Jumping Jack Press, c2010

BOOK ANNOTATION:

Each two-page spread is filled with white pop-up snowflakes of every size and description, set against blue and gray and other muted backgrounds. The text is nominal: "They look like lace" is an example. Occasional use of black and red adds extra contrast. The side flaps reveal other snowflake pop-ups and information about Wilson A. Bentley, who was the first to photograph snowflakes.

MAJOR CURRICULUM AREAS:

All areas

ACTIVITY OVERVIEW:

This presentation assists teachers-librarians in incorporating pop-up books across the curriculum and across interest areas in their planning of lessons plans, activities, programs, and collection development. It can be revised for any grade-level or age-group focus. Simply add more or substitute other pop-up books and additional resources to match the audience interest.

DESCRIPTION OF ACTIVITY:

The program uses an initial theme of winter and related topics but can easily be revised to use any other (especially popular) topic. The pop-ups are presented in a thematic context that can be adapted to include any curriculum or other interest foci, and audience participation encourages the teachers-librarians to share their own ideas for activities.

1. Share the pop-up book with the audience. As it is shared, offer explanations of what a pop-up book is and what paper engineers do. Explain that catching the attention of any audience is always the first step. Also explain that in educational settings, it is critical to link discipline content with real-life experiences.
2. Highlight other pop-up books with winter, climate, environments, penguins and other birds and animals, and related subjects.
3. Ask the audience to brainstorm what the curriculum aspects or interest topics are for these pop-up resources—capture a list of ideas.
4. Introduce the Additional Resources, including showing a clip from *Happy Feet*. Ask the audience to think of topics and activities that can be highlighted from the clip. Offer the idea that the Adelie Amigos group in the film may be seen as stereotypical, which lends itself to a potential discussion area.

5. Divide the audience into pairs to brainstorm specific activities or programs or lessons that could be generated from these and related resources, using their own curriculum or topic interests. If there is access to individual computers, have them do some searching online for other resources, such as websites. Have them share their ideas with the larger audience.

6. Demonstrate how to make a simple pop-up card (see Figure 6.9). Provide supplies so that everyone can make one. Provide stickers (especially effective to offer thematic ones) to use as the illustration that "pops" (simply peel off whatever backing is required to get it to stick to the platform, leaving the part above the platform with its backing intact). Remind the audience of the advantages to students of using paper as a manipulative in a planned project, including the use of geometric principles, and the trial-and-error process of experimentation.

7. Provide a handout of the resources used with websites for favorite pop-up artists (see this book's chapter on Creators) and web and print resources on making pop-ups (see this book's chapter on Creating Pop-Ups).

EXTENSIONS

1. If time allows, provide time for teachers to do a sample lesson plan (provide forms) in small groups, each centering on one pop-up book (bring a selection). If there is computer access, have them add web resources to it. Have them share the plan with the larger group.

2. For librarians, have them design an information-literacy unit (provide forms) in small groups, each centering on one pop-up book of their choice (bring a selection). If there is computer access, have them add web resources to it. Have them share the unit with the larger group.

ADDITIONAL RESOURCES:

Other Pop-Up Books

TITLE: *Oceans: A Journey from the Surface to the Seafloor*

PAPER ENGINEERS: Zerina White and Alan Brown

DESIGNERS: Simon Morse, Jackie Palmer, and Neil Diamond

AUTHORS: Jen Green, Ann Barrett (indexer), and Joe Fullman and Lisa Morris (editors)

ILLUSTRATORS: Sebastian Quigley and Gary Slater

PUBLISHER, COPYRIGHT DATE: Silver Dolphin Books, c2007

ANNOTATION: Great two-page, multi-layered pop-ups and photographs illustrate the substantial informational text of this coverage of the various environments of the earth's oceans. The book is unique among pop-ups for having an index at the back.

TITLE: *Sounds of the Wild: Ocean*

PAPER ENGINEER: Richard Hawke

DESIGNERS: Jonathan Lambert and Caroline Reeves

AUTHORS: A. J. Wood and Valerie Davies

ILLUSTRATOR: Maurice Pledger

PUBLISHER, COPYRIGHT DATE: Silver Dolphin Books, c2007

ANNOTATION: Panoramic, double-page pop-ups capture the variety of wildlife in various areas of the marine world, both above (such as birds) and in it (such as sharks). The book also includes ocean sounds. It concludes with a statement about the necessity to learn how to protect the oceans and these creatures.

TITLE: *Trail: Paper Poetry*

PAPER ENGINEER: David Pelham

PUBLISHER, COPYRIGHT DATE: Little Simon, c2007

ANNOTATION: This book is a unique blending of wheels of movable poetry and stark-white, very complex pop-ups.

TITLE: *The Ultimate Ocean Book: A Unique Introduction to the World Under Water in Fabulous, Full-Color Pop-Ups*

PAPER ENGINEER: James Roger Diaz

DESIGNER: Susan Surprise (book design)

AUTHOR: Maria Rudd-Ruth

ILLUSTRATORS: Virge Kas, Beverly E. Benner and Kristin Kest (cover painting)

PUBLISHER, COPYRIGHT DATE: Artists & Writers Guild Books, Golden Books, c1995

ANNOTATION: Fabulous pop-ups literally rise beyond and outside of the pages of this book. The text was vetted by experts in the field.

TITLE: *Winter in White: A Mini Pop-Up Treat*

PAPER ENGINEER: Robert Sabuda

PUBLISHER, COPYRIGHT DATE: Little Simon, c2007

ANNOTATION: This "mini pop-up treat" is a short poem that is illustrated with white pop-ups of wintery symbols (such as snowflakes) against soft-color backgrounds.

Books without Interactivity

TITLE: *The Missing Snows of Kilimanjaro* (**informational**)

AUTHOR: Rob Waring

ILLUSTRATOR: National Geographic Digital Media (video material)

PUBLISHER, COPYRIGHT DATE: Cengage Learning, c2009

ANNOTATION: Why are the snows of Kilimanjaro disappearing? The book is appropriate for reading level 3.

TITLE: *Mr. Popper's Penguins* (**fiction**)

AUTHORS: Richard Atwater and Florence Atwater

ILLUSTRATOR: Robert Lawson

PUBLISHER; COPYRIGHT DATE: Little Brown, 1938

ANNOTATION: The book has been translated into a movie and the original book remains in print. Mr. Popper is a housepainter who dreams of polar realms, and then he receives a live penguin in the mail.

TITLE: *Through the Eyes of the Vikings: An Aerial Vision of Arctic Lands*

AUTHOR: Robert B. Haas

PUBLISHER, COPYRIGHT DATE: National Geographic, c2010

ANNOTATION: Fabulous aerial views of northern landscapes, photographed by Haas.

DVDs

TITLE: *March of the Penguins* (2005); 80 minutes (**informational**)

DISTRIBUTOR: Warner

ANNOTATION: This documentary follows the life cycle of the emperor penguins who must persevere in the Antactic. Incredible footage.

TITLE: *Happy Feet* (2006); 108 minutes (**fiction**)

DISTRIBUTOR: Warner

ANNOTATION: In this animated movie, Mumble is unique among emperor penguins, who sing. He can't sing, and he lives to tap dance.

Websites

TITLE; AGENCY: *Inuit Gallery of Vancouver* website; Inuit Gallery of Vancouver

URL: http://www.inuit.com

ANNOTATION: From the website: "This gallery showcases serpentine, marble, steatite, stone, musk ox horn, antler, ivory and whalebone carvings. Along with ceramic art, baskets and cloth wall hangings of the Arctic." Great photographs.

TITLE; AGENCY: *Penguins and Puffin Coast*; Saint Louis Zoo

URL: http://www.stlzoo.org/yourvisit/thingstoseeanddo/thewild/penguinpuffincoast.htm

ANNOTATION: In the zoo's Penguin & Puffin Coast, "four different species of penguins, two types of puffins, and various other water birds make their home." Learn facts and see video clips of the birds.

PROGRAM FOR PUBLIC LIBRARY STORY TIMES

THEME: Journeys into the World of Pop-Up Books

CONTRIBUTOR TO ACTIVITY: Stacey Irish-Keffer (See Appendix for Information on this Contributor)

TITLE 1: *Dinosaur Stomp: A Monster Pop-Up*

AUTHOR: Paul Strickland

ILLUSTRATOR: Paul Strickland

PUBLISHER, COPYRIGHT DATE: Dutton's Children's Books, c1996

ANNOTATION:

For the preschool set, this book of giant, colorful pop-up dinosaurs going to a dance combines colors, sizes, and rhymes for discussion with the audience.

TITLE 2: *Encyclopedia Prehistorica: Dinosaurs: The Definitive Pop-Up*

PAPER ENGINEERS: Robert Sabuda and Matthew Reinhart

PUBLISHER, COPYRIGHT DATE: Candlewick, c2005

ANNOTATION:

The older reader will appreciate the amazing pop-ups that come roaring off the page to illustrate the intriguing factual text about dinosaurs.

SUBJECT AREAS:

Depending on the books selected and the emphasis given, this activity can be adapted for all subjects.

ACTIVITY OVERVIEW:

This activity is designed for the public library for children's programming. It can be revised for any age group by adding more or substituting other pop-up books with the same theme or other themes and identifying additional resources, such as DVDs and books without pop-ups, to match the audience interest.

DESCRIPTION OF ACTIVITY:

1. Share one or more pop-up books with the children during story time. For example, listed for this activity are two dinosaur books that can be used with different age groups and interest levels, but there are also many other pop-up books with dinosaur themes.
2. Use the pop-up books to share content (such as rhymes and colors or dinosaur facts) and also to discuss the ways that the books pop-up.
3. At the conclusion of the read-a-loud segment of story time, demonstrate how to fold and cut the paper to create a dinosaur. Robert Sabuda's website (see the Additional Resources) has directions for a v-fold mouth which is easy for elementary school children and makes for a wonderful dinosaur of their own creation. There are also dinosaur pop-up directions on that same site that are appropriate for older participants. Joan Irvine's website (see the Additional Resources) also features a mouth design with additional suggestions for turning it into an animal.
4. Then, direct the children to tables which have already been set up with the materials they will need to create their own pop-ups. Each child's place should have two pieces of eight-by-ten paper, one for creating the pop-up dinosaur and the other for a background to glue it onto. Scissors, glue, rulers, and crayons or color pencils should also be provided. For younger children who might have trouble measuring, draw the lines for cutting on the paper ahead of time.
5. Display the completed pop-ups, along with the book that was read, in the children's section of the library.

EXTENSIONS

1. Talk about the history of pop-up books (see chapters 3 and 4).

2. Talk about the process of making pop-up books (see chapter 9)and their creators: the paper engineers and designers (see chapter 5).

3. Invite the creator of a pop-up book to talk about the process of making the book.

4. Have a special art class for teens on creating a pop-up book. Utilizing library computers, they will choose one of the websites with how-to directions provided by pop-up engineers (see chapter 5). Have a local artist on site to assist.

ADDITIONAL RESOURCES:

Websites

TITLE; AGENCY: *How to Make a Pop-up*; Joan Irvine

URL: http://www.joanirvine.com

ANNOTATION: This website of an author of how-to books on pop-ups demonstrates a talking mouth pop-up, with ideas for converting it to various animals—there's a dinosaur waiting!

TITLE; AGENCY: *Simple Pop-ups You Can Make*; RobertSabuda.com

URL: http://www.robertsabuda.com/popmake/index.asp

ANNOTATION: This page on Robert Sabuda's website starts with Pop-up Basics, which are directions on how to make a basic v-fold mouth pop-up that can be easily converted into a dinosaur or other creature.
For older kids wanting a challenge, scroll down the page to Animals and select Dinosaur.

9

Creating Pop-Ups: Resources That Help

Regardless of their age, once readers (or would-be readers!) discover the wonderful products of paper engineers, they become very interested in how pop-up books are created. There is a wide variety of print and web sources that provide help in creating one's own pop-up books, cards, and other projects. There is a resource for every age group and every level of skill. Oftentimes the ability of younger children to create pop-ups is underestimated. For instance, one of us provided a lesson about pop-ups and how to make them to a class of second graders. For the rest of the year, every note they sent to their teacher had a pop-up! Start simple with demonstrations or sample projects, and then to turn it over to the participants! Their efforts never disappoint!

Also don't forget the templates in the Activities chapter of this book.

BOOKS

Many of these book resources are readily available in libraries or professional development collections. Included are books that appeal to different age groups and skill levels. They are also widely available at book stores or through online sources of used books (check this book's chapter 10, "Finding, Buying, and Housing Pop-ups," for assistance in locating sources).

These recommended titles were selected for their history of appeal to teachers and librarians. They're organized alphabetically by the author's last name. Potential audiences are indicated as guidance for the following resources. Because of their track records, the various authors and publishers in this bibliography are good to follow to identify new publications about creating pop-ups.

Angel, Emma. 2004. *Pop-Up and 3-D Cards: Step-By-Step Projects to Make at Home.* Photography by Chrysalis Image Library/Simon Clay. London: Collins & Brown.

    A British publication, this book has wonderful color photographs illustrating the steps for creating a number of pop-up cards, ranging from fairly simple to rather complex.

Avella, Natalie. 2009. *Paper Engineering: 3D Design Techniques for a 2D Material*. rev., expanded ed. Mies, Switzerland: RotoVision SA.

A beautifully photographed book, Avella's work is not intended to be a how-to. It is a wonderful journey through a photo gallery of paper-engineered products, both commercial and artists' projects. Directed at "students and professionals of graphic design." it should be an inspiration for older students and adults interested in pop-ups.

Barton, Carol. 2005. *The Pocket Paper Engineer: How to Make Pop-Ups Step-By-Step. Vol. 1: Basic Forms*. Glen Echo, MD: Popular Kinetics Press.

This handy, pocket-book sized book has fold-out pages that expand to show in great detail various techniques, which are clearly explained and illustrated step-by-step and also photographed as completed examples. It will appeal to older students and adults.

Barton, Carol. 2008. *The Pocket Paper Engineer: How to Make Pop-Ups Step-By-Step. Vol. 2: Platform Props*. Glen Echo, MD: Popular Kinetics Press.

A great addition to the first volume, this book details "how it's done" for the structures that make the "pop."

Birmingham, Duncan. 2003. *Pop-Up! A Manual of Paper Mechanisms*. Cover by Paul Chilvers. Norfolk, England: Tarquin Publications.

Birmingham teaches pop-up design and engineering at British colleges and universities, and this early guide is illustrated with simple black-and-white line drawings. It is still a useful collection of various pop-up techniques and would appeal to the older child and adult.

Birmingham, Duncan. 2010. *Pop-Up Design and Paper Mechanics: How to Make Folding Paper Sculpture*. Project editing by Gill Parris; managing art editing Gild Pacitti; design by Luke Herriott; photography by Anthony Bailey. Lewes, England: Guild of Master Craftsman Publications.

This new guide from Birmingham presents pop-up engineering from the perspective of theory, including foundation shapes and building techniques. It is liberally illustrated with step–by-step diagrams and photographs of the finished products, rendered in bright contrasting colors that make it easy to see the construction. For the older student and adult.

Bohning, Gerry, Ann Phillips, and Sandra Bryant. 1993. *Literature on the Move: Making and Using Pop-Up and Lift-Flap Books*. Illustrated by Sandra Bryant. Englewood, CO: Teacher Ideas Press.

This is a teacher's guide that combines pop-up-book creation with classroom instruction of reading and writing. Simple line drawings illustrate the directions. About half of the book is arranged by thematic writing and includes classroom activities.

Carter, David A., and James Diaz. 1999. *The Elements of Pop-Up: A Pop-Up Book for Aspiring Paper Engineers*. Assistant design and illustration by Leisa Bentley; photography by Keith Sutter; digital production art by Rick Morrison, White Heat; produced by Intervisual Books; developed by White Heat. New York: Little Simon.

The back cover of this book declares that it is "perfect for aspiring pop-up creators, paper engineers, students, and appreciators," and it's true! This is the must-have book for learning all of the secrets for creating pop-ups. It is a pop-up book format, and each instruction is accompanied by pop-up models of that type of construction. It's both a fun guide for learning "how-to" and a fun pop-up book to explore.

Carter, David A. and James Diaz. 2004. *Let's Make It Pop-Up.* Produced by White Heat. New York: Little Simon.

This is a colorful book, designed for use by younger audiences (older than three years old), from the authors/paper engineers of *The Elements of Pop-up.* As with *Elements,* it is a pop-up book that also provides 3-D instruction for creating pop-ups. The ready-to-use paper pieces to duplicate the models are included in an envelope in the back of the book.

Chatani, Masahiro. 1988. *Paper Magic: Pop-Up Paper Craft: Origami Architecture.* Tokyo, Japan: Ondorisha Publishers.

Designed for the more advanced creator of pop-ups, the 3-D projects require skillful use of a craft knife. Chatani's book is illustrated with small black-and-white photographs of the finished projects.

Chatani, Masahiro and Keiko Nakazawa. 1994. *Pop-Up Geometric Origami.* Translated by Chieko Willemsen and Matt Willemsen. Tokyo, Japan: Ondorisha Publishers.

Small black-and-white photographs, coupled with 20 full-page photographs of the completed projects, illustrate pop-up geometric origami. Not for beginners! But, a great resource for the older student or adult interested in more sophisticated pop-ups. Projects do require a craft knife.

Chatani, Masahiro. 1986. *Pop-Up Greeting Cards: A Creative Personal Touch for Every Occasion: Origamic Architecture.* Tokyo, Japan: Ondorisha Publishers.

A few color photographs and many black-and-white ones illustrate the greeting cards that utilize more advanced techniques for their creation. The projects require use of a craft knife.

Crowther, Robert. 1998. *Robert Crowther's Pop-Up Book of Amazing Facts and Feats: Deep Down Underground.* Cambridge, MA: Candlewick Press.

This pop-up book of facts about underground structures and projects (such as underground lakes and the largest underground garbage dump) is unique in that the backs of the pages reveal the mechanisms that make the pop-ups work.

Diehn, Gwen. 1998. *Making Books That Fly, Fold, Wrap, Hide, Pop Up, Twist, and Turn: Books for Kids to Make.* Art direction and production by Kathleen J. Holmes; production assistance by Bobby Gold; illustrations by Gwen Diehn; photography by Evan Bracken. Asheville, NC: Lark Books.

This book is colorfully illustrated with photographs of the books created. Designed to be used by children, the book includes background and history of unique formats of books.

Fox, Tanya, editor. *Fabulous Folds for Card Making.* Berne, IN: House of White Birches. Art direction by Brad Snow; copy supervision by Michelle Beck; technical editing by Lana Shurb; photography supervising by Tammy Christian; photography styling by Tammy Steiner; graphic arts supervision by Ronda Bechinski; technical art by Nicole Gage.

This spiral-bound book is liberally illustrated with color photos of all of the completed projects. It includes a short appendix of templates. Each of the six chapters is built around a particular technique, including gatefolds, iris folds, tea-bag folds, and true pop-ups.

Hiner, Mark. 1985. *Paper Engineering for Pop-Up Books and Cards.* Design by Wilson Smith. Norfolk, England: Tarquin Publications.

The book has color templates that are to be cut out to build 10 pop-up-book and card projects. Simple line drawings illustrate the necessary steps.

Hiner, Mark. 1996. *Up-Pops: Paper Engineering with Elastic Bands.* Design by Susan Apling. Norfolk, England: Tarquin Publications.

> Color templates are designed to be scored and cut out to complete the projects. Paper bands are intended to be the mechanism for providing the rapid motion of the models.

Irvine, Joan. 1992. *How to Make Super Pop-Ups.* Illustrated by Linda Hendry. New York: Beech Tree Books.

> A familiar name to teachers and school librarians, Irvine's books for creating pop-ups are directed at younger audiences. Black-and-white line drawings illustrate the step-by-step directions for "toys, cards, and masks that slide, spring, and snap."

Ives, Rob. 2009. *Paper Engineering & Pop-Ups for Dummies.* Hoboken, NJ: Wiley Publishing.

> The author of this recent edition to the popular "Dummies Guide" series started his full-time design and paper engineering career as a primary school teacher. It follows the series' standard format, with black-and-white line and photographic illustrations. It has templates, with dimensions added, for projects that cover a range from basic (pop-up card) to complex (3-D animals that owe their movement to crank shafts).

Jackson, Paul. 1993. *The Pop-Up Book: Step-By-Step Instructions for Creating Over 100 Original Paper Projects.* Photography by Paul Forrester; project editing by Clare Nicholson; design by Michael Morey; illustration by John Hutchinson; hand model by Paul Austin; editorial direction by Joanna Loenz. New York: Henry Holt.

> The large, clear color photos in this book illustrate the step-by-step instructions for creating a wide variety of pop-ups. The pop-ups are featured as pop-up cards in the photographs but would also work nicely as book pages.

Jacobs, Michael. 2006. *Books Unbound: 20 Innovative Bookmaking Projects.* Editing by Jennifer Fellinger; cover designer by Lisa Buchanan and Brian Roeth; interior design by Brian Roeth; layout art by Kathy Gardner; production coordination by Robin Richie; photography by Christine Polomsky and Tim Grondin; photography styling by Jan Nickum. Cincinnati, OH: North Light Books.

> Unique, handmade books are known in the art world as artists' books. This compilation of directions for creating remarkable three-dimensional books is illustrated with colorful photographs. Many of the construction techniques are what create pop-ups. This resource is geared to the older youth or adult.

Jacobs, Michael. 2005. *Cards That Pop Up, Flip & Slide.* Editing by Christa Hamilton; design by Stephanie Strang; layout art by Jessica Schultz; photography by Tim Grondin, Christine Polomsky, and Greg Grosse Photography. Cincinnati, OH: North Light Books.

> Color photographs illustrate the step-by-step instructions for creating action cards. A useful aspect of this book is that all of the cards are designed to fit into standard-size envelopes. This resource is for the older youth or adult.

Johnson, Paul. 1992. *Pop-Up Paper Engineering: Cross-Curricular Activities in Design Technology, English and Art.* Designed and illustrated by Benedict Evans; photography by Bernie Ross and Jez Lugg; cover design by Caroline Archer. London: Falmer Press.

> A British publication, this teacher's guide is distinguished by using color photographs of work by students, and credits include their names and ages. Line drawings illustrate the steps for creating the various projects.

Lombardo, Mary A. 2003. *Poetry and Pop-Ups: An Art-Enhanced Approach to Writing Poetry.* Worthington, OH: Linworth Publishing.

This book is a classroom teacher's guide to combining writing poetry with the student creation of pop-ups. It includes student worksheets, classroom activities, and simple drawings to illustrate the steps for producing the pop-ups.

Mathieson, Jo F. 2008. *Pop-Up Cards.* 1st U.S. ed. New York: St. Martin's Griffin.

Instructions for creating 18 themed greeting cards are provided in color photographs and step-by-step layout. Each of the finished product photographs covers almost an entire page.

Maurer-Mathison, Diane. 2006. *Paper in Three Dimensions: Origami, Pop-Ups, Sculpture, Baskets, Boxes, and More.* Senior editor Joy Aquilino; editing by Holly Jennings; designer by Aret Buk/Thumb Print; production managing by Hector Campbell. New York: Watson-Guptill Publications.

While this book covers more projects than pop-ups, its Chapter 3 is devoted to pop-ups. It is unique for covering more advanced techniques, such as origamic architecture, slice-form pop-ups, and amazingly, wearable pop-ups by artist Susan Share. Wonderful photographs illustrate the final products and essential steps in their creation.

McNeill, Suzanne, Danielle Harris, and Delores Frantz. 1999. *The Scrap Happy Guide To: Peek & Pull Motion Pages.* Art coordination by Kathy McMillan; art direction by Laurie Rice; art by Janet Long; photography by David and Donna Thomason; editing by Wanda J. Little and Colleen Reigh. Fort Worth, TX: Design Originals.

This guide is for the scrap-booker, and drawings and photographs illustrate the instructions and the completed scrapbook pages.

Miller, Tamara B. 2005. *Pop-Up Activities to Teach Genre.* Cover design by Jason Robinson; color photography by Studio 10; cover and interior illustrations by George Ulrich; interior design by Sydney Wright; genre introduction pages edited by Betsy Yarbrough. New York: Teaching Resources.

The cover blurb explains the contents: "18 unique pop-up projects with templates, story starters, and graphic organizers that motivate kids to write in different genres." Genres include: "mystery, science fiction, tall tales, historical fiction, fairy tales, humorous fiction, personal narrative, expository writing, adventure."

Pridemore, Heidi. 2007. *Pop-Up Paper Structures: The Beginner's Guide to Creating 3-D Elements for Books, Cards & More.* Editorial direction by Gailen Runge; editing by Stacy Chamness; cover designer/book designer by Christina D. Jarumay; illustration by Tim Manibusan. Lafayette, CA: C & T Publishing.

Color photographs of the finished products and of major construction steps, coupled with line drawings of assembly steps, make this user-friendly guide to creating the pop-up elements that can be incorporated into books, cards, or other projects.

Uribe, Diego. 1998. *Fractal Cuts: Exploring the magic of Fractals and Pop-Up Designs.* Design by Magdalen Bear; cover by Paul Chilvers. Norfolk, England: Tarquin Publications.

Illustrated in black-and-white line drawings, this resource provides guidance on creating the 3-D geometric objects termed fractals. The first 16 pages of the book are an easy-to-understand explanation of fractals, including the history of their discovery. Creating the products in the book requires the use of a craft knife.

Watt, Fiona. n.d. *The Usbornebook of Paper Engineering.* Design by Vicki Groombridge; paper engineering consulting by Iain Ashman; illustration by John Woodcock; photography by Howard Allman; models made by Tamsin Howe, Jan MaCafferty, and Zoe Wray; series editing by Cheryl Evans. Tulsa, OK: EDC Publishing.

Geared to younger readers, this colorful 32-page guide has step-by-step instructions for cards and for stand-alone figures. The techniques are fairly sophisticated and the illustrated figures require an artistic flair, so this resource would be just as appealing for older and adult creators.

Wickings, Ruth. 2010. *Pop-Up: Everything You Need to Know to Create Your Own Pop-Up Book.* Paper engineering by Ruth Wickings and Alan Brown; illustration by Frances Castle and Andrew Crowson; design by Laura Hambleton; managing editing by Pauliina Teodoro; art direction by Jonathan Gilbert; published by Sue Grabham. Somerville, MA: Candlewick Press.

This guide for youthful audiences starts with explanations of general pop-up techniques, includes a two-page spread of a pop-up robot with specific techniques used, and then presents pop-ups that can be assembled, including punch-outs and instructions. The do-it-yourself projects are a dragon, castle, Frankenstein's lab, and a jungle scene. The clever lift flap on the book's cover is a lagniappe!

Yoshida, Miyuki. 2008. *The Art of Paper Folding for Pop-Up.* Jacket design by Hajime Kabutoya; editing by Kaori Saito. Reprint of *Paper Folding for POP-UP* (2008). Tokyo, Japan: Pie Books.

This uniquely formatted book has 30 pages of fold outs on heavy white stock, each of which opens to reveal a colored pop-up in combinations of red, yellow, and blue. There is no text for the pop-ups, but the simplicity of the wonderful pop-ups makes them self-explanatory. The book covers have removable brads, so the pages can be extracted for closer examination or, as the cover blurb says, for use as "greeting cards, ornaments, and more."

NEED MORE BOOKS?

Need more examples of how-to books? A favorite bibliography is available on the web, on the site of famed paper engineer Robert Sabuda. It is arranged by beginner, intermediate, and advanced levels and includes his annotations of each book. The bibliography is titled, "How to Make Pop-Ups: A Guide to Books about Making Pop-Ups," and it is available at: http://robertsabuda.com/popupbib.html.

WEBSITES

Most of the websites below are the products of established paper engineers or pop-up-book designers, and thus offer the added appeal of letting the audience see techniques favored by their favorite paper engineers and designers.

Carter, David A. http://www.popupbooks.com.

Go to David A. Carter's home website and click on the "Make It" link. Here are video clips showing how various pop-ups are created. Also in this area are links to templates of pop-ups featured in the movies. The site is a wonderful accompaniment to any of David Carter's pop-up books!

Dorota. Make your own pop-up froggy card! http://allaboutfrogs.org/funstuff/holidays/valentines/popupcard.html.

Color photographs provide step-by-step instructions for making a fairly simple pop-up frog card.

HGTV. http://www.hgtv.com.

Do a search for pop-up cards or pop-up books and locate links to instructions and templates for projects featured on the cable television network, HGTV.

Irvine, Joan. How to make a pop-up. http://joanirvine.com/default.aspx.

   Author Joan Irvine, who styles herself the "pop-up" lady and has authored books on making pop-ups for young readers, provides line drawing illustrations of the directions for making a pop-up mouth that can easily be transformed into several different animals.

Reinhart, Matthew. Make a pop-up! http://www.matthewreinhart.com/popmake.php.

   Renowned paper engineer Matthew Reinhart offers illustrations that can be downloaded and instructions for creating pop-ups from his books, including figures from Star Wars.

Sabuda, Robert. Simple pop-ups you can make! http://www.robertsabuda.com/pop-makesimple.asp.

   On famous paper engineer Robert Sabuda's website is this page with illustrations of pop-ups that can be made. Just click on the photos to access the instructions and the templates.

Scholastic. Make your own pop-up book. http://www.scholastic.com/titles/alice/index.htm.

   A PDF link provides access to cut-out characters (that can be colored) and a background to use in creating a pop-up page based on Otto Seibold's *Alice in Wonderland* pop-up book.

Smithsonian Institution. History on stage pop-up lesson plan. http://www.sil.si.edu/pdf/Paper_Engineering_Lesson_Plan_Final_rev.pdf.

   To accompany the Smithsonian Institution's Libraries 2010–2011 exhibit at the National Museum of American History, *Paper Engineering: Fold, Pull, Pop & Turn*, is this lesson plan (PDF) for grades 5 to 8. It provides photographs of step-by-step instructions for making a pop-up that "illustrates a topic in American history."

10

Finding, Buying, and Housing Pop-Ups

HOW WILL I KNOW WHAT'S OUT THERE?

For the librarian, the good news is that with the increased popularity of pop-up books, more of them are appearing in standard review sources: *Booklist, Bulletin of the Center for Children's Books, Horn Book, New York Times Book Review, Publishers' Weekly,* and *School Library Journal.*

However, because of the unique physical nature of pop-up books, perhaps more useful are various sources that regularly list and describe pop-up books. It is important to discuss both the features that pop-up books have in common with regular books and those that are different. Of course, as with any other book, any one aspect of a pop-up work can be more or less important, depending on the intended use of the book. These factors include such things as the sort of movable components in the book, the overall layout and presentation of the book, the identity of the paper engineer or designer, the content of the textual matter, and so on. Either having as much access as possible to such details, or being able to personally see and handle the book, can be critical for making a selection decision. Here are some of suggestions for accessing descriptions of pop-up books:

Alibris. http://www.alibris.com.
> This is a popular site for locating and buying used, new, and out-of-print books from a huge number of independent sellers. The advanced search function (for books) allows the addition of keywords, such as "pop-up." This site also has a glossary of book terms (http://www.alibris.com/glossary/glossary.cfm?S=R) that can be very useful in understanding the descriptions provided by book sellers.

Amazon.com. http://www.amazon.com.
> This online bookseller, around since 1995, sells not only new books, but also provides access to third-party sellers of primarily used books (some the items listed by third parties are new), with payment going to those sellers through Amazon. Use the advanced search function with terms such as "movable book" or "pop-up book" in the subject field to limit search results. Many listings on Amazon will provide views of the covers and interiors of books.

Also, Amazon.com provides a service to potential readers, called Listmania. It contains listings of favorite books, and so forth (the limit is 40 per list) that can be purchased on Amazon.com, with descriptions and commentary. These lists are contributed by the website's visitors. There are always many of them for pop-up books, and they provide insight about which titles are popular with readers.

eBay.com. http://www.ebay.com.

The favorite site for those individuals who enjoy the auction world, eBay also provides the opportunity to do free searching, with the ability to limit searches to categories of items, such as books. Because these items are for sale, they are usually accompanied by detailed descriptions and photos, making this a good site for "getting the facts" on an item under consideration.

Movable Book Society. http://movablebooksociety.org/newsletter.html.

For $30 per year, members of the Movable Book Society receive the color illustrated quarterly newsletter, which offers detailed coverage of new and classic pop-ups through articles, reviews, and announcements. On the website are links to indexes for the society's publication, *Movable Stationary*, beginning with volume 1 (1993).

One good source for information about titles for retrospective collecting are librarian/collector Ann R. Montanaro's two definitive bibliographies of pop-up books (1993, 2000), which contain descriptions as well as credible citations.

Finally, for more assistance in retrospective collecting, see the descriptions of pop-up books in "The FAVES" chapter of this book!

WHERE DO I GO TO GET THEM?

One of the most common questions that is asked is where to obtain pop-up books, and the response is: almost everywhere! The following sources are fruitful.

Bookstores that sell new and/or used books, both chain and independent, almost always have pop-up books, often shelved in a special section such as in a children's books area. If you don't see them, ask! Also, it's common to find pop-up books at greatly reduced prices on the remainder (new books greatly reduced for quick sale) and bargain shelves of chain bookstores.

Garage or tag sales, thrift stores, and flea markets can also prove to be good sites for finding cheap and even collectible pop-up books. Inexpensive versions of pop-up books are often available at discount stores, and these can be affordable giveaways in reading programs or as classroom rewards. Large retail stores that sell a variety of merchandise usually have some pop-up books in the children's sections.

Online vendors are one source of pop-up books that provides a wide range of book titles and price ranges, and they offer the advantage that descriptions and pictures of covers, and sometimes interiors of the books, are commonly provided. Some of the more popular vendors (and there are others) for individuals are listed in the previous section titled "How Will I Know What's Out There?" School and library purchasers should visit with the book vendors that they already use.

Pop-up books have many moving parts, so potential buyers are urged to carefully examine books before purchasing (unless the item is in its original shrink wrap). For online purchases, buy from reputable vendors who will allow returns for unsatisfactory items. Also, carefully read the descriptions for online sales and then thoroughly examine and compare the items immediately upon receiving them.

And, of course, becoming familiar with the creators of pop-up books who are producing works that one particularly likes is another great way to assist in the selection of items for purchase. Check out the Creators chapter of this book for information on a selection of these individuals. Some paper engineers also sell their own pop-up works (books, cards, etc.) on their websites.

Finally, for the teacher or librarian who is interested in building a personal collection of pop-up books, tell family and friends that a gift of a pop-up book will be greatly appreciated!

THE VENDOR, THE POP-UP BOOK, AND THE SCHOOL LIBRARY

School library media specialists and teachers will quickly discover that they won't generally see pop-up books listed in the catalogs and on the websites of the mainstream book jobbers/vendors who typically supply the school market. Those publishers that work directly with the most prestigious paper engineers are most likely to consistently offer new titles of pop-ups, and beginning with their catalogs and websites can be an effective strategy for becoming familiar with this area of the market. Following is a limited selection of publishers that we offer as a starting list.

Dorling Kindersley (http://www.dk.com) publishes worldwide and is perhaps best known to educators and librarians for its "Eyewitness Guides" series. It also publishes pop-up books—when searching, it's necessary to search several geographic areas (United States, United Kingdom, etc.) to identify titles.

Little Simon (http://www.simonsays.com/content/index.cfm?sid=183), an imprint of Simon & Schuster Children's Publishing Division, has been the publisher for paper engineer superstars such as Robert Sabuda, Matthew Reinhart, David A. Carter, Bruce Foster, David Pelham, and others.

The National Geographic Society (http://shop.nationalgeographic.com), long respected for its informational magazines, books, and videos and DVDs, continues to uphold its reputation with accurate and appealing pop-ups. Use the search function to locate current "pop-up" book titles.

Scholastic (http://www2.scholastic.com/browse/home.jsp) is another mainstream publisher well-known to teachers and librarians. It offers pop-up books fairly frequently, often under one of its imprints such as Orchard Books.

Currently gaining popularity are pop-ups geared to very young children. Producers of those include Piggy Toes Press (an imprint of Intervisual Books, a subsidiary of Dalmatian Press, http://piggytoespress.com/). Also, titles are still available from BumbleBee Books and Backpack Books. Popular series of pop-up books may remain in print under a number of imprints. For example, the "Snappy" pop-up books illustrated by Derek Matthews have been published by Templar, Millbrook Press, Silver Dolphin, and others.

Those who locate pop-up books for use in the school setting will occasionally recognize the names of other publishers, but not with great regularity, and librarians should be observant in noting the names of the publishers producing favorite titles and paper engineers.

In the past the prevailing thought, incorrectly in these authors' opinion, was that pop-ups were too fragile for young children. It has been interesting to observe the trend of increasing popularity of pop-ups geared to a wide range of ages, including young children. As mainstream publishers increasingly become producers of pop-ups, this format will become much more familiar to schools and public libraries purchasing for early childhood programs.

FINDING A HOME FOR POP-UPS IN THE LIBRARY

As with another popular format of books, graphic novels, there is much discussion and many ideas among librarians regarding the shelving of pop-up books. The conversation is reminiscent of the questions once raised regarding media: Should it be shelved in a separate section or interfiled with the books on the same subject? If the decision is made to shelve them separately, more questions need to be answered. Should all pop-up books be shelved together or should they be divided into fiction and informational? Should the easy books be in a separate area, as they often are in picture book collections? And, as with media, the answers will depend upon each library and the needs of its patrons.

Because of the format of pop-ups, some circulation considerations may also be different from those regarding graphic novels and media. Should the books be shelved in the circulating collection at all or should they be noncirculating so that little hands can't touch them without the permission of the librarian? Should they be housed in the professional/curriculum collection from which only teachers will be able to check them out? Once again, the answers depend on the situation, but accessibility has always trumped dwelling too much on preservation, exempting rare and special book collections.

For a method of circulating pop-up books in a school setting, in a way that helps to protect them and alerts the child to handling them properly, see librarian Karen Criscillo's idea, with illustrations, on Robert Sabuda's website: http://www.robertsabuda.com/everythingpopup/0709_bells-library/index.asp.

Librarians in public libraries will face not only the same circulation and shelving issues as school librarians, but they must also take into account circumstances particular to their libraries' roles as public service institutions. For example, circulating collections in public libraries are meant to circulate. Many public libraries don't have large closed areas such as professional collections in school systems, reference sections are not appropriate placement for most pop-up books, and as there is no "class time" similar to that in school libraries, using a noncirculating policy to keep the books under the watchful eye of the librarian is not generally feasible or preferable. A potential compromise is having a collection of pop-ups set aside for use by the children's librarian during story times and programs, an approach that is parallel to placing pop-ups in a school's professional collection.

There are no hard and fast rules for shelving pop-up books. As has always been the case with other resources, librarians must consider the expectations and needs of the patron, whether that individual is a child, a teacher, or a member of the public. Weigh that "prime directive" against the options that may be affected by space or staff. The ultimate solution may not be perfect, but it should be workable. And, it should never prevent pop-up books from becoming a viable part of the library collection!

CATALOGING THOSE POP-UPS

Increasingly, pop-up books carry Cataloging-in-Publication (CIP) data. Librarians should add a format subject heading to bibliographic/surrogate records, using standard tools such as *Library of Congress Subject Headings* (32nd edition, 2010) or the *Sears List of Subject Headings* (20th edition, 2010), which is also available in a Spanish edition (19th edition, 2008). Adding a form subject heading such as "toy and movable books" (Library of Congress subject heading for children's literature) will enable easier access for the individual looking specifically for pop-up books.

For those situations in which cataloging and the book are not purchased from a vendor and original cataloging must be provided, the good news is that increasingly pop-up titles can be located on OCLC. Easy and free public access to OCLC's WorldCat ("the world's largest network of library content and services") is available at http://www.worldcat.org. This resource has the advantages of allowing simple and advanced searching, providing access to credible bibliographic records (description) that can offer guidance for original cataloging, and listing the libraries that hold the pop-up books.

DEVELOPING PROFESSIONAL COLLECTIONS FOR TEACHERS

Pop-up books (and books about making and using pop-ups) can be greatly appreciated additions to professional development collections that are accessible to teachers within a school district and to curriculum centers and libraries used by future teachers. Assuming that there are not pop-up books in the professional collection, there are decisions to be made. First, a needs assessment is always helpful. Use those curricular and collection needs to guide compilation of a list of some pop-up books considered to be truly outstanding and which can be located for purchase. If there are pictures in a catalog or on a website, have them available for sharing so that the quality and appeal of the paper engineering will be readily apparent. Librarians should discuss the list with teachers (teachers should discuss with colleagues), grade level or subject team leaders, and curriculum coordinators. Start with those selections that fit into the school's curriculum and that people are excited about having available for their use. Make those titles the first purchases. The success of any project is greatest when all potential users know that they have helped with the end product.

Some districts or administrators make extra funding available to get new projects started, and some even have local grants that favor innovative ideas. Don't forget parent organizations that often have fundraisers for special projects. If those monies can be tapped, it will alleviate some of the stress of deciding how much of the annual budget can be allocated to purchase these new resources.

When the new pop-ups arrive, it is best to shelve them alongside the other resources teachers use regularly for their lessons so that they won't be overlooked. Be sure to make everyone aware of these new additions with displays, signage, and announcements. It is true that food is a sure way to get people's attention. Consider a brief after-school event or an all-day come-and-go to showcase the books—with cookies provided, of course!

It may take a while to change perceptions of the value of using pop-ups in the classroom. Ask the administrator for time to make a brief presentation at a staff development or a faculty meeting. If teachers have department curriculum or grade level meetings, ask to speak at several of those occasions. If there are local professional organizations for teachers and/or administrators, be available to do a short program. Always make the presentation as succinct as possible. Don't turn people off to the idea simply because the presentation is taking valuable time that they have allotted for other pressing matters. As when giving a booktalk, show one or two fabulous books and give a mini-lesson on how they can be incorporated into the curriculum. For future meetings, ask some of those who have experienced success using pop-ups to share their experiences. Or, consider putting together a newsletter with plans and activities that individuals are willing to share. Or, add this information to a school website area geared to teachers.

Adding pop-ups to the collection, as with adding any new resources, will take planning, effort, cooperation, and public relations. The payoff will be putting pop-ups books into a school's professional/curriculum collection and into the hands of teachers and students, and then listening to the thank yous!

REFERENCES

Montanaro, Ann R. 1993. *Pop-Up and Movable Books: A Bibliography*. Metuchen, NJ: Scarecrow Press.

Montanaro, Ann R. 2000. *Pop-Up and Movable Books: A Bibliography, Supplement 1, 1991–1997.* Lanham, MD: Scarecrow Press.

11

The FAVES: The Books for Our Dream Pop-Up Libraries

Pretend! Pretend that you could choose any pop-up books in the world for your own "dream" library. We've gone there, and here are the results!

Each of us describes our dream library of pop-up books that could be used for recreational reading, taking advantage of teachable moments in working with others; our own lifelong learning; art appreciation; and modeling paper engineering techniques useful for our own creations.

A few of the book titles are duplicated across our dream libraries, but each of us loves them for different reasons, which is one of the wonderful things about pop-up books! They appeal to people for a variety of reasons. Thus, what is very clear to us is that any pop-up book, or any collection of pop-up books, can serve many purposes—imagination is the only limit!

We've come full circle as we began this book with a conversation about our collecting of pop-ups, and we are ending by sharing our favorite pop-ups. We hope that this very enjoyable exercise, for which we considered the various engaging aspects of each of these titles that we love, will spur you to think about selections for your own dream library, which can be as large or as small as you wish it to be. And, for guidance once you've acquired them, don't forget to visit the chapter "Finding, Buying, and Housing Pop-ups."

Finally, thinking about what titles should be included in a "dream library" of pop-up books is also a great brain-storming activity for students and other young audiences. Comparing dream lists with fellow students provides insights into others' interests. For older students, the activity can be an interesting variation on the Library Thing social website (http://www.librarything.com), where individuals share and store information about their own books and reading. It boasts of being "a community of 1,200,000 book lovers."

ARRANGEMENT OF THE LISTS OF DREAM LIBRARIES

The titles in each of the "libraries" are arranged alphabetically by the author's last name. As with other sections of this book, in the bibliographic entries we have included extra information about the various individuals and entities playing major roles in the creation of these pop-ups, since this information is not usually present in bibliographic citations in tools that might be accessed for information about potential purchases.

TAGS IN THE LISTS

After the annotation for each of the pop-up selections, we have added a list of **tags** to provide clues about elements (whether content elements, format, or curriculum areas) that might be important to teachers, librarians, and others who are considering selecting titles from our compilations. The tags are also a gentle reminder that any one pop-up book can be approached from many directions, which makes them very useful for instructional purposes.

For each pop-up book title, the tags are arranged alphabetically.

RHONDA'S DREAM LIBRARY OF POP-UPS

Rhonda's choices for her dream library of pop-ups focus on popular culture, science, math, belief systems, technology, and unusual formats. These topics reflect both personal interests as well as the professional interests that she has often incorporated into her writing, teaching, and workshop presentations.

Anderson, Wayne. 1995. *The Perfect Match.* 1st U.S. ed. New York: Dorling Kindersley Publishing.

I love pop-up books that use paper engineering to transform illustrations from one thing to another. This clever book uses the theme of a "fantastic wedding," and the flaps transform the fantasy characters of troll, ogre, princess, and so on, into "8,000 guests"—I confess that I've never actually counted them! This book is a great resource to use in prediction for math lessons.

TAGS: fairy tales; fantasy; humor; weddings

Alexander, Cecil F. 1995. *All Things Bright and Beautiful.* Design and paper engineering by Keith Moseley; illustration by Linda Birkinshaw. Wheaton, IL: Tyndale House Publishers.

The inspirational poem, now more than a century old, is beautifully updated with illustrations of diverse and smiling children and happy animals, all of whom seem to actually move as the pages open to reveal idyllic natural settings. The format does justice to the flow of the words that affirm "all things bright and beautiful."

TAGS: animals; inspirational literature; nature; poems

Anno, Mitsumasa. 1985. *Anno's Sundial.* New York: Philomel Books.

I have long been a fan of the works of author/illustrator Mitsumasa Anno, who was a former math teacher. Not surprisingly, his books are perfect tie-ins for math instruction, and this one, his first pop-up book, is a great resource for bringing together concepts of measurement and natural cycles and history around the topic of sundials.

TAGS: cycles; latitude and longitude; math; measurement; sun; sundials; timekeeping

Bantock, Nick. 1990. *Wings: A Pop-Up Book of Things that Fly.* 1st U.S. ed. Illustrations by Nick Bantock; design by Nick Bantock and Doug Bergstreser; paper engineering by Rodger Smith; production by Intervisual Communications. New York: Random House.

Who would not be delighted by a pop-up book that has butterflies, birds, bats, and planes flying off the pages? A variety of paper engineering mechanisms are used to illustrate the topics of wings and flying, which are enhanced with authoritative discussion.

TOPICS: flying; nature; wings

Barklem, Jill. 1992. *The World of Brambly Hedge: A Pop-Up Book.* Paper engineering by Damian Johnston. New York: Philomel Books.

Barklem's world of Brambly Hedge, inhabited by mice reminiscent of Beatrix Potter's characters, is brought to life in domestic vignettes that are "framed" in multilevel pop-ups. It is irresistibly charming!

TAGS: Brambly Hedge; children's literature

Bataille, Marion. 2008. *ABC3D.* 1st U.S. ed. Book design by Marion Bataille; cover design by Michael Yuen. New York: Roaring Brook Press.

I am always entranced by pop-up books that focus on language and letters. On each two-page spread, a 3-D letter of the alphabet jumps from the page. The presentation of the pop-ups seems very "modern art" and is a wonderful example of displaying simple information in complex ways.

TAGS: alphabet; language; letters

Bemelmans, Ludwig. 1987. *Madeline: A Pop-Up Book Based on the Original by Ludwig Bemelmans.* Pictures by Ludwig Bemelmans; art adapted by Jody Wheeler; design and paper engineering by David A. Carter. New York: Viking Kestrel.

The little French girl with a mind of her own has always been one of my favorite characters in children's literature. The paper engineering in this classic book works so well with the illustrations that the presentation is seamless. My favorite pop-up is the last one, of the imposingly blue-caped Miss Clavel framed in an open door.

TAGS: children's literature; France; Ludwig Bemelmans; *Madeline*

Bender, Michael. 1999. *All the World's a Stage: William Shakespeare: A Pop-Up Biography.* Book design by Vandy Ritter. San Francisco: Chronicle Books.

Shakespeare is as intriguing to me as it has been to millions of people over the past five centuries! This biographical treatment, enhanced with a chronology and a glossary, is brought to life with pop-ups, flaps, and tabs.

TAGS: acting; biographies; drama; Elizabethan history; the Globe Theatre; theaters; William Shakespeare

Brown, Marc. 1989. *Marc Brown's Play-Pops: Two Little Monkeys.* 1st ed. Illustrations by Marc Brown; designed by Jon Z. Haber. New York: E.P. Dutton.

This small book has only four double-page spreads, each with a pop-up that moves to duplicate an updated version of "Two Little Monkeys" and that also reflects hand movements matching the rhyme. It impresses me because it is both simple and sophisticated in technique.

TAGS: rhymes; "Two Little Monkeys"

Burroughs, Edgar Rice. 1984. *Tarzan: A Pop-Up Book*. Illustration by Jon Townley and Bill Selby; paper engineering by Ib Penick. New York: Random House.

    For over 70 years, the character of Tarzan has continued to be popularized by what must be every possible format delivery, from books to movies to graphic novels. I am fascinated by why it remains intriguing to so many. This simple retelling of the storyline is illustrated with great pop-ups which are enhanced with tabs that accentuate their motion.

TAGS: popular literature; Tarzan

Buxton, John. 1997. *Secret Treasures*. Illustration by John Buxton; paper engineering by Tor Lokvig; text compilation by Catherine Herbert Howell; scientific consultation by Catharine H. Roehrig, Metropolitan Museum of Art, Michael Nylan, Bryn Mawr College, David L. Thompson, Howard University, George E. Stuart, National Geographic Society, Dan Fiero, Linda Martin, and the staff of the Mesa Verde Museum; reading consultation by Elaine Liebesman and Veronica Dannerhoj's second graders at Oakridge Elementary School, Arlington, Virginia. Washington, D.C.: National Geographic Society.

    All of the pop-ups in National Geographic's "Action Book" series are excellent! I am particularly fond of this one because it presents the diversity of societies and cultural treasures around the world.

TAGS: Anasazi; anthropology; archaeology; Central America; China; Egypt; Italy; Maya; Mesa Verde; Pompeii; Southwestern United States; Tutankhamun; Xi'An

Carter, David A. 1988. *How Many Bugs in a Box? A Pop-Up Counting Book*. Design and illustration by David A. Carter; production by Intervisual Communications. New York: Simon & Schuster Books for Young Readers.

    This is only one title in the very popular "Bugs" series of pop-up books created by David Carter, and it is a wonderful concept book that combines counting, prediction, and humor in a way (watch the fantasy bugs!) that has universal appeal to kids.

TAGS: bugs; counting; fantasy; humor; math; prediction

Cerf, Chris. 2000. *Un People vs. Re People: A Super Pop-Up Book*. 1st ed. Design and production by Brown Wells and Jacobs. London: Golden Books Publishing Company.

    One of my favorite educational television series for children was always the Emmy Award–winning PBS series "Between the Lions," which promoted reading. This pop-up version of a recurring segment on the series focuses on Monica Maxwell, who navigates a world of words prefaced by "un-" and "re-."

TAGS: "Between the Lions"; children's television series; language; prefixes; words

Clarke, Sue, and Hilary Arnold. 1995. *Heaven and Earth: A Jacob's Ladder Book*. New York: Hyperion Books for Children.

    In movable books, a Jacob's ladder technique allows the reader to move forward in a linear fashion through the story. Then, by holding one of the book's panels, hidden scenes are revealed. This small (4.5-by-5-inch) book tells the story of a great flood that threatened to destroy the world and of a dragon's role in saving it. I am particularly fond of the intricate illustrations with their use of bright color.

TAGS: China; dragons

Crowther, Robert. 2000. *Amazing Pop-Up House of Inventions.* 1st U.S. ed. Cambridge, MA: Candlewick Press.

Inventions are one of the pop-up book topics that always delight me. Each two-page spread of this book is one room of a house, and each is filled with the facts about the inventions that make life easier, efficient, and comfortable.

TAGS: inventions; technology

Crowther, Robert. 1981. *The Most Amazing Hide-and-Seek Counting Book.* Paper engineer James R. Diaz. London: Penguin Group.

I love this book's variety of paper engineering techniques that are used to reveal the number of trees and plants and animals that are being counted.

TAGS: animals; counting; games; hide-and-seek; math; nature; plants; numbers

Crowther, Robert. 1995. *The Most Amazing Night Book.* London: Viking Children's Books.

I love the works of Robert Crowther! They always have great topics selected to appeal. Plus, they are filled with small flaps and tabs that transform and inform, and this book is a perfect example, revealing what's behind the dark scenes in the urban night. The text consists of the balloon dialogs of the people and animals dwelling in the city.

TAGS: cities; nighttime

Crowther, Robert. 1996. *Pop-Up Olympics: Amazing Facts and Record Breakers.* 1st U.S. ed. Cambridge, MA: Candlewick Press.

The Olympics provide opportunities to work with topics such as history, games, record-keeping, math, measurements, and so on. This book is one of my favorites because the tabs and pop-ups capture the sense of motion of the Olympic Games, and the informative details provide insight into records and the rules and equipment of the games.

TAGS: games; math; measurement; Olympic Games; records (sports); sports

Crowther, Robert. 2002. *Shapes.* Cambridge, MA: Candlewick Press.

Many of my own pop-up books focus on math concepts such as counting, shapes, and calculations. I am also especially fond of pop-up books that transform one shape or image into another. Thus, it's no surprise that this is one of my dream books. Each page is a shape in a solid, bright color that transforms, via tags and flaps, into a familiar object. For example, an orange oval becomes a fish.

TAGS: colors; shapes

Diaz, James, and Francesca Diaz. 2007. *Popigami: When Everyday Paper Pops*! Paper engineering by James Diaz; illustration by Francesca Diaz. Atlanta: Intervisual Books.

This fantastic book blends what Nancy and I have often suggested to teachers would result in a perfect pairing: pop-ups and origami. It uses the paper products of ordinary life, such as gum wrappers, to create pop-ups that match the clever verses in rhyme.

TAGS: origami; rhymes; verse

Drescher, Henrik. *Pat the Beastie: A Pull-and-Poke Book*. Paper engineering by Dennis K. Meyer; production by Intervisual Books. New York: Hyperion Books for Children.

This six-inch-tall book manages to combine pop-ups, touch-and-feel, and flaps to convey the story of two children who are guilty of not being kind to their pet beastie. Needless to say, "when you cross a beastie, then he'll feastie." Maybe my fondness for this book is because of its inclusion of a small book created by the children, with the side comment that "reading is gastronomical"!

TAGS: animals; fantasy; reading; treatment of pets

Ellis, Jon. 1995. *The Pop-Up Book of Long and Tall Animals*. Illustration by Jon Ellis; production with the cooperation of the Philadelphia Zoo, Karl Kranz, curator; design and paper engineering by Roger Culbertson; cover design by Carolyn Keer and Cristina Culbertson. New York: Little Simon.

I love the size of this book! It's not quite five inches wide and is more than a foot tall, which makes it a perfect carrier for the loooong animal pop-ups. The blue whale pop-up at the end is especially memorable. Each pop-up is accompanied by a short, fact-filled introduction.

TAGS: animals; nature; science

Faulkner, Keith, and Jonathan Lambert. 1998. *Crazy Pops: Silly Rhymes and Crazy Pop-Ups*. [Reigate, Surrey, England]: Borders Press.

This tall book is a very humorous presentation of clever pop-ups that illustrate the silly rhymes about animals.

TAGS: animals; humor; rhymes

Faulkner, Keith. 2005. *Extreme Machines*. 1st ed. Illustration by Adrian Chesterman. New York: Barron's.

I can't resist pop-ups about technology! This book uses tabs (think gearshifts) to create the motion of the powerful machines that it illustrates. An especially fascinating technique is that each tab serves to create the motion on both the front and back of the page.

TAGS: inventions; machines; technology

Fischer, Chuck. 2005. *Christmas in New York: A Pop-Up Book*. New York: Bullfinch Press.
I love all of Chuck Fischer's books, but this one is particularly special! The colorful and astounding pop-ups capture the landmarks and activities that one should not miss if spending Christmas in New York.

TAGS: celebrations; Christmas; holidays; New York; travel

Fischer, Chuck. 2004. *The White House*. New York: Universe Publishing.
This pop-up book is almost as good as a trip to the White House, and I enjoy it because it reminds me of my own tour of the "People's House." Oversized and filled with colorful pop-ups and tabs and fold-outs and explanatory text, it covers the more than 200 years of this icon of American architecture.

TAGS: American history; architecture; tours; presidents of the United States; Washington, D.C.; the White House

Freedland, Sara. 1999. *Hanukkah! A Three-Dimensional Celebration.* 2nd U.S. ed. Illustrations by Sue Clarke; paper engineering by David Hawcock, Jerome Bruandet, and Mat Johnstone. London: Tango Books.

> This introduction to Hanukkah has illustrations reminiscent of textured collage, and the pop-ups enhance that presentation.

TAGS: Festival of Lights; Hanukkah; Jerusalem; Judaism

Hague, Michael. 1986. *Michael Hague's World of Unicorns.* Paper engineering by John Strejan and Rodger Smith. Henry Holt.

> The ever-popular unicorn pops gloriously from the very first page of this retelling of the saga of this beloved fantasy creature. The use of muted color so typical of Hague's works is particularly effective for portraying the other inhabitants of Fairyland, who fly from the pages.

TAGS: fairies; fantasy; unicorns

Harris, John, and Calef Brown. 2005. *Pop-Up Aesop.* Written by John Harris; illustration by Calef Brown; editing by John Harris; design by Kurt Hauser; production coordination by Elizabeth Zozom; paper engineering by Arty Projects Studio, Sally Blakemore, and Eileen Banashek; engineering refinements and production by Andy Baron. Los Angeles: Getty Publications.

> The first fable in this book is about the familiar tortoise and the hare; the other four are designed to encourage younger readers to create their own fables, which I find to be an appealing aspect of this book. The pop-ups are sophisticated in movement, reminding one of puppets.

TAGS: Aesop's Fables; creative writing

Hargreaves, Roger. 1983. *Mr. Happy Goes to a Pop-Up Dinner.* Paper engineering by Dick Dudley. Los Angeles: Price/Stern/Sloan Publishers.

> There is just something so enticing about a cast of characters who look like colored eggs and have names like Mr. Happy, Miss Shy, and Mr. Clumsy! I like the primary colors, simple lines, and combination of a variety of movable book techniques in this small book with a humorous plot.

TAGS: humor; meals

Harrison, James. 2003. *Amazing Vehicles: A Magic Skeleton Book.* Art direction by Ali Scrivens; managing editing by Ruth Hooper; story illustration by Jan Smith; cross section illustration by Peter Bull. New York: Sterling Publishing.

> I love this book because of its "amazing cross sections"! When tabs are pulled, the line drawings of everyday vehicles are transformed into full-color images. Really, truly amazing! The storyline is a field trip, and the narrative provides ample details about the workings, history, and purposes of the vehicles.

TAGS: field trip; technology; vehicles

Hawkins, Emily, and Sue Harris. 2007. *Human Body: Pop-Up Facts Bring the Body to Life.* Design and paper engineering by Andy Mansfield; illustration by Kim Thompson; front cover illustration by Steve Kingston; consultation by Dr. Ross Francis and Dr. Rachael Pery-Johnston. [New York]: Barnes & Noble.

One of the most intriguing aspects of this clever pop-up book is its arrangement by body functions: heartbeats, deep breaths, headquarters, making sense, and down the hatch. Mansfield's pop-ups are notable for their intricate movement.

TAGS: anatomy; biology

Israel Museum and Koren Publishers. 1997. *The Haggada of Passover: With Pop-Up Spreads.* Design and paper engineering by Keith Moseley; illustration by Linda Birkinshaw; Hebrew text and English translation are from the original Haggada published by Koren Publishers, Jerusalem; production by Compass Productions. Jerusalem: Israel Museum; Chicago: Kidsbooks.

This wonderful version of the Bird's-head Haggada, which was published in Germany in the 14th century, recounts the story of the Passover in both Hebrew and English. The flaps, tabs, and pop-ups add dimension to the reproduction of the original images.

TAGS: Germany; Haggada; Judaism; Passover; Seder

Johnson, Jinny, and Roland Lewis. 2007. *Frank Gehry in Pop-Up.* Design by Martin Hendry; picture researcher by Carrie Haines; paper engineering by Keith Finch and Neal Manning; illustration by Philip Jacobs. San Diego: Thunder Bay Press.

The work of award-winning Canadian architect Frank Gehry is the focus of this oversized and stunning book that captures five of his most notable projects. This book is a real treat for anyone who is fascinated by design and/or architecture.

TAGS: architecture; design; Frank Gehry; landmarks

Jordan, Carrie. 2002. *Pop-Up Farm Equipment.* Concept, illustrations, and paper engineering by Carrie Jordan. Bedford, TX: Carah Kids.

Designed for younger readers, the pop-ups and slides in this sturdy book are simply constructed. What I love about it is the topic of farm equipment, with the various types of machinery illustrated and explained.

TAGS: farms; farming; tractors

Kelly, Margaret. *Imperial Surprises.* 1994. Concept by Mary Ann Allin; design and paper engineering by Keith Moseley; illustrations by Stef Suchomski; photography by Larry Stein, Otto Nelson, Robert Forbes, and Steven Mays. New York: Harry N. Abrams.

This book is unique in its art topic: Fabergé eggs. Photographs of the actual eggs become truly three-dimensional as breathtaking pop-ups—which always make me wish to see them in real life! The text provides authoritative information about the eggs.

TAGS: art; Fabergé eggs; Russian art; Russian history

King, Celia. 1990. *The Seven Ancient Wonders of the World.* San Francisco: Chronicle Books.

It's both the size and the topic of this book that have always intrigued me. This delightful little book (just about hand size) uses pop-ups to introduce the seven ancient wonders of the world. Each "wonder" fits into a two-page spread and is preceded by a short history of it and a map pinpointing its location. This title is part of a series that includes mysterious wonders, modern wonders, and natural wonders.

TAGS: geography; history; landmark; seven wonders of the ancient world

Kirk, David. 2005. *Nova the Robot Super-Galactic Pop-Up.* Paper engineering and design by
   Phillip Fickling. New York: Callaway & Kirk Company.
   David Kirk's Nova the robot is a futuristic boy with equally mechanical friends.
   It is the paper engineering of this book that really captured me—the motion is both
   intricate and smooth.

TAGS: children's literature; robots

Knight, Joan. 1986. *Journey to Egypt.* 1st ed. Illustration by Piero Ventura; conception by
   Joan Knight; design and paper engineering by Dick Dudley and David A. Carter.
   New York: Viking Penguin.
   One of the reasons that I like this book is because it presents a historical and contemporary look at the culture, history, and landmarks of Egypt without focusing on
   pyramids and mummies. This pop-up book was one of a series of books by UNICEF
   intended to facilitate understanding of world diversity.

TAGS: Egypt; Egyptian history; life in Egypt

Kondeatis, Christos. 1994. *Scenes from the Life of Jesus Christ: A Three-Dimensional Bible Storybook.* Design, illustration, and paper engineering by Christos Kondeatis. London:
   Studio Editions.
   The wonderfully illustrated and complex pop-up scenes in this book highlight
   critical episodes in the life of Jesus Christ. The text is taken from the King James version of the Bible.

TAGS: Christianity; Jesus Christ

Lewis, C.S. 2007. *The Chronicles of Narnia.* Paper engineering by Robert Sabuda; full-color
   art by Matthew Armstrong. New York: HarperCollins Children's Books.
   Each two-page spread is filled with a magnificent pop-up that illustrates one of
   the books in the Narnia series. My favorite is the lion—magnificent!

TAGS: C.S. Lewis; *The Chronicles of Narnia*

Lockheart, Susanna. 2007. *If You See a Fairy Ring.* 1st ed. Illustration by Susanna Lock-
   heart; paper engineering by Alan Brown; design by Laura Hambleton; editing by
   Meg Wang; art direction by Rosamund Saunders and Jonathan Gilbert. Hauppauge,
   NY: Barron's.
   Poems about fairies, written by Robert Graves, Rose Fyleman, Annie Rentoul,
   Laura Ingalls Wilder, and Steven Kroll, are illustrated in a style charmingly evocative
   of Cicely Mary Barker Warne. But it is the construction of the movement in this book
   that attracts me: As each page is turned, the illustration in a centered oval is trans-
   formed into action.

TAGS: fairies; fairy tales; poetry

Los Angeles County Museum of Art and Universe Publishing. 2000. *The California Pop-
   Up Book.* Paper engineering and design by David Hawcock and Lesley Betts. New
   York: Universe Publishing.
   The librarian in me loves any book that whispers "reference"! Presented chrono-
   logically, beginning with the Gold Rush, this wonderful pop-up book uses pop-up
   and pull tabs to capture California's major landmarks and historical events. The text

is provided by the words of famous Californians, such as multiple-term Governor Jerry Brown, the authors of *Farewell to Manzanar* (James D. and Jeanne Wakatsuki Houston), and actor/artist Dennis Hopper.

TAGS: American art; American history; American literature; California; landmarks

Maizels, Jennie, and Kate Petty. 1996. *The Amazing Pop-Up Grammar Book.* Illustrations and letter **by** Jennie Maizels; text by Kate Petty; paper engineering by Damian Johnston; language consultation by Duncan Forbes; educational consultation by Tatiana Wilson.

I really enjoy the series of "Amazing Pop-up" books which introduce concepts, and this one focuses on grammar, which isn't a common topic for pop-up books. I am always entranced by the illustrations that somehow remind me of Martin Handford's "Waldo" books.

TAGS: grammar; language

Marceau, Fani, and Joëlle Jolivet. 2009. *Panorama: A Foldout Book.* New York: Abrams Books for Young Readers.

Some pop-up books just capture your imagination and never let go! This title, while relying on the simplicity of a "foldout," is one of those! This oversized book, rendered in black-and-white woodcuts with a touch of yellow at the bottom of the "pages" to serve as backdrop for the flowing descriptive prose, folds out as the tableau moves across memorable locations (such as mountains, deserts, seas, islands) around the world, highlighting native wildlife. The reverse of the pages reveals the same locations at night.

TAGS: animals; geography; history; nature; night; travel

Messenger, Norman. 1995. *Famous Faces.* 1st U.S. ed. New York: Dorling Kindersley Publishing.

This book uses one of my favorite formats for movement: simple flaps. They are used to transform the faces of the famous, such as Groucho Marx, Prince Charles, and Clint Eastwood.

TAGS: fame; movie stars; heads of state; rock stars

Moore, Patrick, and Heather Couper. 1985. *Halley's Comet: Pop-Up Book.* Illustration by Paul Doherty; paper engineering by Vic Duppa Whyte. New York: Bonanza Pop-up Books.

All aspects of "the most famous of all comets" are revealed in this very informative book which exhibits a wide variety of paper engineering methods.

TAGS: astronomy; Halley's Comet; science

Moseley, Keith. 1984. *The Bible Alphabet: A Pop-Up Book.* Pop-up engineering by Keith Moseley; cover and interior design by Michael J. Young. Nashville: Broadman & Holman Publishers.

Keith Moseley is another one of my favorite paper engineers, and this colorful pop-up book is filled with four-inch squares that open to reveal pop-ups corresponding to each letter of the alphabet. The text is from the New International Version of the Bible.

TAGS: alphabet; Bible; letters

Murray, Elizabeth. 2005. *Popped Art.* Pop-ups designed by Bruce Foster. New York: Museum of Modern Art.

I am always fascinated by the translation of art into the three-dimensional presentation of pop-ups. These pop-ups of the relief paintings of modern artist Elizabeth Murray add a new perspective to the original art.

TAGS: art; Elizabeth Murray; Museum of Modern Art; paintings; relief paintings

Paul, Korky. 1991. *The Pop-Up Book of Ghost Tales.* Illustration by Korky Paul; paper engineering by David Hawcock; created and production by Sadie Fields Productions. Orlando: Harcourt Brace Jovanovich.

Excerpts from famous horror stories, and background information about them, are illustrated with well-designed flaps, pull tabs, and pop-ups that capture the terror, but that also add a humorous element in the outlandish people, animals, and otherworldly creatures. It's always intriguing to revisit Poe, James, and Stoker in new treatments.

TAGS: Bram Stoker; *Dracula*; "Dracula's Guest"; Edgar Allan Poe; The Flying Dutchman; F. Marion Crawford; ghost stories; horror literature; M.R. James; "The Masque of the Red Death"; "Room 13"; "The Upper Berth"

Petty, Kate, and Jennie Maizels. 1999. *The Amazing Pop-Up Music Book.* Illustrations and lettering by Jennie Maizels; text by Kate Petty; paper engineering by Damian Johnston; music consultation by Jonathan Cooper, Stephen Lustig, and Diana Tejada; educational consultation by Helen Dooley. New York: Dutton Children's Books.

I really enjoy pop-up books that focus on songs and/or music, and each page of this pop-up book is filled with tabs and flaps that draw attention to the fundamentals of music. It ends with a 3-D piano keyboard that is operated with batteries.

TAGS: music

Potter, Beatrix. 2005. *The Tale of Peter Rabbit: A Pop-Up Adventure.* Conception, creation, and design by Brushfire; paper engineering by Keith Finch; additional illustration by Richard Cooper. London: Frederick Warne.

There are many pop-up renditions of Beatrix Potter's work. *Peter Rabbit* is my favorite of her stories, and this pop-up of that story is my favorite of the many versions that exist. Each two-page spread has multiple pop-ups that do justice to the original illustrations.

TAGS: animal characters; children's literature; Beatrix Potter; *The Tale of Peter Rabbit*

Reeve, Tim, and Gavin MacLeod. 1995. *Action Robots: A Pop-Up Book Showing How They Work.* 1st ed. Text nu Tim Reeve; illustration by Gavin MacLeod; paper engineering by David Hawcock; developed and production by Sadie Fields. New York: Dial Books for Young Readers.

Who isn't fascinated by robots? It is the content of this book that intrigues me—this presentation of pop-up robots is enhanced with such additions as a history of robots and (Isaac) Asimov's Three Laws of Robotics.

TAGS: invention; technology; robots

Reeve, Tim. 1993. *Machines: A Book of Moving Pop-Ups*. Illustrations by Robert Andrew; paper engineering by David Hawcock. New York: Philomel Books.

> In this wonderful book, each of the double-page spreads captures an important invention in the history of machines. And, these pop-up models work! There is ample explanation of each of the machine's workings, such as levers and gravity and power sources.

TAGS: invention; machinery; technology

Rojany, Lisa. 1993. *The Story of Hanukkah: A Lift-the-Flap Rebus Book*. Illustration by Holly Jones; design by Leslie McGuire; paper engineering by Jose R. Seminario and Ariel Apte; consultation by Camille Shira Angel; production by Intervisual Books. New York: Hyperion Books.

> I really enjoy the fact that this book has combined a rebus format with the story of Hanukkah. It also has pop-ups. The small flaps of the rebus enliven the text that introduces Hanukkah, the Festival of Lights.

TAGS: Hanukkah; Judaism; rebuses; Festival of Lights

Reinhart, Matthew. 2007. *Star Wars: A Pop-Up Guide to the Galaxy*. 1st ed. New York: Orchard Books.

> I still remember when I saw the first *Star Wars* movie, so this book is a real treat! Produced on the 30th anniversary of the movie, each page is a wonderfully constructed pop-up, and astoundingly, it includes light sabers that actually glow.

TAGS: movies; *Star Wars*; science fiction

Seder, Rufus Butler. 2007. *Gallop!* New York: Workman Publishing Company.

> How could you not love a book as clever as this one! As each page is opened, tabs that connect each spread create animals in motion—open the book faster, and they run faster! The flavor is similar to black-and-white movies, not surprisingly, since "the author acknowledges some illustrations in this book are based on the motion photography pioneered by Eadweard Muybridge."

TAGS: animals; Eadweard Muybridge; motion; photography

Seibold, J. Otto, and Vivian Walsh. 1997. *Olive, the Other Reindeer*. San Franciso: Chronicle Books.

> This book is the charming story of Olive, a dog who decides that she is a reindeer. I love the use of muted colors and illustrations similar to cartoons, as well as the wonderful pop-up of Santa's castle. Also, unusual in a pop-up book, it has scratch-and-sniff areas.

TAGS: Christmas; dogs; reindeers; Santa Claus

Serrano, Francisco. 1998. *Our Lady of Guadalupe*. Pictures by Felipe Davalos; paper engineering by Eugenia Guzman; translation by Haydn Raulinson and Groundwood Books. [Canada]: Groundwood Book.

> I really like this colorful pop-up book because it beautifully presents the 16th-century story of Our Lady of Guadalupe, whose miraculous appearance to Juan Diego culminated in a church being erected on Tepeyac Hill. The pop-ups and the illustrations are equally sophisticated.

TAGS: Christianity; the Madonna; Mexico; the Immaculate Virgin Mary of Guadalupe; Our Lady of Guadalupe; the Virgin Mary; Saint Juan Diego

Sommers, Joan. 2006. *Henri Rousseau's Tunnel Book.* 1st ed. Design by Joan Sommers Design. [Chicago]: Tunnel Vision Books.

One technique for a movable book that is fairly uncommon today is the "tunnel," which requires the reader to lift the accordion format to create the three-dimension scene. I never fail to be entranced by this presentation of Rousseau's 1908 painting *Fight Between a Tiger and a Buffalo.* The lushness of the jungle scene comes to life in this format, which is accompanied by an informative booklet. This same independent publisher has also produced an equally masterful rendition of Mexican printmaker Jose Guadalupe Posada's "dancing skeletons" in *The Dancing Skeletons Tunnel Book* (same imprint information).

TAGS: art; French art; Henri Rousseau; *Fight Between a Tiger and a Buffalo*

Strickland, Paul. 2005. *Big Dig: A Pop-Up Construction!* New York: Backpack Books.

Watch out! Construction in progress! This is a notable book for the topic (heavy machinery) and the three-dimensional capture of powerful movement.

TAGS: building; construction; machines

Symes, Sally, and Steve Lavis. 2005. *Who's Been Walking on My Floor?* Paper engineering by Corina Fletcher. Hauppage, NY: Barron's.

Remember Old MacDonald and his farm? Well, Mrs. MacDonald has to track down which of the farm's many animals have been walking on her clean floor. Flaps reveal the pops of the animals. This storyline is a clever twist on a familiar set of characters, and the ending, with its large fold-out of a joyous meal, would have pleased the overburdened Little Red Hen!

TAGS: animals; farms; tracks

Van der Meer, Ron. 2007. *How Many? Spectacular Paper Sculptures.* Design and paper engineering by Ron van der Meer and Graham Brown; production and manufacturing by Graham Brown; text by Yvette Lodge; graphics by Tim Dyer. New York: Robin Cory Books.

I love this book because it *really* is filled with "spectacular paper sculptures." Each of these masterpieces of paper engineering is accompanied by questions that ask about the numbers of shapes (not as easy as you think!), and there's a website where the answers can be double-checked.

TAGS: counting; lines; math; numbers; shapes

Van Fleet, Matthew. 2003. *Tails.* Editing and art direction by Skip Skwarek. San Diego: Red Wagon Books, Harcourt.

This is a sturdy book that uses vocabulary, tabs, flaps, and fabric to demonstrate the wide range of animals' tails and their purposes, while also introducing concepts of numbers, animal names, and size. It's a wonderful work that can be used to teach many basics, plus it's just fun to read!

TAGS: adjectives; animals; counting; math; nature; numbers; size; tails

Weeks, Sarah, and David A. Carter. 1996. *Noodles: An Enriched Pop-Up Product*. Text by Sarah Weeks; illustration by David A. Carter; production by White Heat. [New York]: HarperFestival.

As a fan of cookery, I've always been enchanted by this now-classic pop-up by David A. Carter. It has pop-ups and tabs that enable the pasta characters to be introduced as lively figures. The text is in verse, which adds another dimension to the book's humor. I also love the fact that the cover of this book has its net weight listed (11 ounces or 312 grams)!

TAGS: food; humor; pasta; shapes; verse

Willis, Jeanne. 2004. *Operation Itchy*. 1st U.S. ed. Illustration by Penny Dann; adapted from an idea by Paul Cottington. Cambridge, MA: Candlewick Press.

As a fan of mysteries and suspense, I can never resist a pop-up book that evokes those genres! This book, for a younger audience, has a dog as a secret agent with a mission to thwart megafleas.

TAGS: dogs; fleas; mysteries; secret agents

Woelflein, Luise. 1992. *A Larger-Than-Life 3-D Look at the Spider*. Illustration by Tomo Narashima; paper engineering by James Diaz; book design by Lynette Ruschak. Santa Monica, CA: Piggy Toes Press.

I really like books about nature and its creatures, and this title is one in a series linked to *Nature*, the Emmy Award-winning public television series. Open it, and you are instantly confronted with a much larger-than-life pop-up tarantula! Side bars are actually pages of informative text, enhanced with their own pop-ups and flaps.

TAGS: arachnids; insects; nature; spiders

Young, Jay. 1994. *The Most Amazing Science Pop-Up Book*. 1st U.S. ed. Paper engineering by Jay Young. [New York]: HarperFestival.

This pop-up book is notable for its interactive nature, using working models to highlight important inventions. It has abundant text that explains and provides historical background and profiles notables in the world of science.

TAGS: experiments; history of science; science; scientists

NANCY'S DREAM LIBRARY OF POP-UPS

Selections for Nancy's dream library reflect her belief that movable books are works of art as well as literature and should be considered as such. The paper engineer is truly an artist, creating with paper as other artists create with a variety of mediums such as paint, clay, and fiber. When making purchases, among the things she considers are the style of the illustrations, the use of color, intricacy or boldness of design, use of unusual materials, unique formats or approaches to the topic, and how movement adds to the story or imparts information.

Personal interests also played a big part in how books were selected for inclusion in the dream library. They may reflect Nancy's love of traditional literature or her passion for art, music, theater, history, and travel. Some invoke a sense of nostalgia. Most of all, she picked them because every time she opens each and every one of them, she smiles!

There are some items that would definitely go into Nancy's dream library but the titles are omitted because they have been acquired in her travels abroad and would be difficult to find. They include a book in verse in the shape of a Leprechaun with arms that move (*The Leprechaun* 2000), a flea market acquisition of a French version of the book *When Sue Pretends* (*Si J'Etais* 1990), and a Russian pop-up whose translated title is *The Priest and His Workman Balda* (ISBN 5–7341–004–8).

Artist to Artist: *23 Major Illustrators Talk to Children about Their Art.* 2007. New York: Philomel Books.

    Technically this book might not belong in a list of movable books. It is an anthology of writings in which some of the world's most honored picture book artists talk to children about their art. Foldout spreads feature photos of the artists, their studios, and their work. There is only one pop-up: A Robert Sabuda and Matthew Reinhart collaboration is included. It is wonderful to see these renowned paper engineers receive recognition as artists, a distinction that is often overlooked and that many others in the field have also long deserved. Works of several of the featured illustrators, such as Eric Carle, Tomie DePaola, Maurice Sendak, Paul O. Zelinsky, and others, have been adapted as pop-up books. As a collector, librarian, and adjunct professor of children's literature, this book had to be included in my dream library as a valuable resource for further study. An interesting note: Sales of the book benefit the Eric Carle Museum of Picture Book Art.

TAGS: artists; children's book illustrators; illustrators

Base, Graeme. 1996. *Lewis Carroll's Jabberwocky: A Book of Brillig Dioramas.* Design by Graeme Base; retouching and color separations by Ross McCartney & Associates; production by Compass Productions. New York: Harry N. Abrams.

    Three-D diorama pages entice the reader to enter the fantasy world created in Lewis Carroll's poem, "Jabberwocky." The depth of the dioramas and the bold, detailed artwork of Australian Graeme Base are the perfect combination for bringing to life this classic bit of nonsense verse. An internationally acclaimed illustrator, Base was the recipient of the Australian Children's Book Award Picture Book of the Year, 1989, for *The Eleventh Hour: A Curious Mystery.*

TAGS: dioramas; British literature; "Jabberwocky"; Lewis Carroll; verse

Bantock, Nick. 1994. *Kubla Khan: A Pop-Up Version of Coleridge's Classic.* Text by Samuel Taylor Coleridge; illustration by Nick Bantock; design by Barbara Hodgson and Nick Bantock; paper engineering by Nick Bantock and Dennis K. Meyer. New York: Viking Penguin.

    Bantock uses collage to create images of Xanadu and the stately pleasure dome of Coleridge's poem across double-page spreads. It is not the literary content that attracts here. It is the exotic images that draw me into this dark, rich pop-up. It was a long while before I realized that I had never even read the verse—from the start I was mesmerized by the evocative art.

TAGS: British literature; British poetry; "Kubla Khan"; poetry; Samuel Taylor Coleridge; Xanadu

Bonn, Franz. 1978. *The Children's Theatre: A Reproduction of the Antique Pop-Up Book.* Production by Intervisual Communications. London: Kestrel Books; New York: Viking Press.

    This title is a reproduction of a pop-up book first published in 1878 in Germany. It opens from the top to reveal pop-up stage scenes. Depth is achieved by placing the figures at three intervals in front of a backdrop. The "plays" include two classic folk tales, a nativity scene, and an old-fashioned family Christmas. Child musicians who pop-up in front of each stage add charm as do instrument-playing angels in front of the nativity scene. Text written in verse describes the action in each theater setting.

First published by J. F. Schreiber of Esslingen, Germany.

TAGS: Fairy tales; Hansel and Gretel; Little Red Riding Hood; the Nativity; plays; theater

Brown, Harriet, and Teri Witkowski. 2008. *Kit's World: A Girl's-Eye View of the Great Depression.* Design and art direction by Chris David and Susan Walsh; production by Jeannette Bailey, Julie Kimmell, Judith Lary, Gail Longworth, Kendra Schulter, and Sally Wood; paper Engineering by Shawn Wilder Sheehy; color illustration by Walter Rane; interior illustration by Philip Hood, Susan McAliley, Susan Moore, Walter Rane, and Jean-Paul Tibbles. Middleton, WI: American Girl Publishing.

This treasure was discovered when I was shopping for a birthday present, but it ended up being a gift to me from me! American Girl's historical fiction books (for ages 8 to 13) place girls from various cultural and ethnic backgrounds as key characters in major events in American history. The saying "Don't judge a book by its cover" doesn't apply in this case because that is what makes the shopper reach up and take it from the shelf. A portrait of Kit changes to a picture of her sliding down the banister, clothes basket tucked under one arm when a tab is pulled. Inside, this very educational interactive book is full of period photos of people and objects, facts and anecdotes revealed through the use of lift-the-flaps, wheels, and pop-ups. The book was the 2008 Gold Award winner from the National Parenting Publication Awards (NAPPA).

TAGS: American history; the Great Depression; women and history

Carle, Eric. 2009. *The Very Hungry Caterpillar.* Pop-up design by Brushfire; paper engineering by Keith Finch. New York: Philomel Books.

Many children learned their numbers and first heard about metamorphosis from a hungry little caterpillar. That world famous, award-winning muncher turned 40 in 2009. In honor of the occasion, a first-ever pop-up edition was released. From the opening pop-up of a little egg on a leafy branch in the moonlight to the shimmering butterfly that pops across a double-page spread on the final pages, this book is a wonderful 40th anniversary tribute to the original. The caterpillar's transformation is made all the more fun and breathtaking by the dimension and movement achieved with great paper engineering.

TAGS: caterpillars; children's literature; counting; Eric Carle; math; geometry; metamorphosis, *The Very Hungry Caterpillar*

Carter, David A. 2004. *One Red Dot: A Pop-Up Book for Children of All Ages.* New York: Little Simon.

This is my favorite in Carter's series of non-bug books that focuses on math concepts. At first look of this very intricate pop-up, I thought: modern art. But it is more than that. It is color and counting at the most basic level; geometry and other math concepts at more sophisticated levels. It takes visual acuity to keep locating that red dot!

TAGS: color; counting; geometry; math

Crespi, Francesca. 1992. *A Walk in Monet's Garden*. 1st North American ed. Text by Frances Lincoln; illustration by Francesca Crespi. Boston: A Bulfinch Press Book, Little Brown and Company.

> This is a book that isn't actually a book. Unfold it and it becomes an almost three-square-foot replica of Monet's Garden in Giverny, France. The plants, the farmhouse, the Japanese-style bridge over the pond, Monet's studio—all come to life. The pop-up book includes a small guidebook that links the garden, Monet's artwork, and his life in Giverny. This Impressionist painter is one of my favorite artists and what a dream come true it was to visit this garden! Now I can return anytime I wish without ever leaving my kitchen table.

TAGS: art; art appreciation; Claude Monet; famous gardens; gardening; Giverny, France

De Borchgrave, Isabelle. 2000. *Fashion a' La Mode*. Text by Dorothy Twining Globus; design and paper engineering by David Hawcock; editing by Ellen Cohen. New York: Universe Publishing.

> I am enthralled by this coverage of fashion through history which spans many eras and cultures. The figures, which pop up in appropriate settings, capture the flavor of each time and place providing a context for the fashion. Removable interactive accessories, such as a fan from the court of Marie Antoinette, are cleverly included. Essays by notable names in the world of fashion add text to a book whose information is imparted largely through visual images. The design of this book makes it a work of art in itself!

TAGS: art; fashion; costumes; history

Denchfield, Nick, Sue Scullard. 2003. *The Nutcracker: A Magical Pop-Up Adventure*. Paper engineering by Nick Denchfield; illustration by Sue Scullard. London: Macmillan Children's Books.

> Nutcrackers adorn my kitchen during the entire holiday season from just after Thanksgiving into the New Year. Among them, I place a few of my favorite Nutcracker pop-up books. The popular ballet, with its roots in the 1816 story by E.T.A. Hoffman ("The Nutcracker and the King of Mice") translates wonderfully into the movement of a pop-up presentation. Denchfield's version with impressively large double-page scenes and surprises hidden in tiny presents and beneath snowflakes always gets a prominent place in the display.

TAGS: ballet; Christmas; dance; E.T.A. Hoffmann; music; nutcrackers; *The Nutcracker*

DePrisco, Dorothea. 2005. *Bluebird's Nest*. Illustration by Jo Parry; design by Melanie Random; production by Intervisual Books. Los Angeles: Piggy Toes Press.

> The use of an unusual material is what initially caught my attention when I saw this book. Bluebird builds her nest throughout the seasons and to show its growth, raveling strings of yarn are added one at a time. They stretch across the center of the book as each page is turned. With the help of her friends who contribute other materials, the nest is ready to welcome her babies in the spring. This sturdy board book is a delightful way to teach preschool age children about working together, and about nature, including the cycle of seasons and the materials that can be used in building a nest.

TAGS: birds; bluebirds; cycle of seasons; nature; friendship, cooperation

Dr. Seuss Pops Up! *A Celebration of Seven Seuss Classics.* 2005. Paper engineering by Keith Finch; original conception, design, and production by Brushfire Publishing. New York: Random House Children's Books.

Pop-ups, pull-tabs, gatefolds, a juggling cat in the hat! If you find, as I do, the verse and art of Dr. Seuss to be both amusing and thought-provoking, just imagine the reaction when movement is added to these excerpts from seven of his most well-known stories!

TAGS: Dr. Seuss; humor

Escher, M.C. 1991. *The Pop-Up Book of M.C. Escher.* Production by Blaze International Productions; engineering by John J. Strejan; design by Bonnie Smetts Design. Petaluma: Pomegranate Artbooks.

Looking at the complex artwork of Escher can keep me occupied for hours. The detail, the perspective, and the visual puzzles are impossible to take in with a quick glance. His two-dimensional works, which give the illusion of being three-dimensional, are truly brought to life when placed in the 3-D format of pop-ups. There is just enough text, much of it quotes from Escher himself, to aid in understanding his intriguing work.

TAGS: architecture; art; art appreciation; art techniques; illusions; lithographs; math; M.C. Escher; three-dimensional; woodcuts

Fischer, Chuck. *Great American Houses and Gardens.* 2002. Design by David Hawcock. New York: Universe Publishing.

Fischer combines pop-ups, a concertina, carousels, photography, and his own painting to bring the architecture and history of the great estates of America to life. As a person who has planned vacations around the dates of historic home and garden tours, I've realized that this magnificent book was destined to be a favorite of mine. It allows me to relive trips to those places I have already seen and inspires me to keep those that I have not visited on my "must go to" list.

TAGS: famous houses

Foreman, Michael. 1997. *Ben's Box: A Pop-Up Fantasy.* Paper engineering by David A. Carter and David Pelham. Kansas City, MO: Piggy Toes Press.

It is wonderful to observe the imagination of a child when it is not inhibited by the structure of instructions from an adult. For years I walked around forts that sprang up in my living room floor. Now my granddaughters have grand tea parties in the castle (in reality, a blanket-covered card table) in my living room. Similarly, marvelous adventures take place in Ben's kitchen when his mother gives him the box from a new washing machine. What a nice trip down memory lane this book provides—and a reminder for us adults so rooted in reality to think outside the box once in a while.

TAGS: children's literature; children's play activities; creative writing; creativity

Forward, Toby. 2005. *Shakespeare's Globe: An Interactive Pop-Up Theatre.* Text by Toby Forward; illustration by Juan Wijngaard; back cover photography by Mike Galletly. Cambridge, MA: Candlewick Press.

Rhonda and I used this book in a presentation on Shakespeare given to a group of senior citizens participating in a workshop at a university. They loved it, reaffirming to me my belief that pop-ups are not just for children. A model of the Globe

Theatre rises from the pages allowing the viewer both exterior and interior views. The text is a first person narration in the words of an Elizabethan actor telling about the Globe—its history, the plays, what the audience can expect at a performance. Also included are short scripts of scenes from several plays to be read aloud or to be "performed" by the paper characters provided.

TAGS: Elizabethan history; Globe Theatre; plays; theater; William Shakespeare

Gallagher, Derek. 2004. *Ancient Dwellings of the Southwest*. Illustration by Sally Blakemore; paper engineering by Eileen Banashek, Sally Blakemore, and Anthony Esparsen; pop-up book design and production by Arty Projects Studio. Tucson, AZ: Western National Parks Association.

Pop-up books about cultures, especially those of a regional nature, are not often seen. This book, acquired on a trip to New Mexico, is not only an unusual find but also is very well executed. Through the use of pop-ups and pull-tabs which accompany an informative text, it is possible to see that which is generally hard to visualize when reading about unfamiliar cultures and time periods. Several national historical parks, monuments, and the contemporary World Heritage Site at Taos Pueblo are featured. At the end of each section, turn the book around so it faces away from you to discover more narrative and pop-ups.

TAGS: housing; multiculturalism; Native Americans; Southwestern United States

Gruelle, Johnny. 1924; (abridged text and altered illustrations) 2003. *Raggedy Ann and Andy and the Camel with the Wrinkled Knees*. 1st ed. Paper engineering by Kees Moerbeck; text adaptation by Melissa Eisler. New York: Little Simon.

Raggedy Ann and Andy have resided in generations of children's nurseries since the publication of Gruelle's first story about them in 1918. Today's youngsters who have grown up with the fast paced action and animation of television and video games may be harder to hook on the adventures of two rag dolls. This pop-up adaptation of the classic has large, colorful center-of-the-page pop-ups in the original style. The text and smaller pop-ups are concealed under side book pages. It should win over even the most skeptical child when a parent or grandparent says, "You'll love this book about Raggedy Ann and Andy." This version is so well done that I think it is destined to become a classic itself.

TAGS: *The Camel with the Wrinkled Knees*; classic children's literature; dolls; Johnny Gruelle; Raggedy Ann; Raggedy Andy

Hawcock, David. 1994. *Making Tracks: A Circular Pop-Up Story*. Illustration by Jan Lewis; creation and production by Sadie Fields. [New York]: Hyperion Books for Children.

This pop-up has one of those unusual formats that always attracts my attention. Turn the pages to read this book. At the end, place it on a large flat surface, lift the last page and pull it out until it forms a large circle. Then enjoy reading this circular story again as you follow the animals leaving footprints in the snow and leading to . . .?

TAGS: animals; nature; snow; tracks

Hong, Seonna. 2005. *Animus: A Moving Picture Book*. 1st ed. Images by Seonna Hong; text by Seonna Hong with Shenne Hahn. Van Nuys, CA: Baby Tattoo Books.

This simple little book struck a chord with me the first time I read it. The strong storyline, written in verse, is about knowing oneself. A small girl who is afraid of a large dog learns to confront her fears and discovers an important life lesson—it is what we do to ourselves that causes the dread and thus, we must look to ourselves to find peace. It is unusual to see ethnic diversity in pop-ups and this author and artist of Korean descent has used a small Asian girl to illustrate a story that could happen to any child of any race. I like that. It is worth noting that Hong is an Emmy Award–winning (for Nickelodeon's *My Life as a Teenage Robot*) animation artist whose credits also include the Cartoon Network's Emmy Award–winning *Powder Puff Girls*.

TAGS: dogs; fear; self-discovery; verse

Ives, Penny. 1994. *Santa's Christmas Journey: A Scrolling Picture Book*. Illustrations by Penny Ives; design by David Hawcock. [S.l.]: Hyperion Books for Children.

How could I not love this book?! It combines two of my favorite things—a unique format and travel! Turn the handle of a scroll to get a bird's-eye view of the cities below as Santa flies from the North Pole around the world to deliver his gifts. With each turn, the picture rolls forward to reveal another city and country. It is fun to try to identify the famous landmarks shown in each location. Going a step further, Santa's journey can be plotted on a globe—and the book is a great springboard for a discussion of Christmas customs in other countries. There is no "pop" in this book, but it is a very interesting movable book that encourages skills of keen observation and critical thinking.

TAGS: Christmas; geography; landmarks; Santa Claus; scrolls; travel

Jakubowski, Maxim, and Ron Van der Meer. 1987. *The Great Movies Live!: A Pop-Up Book*. Design and editing by Ebury Press; production by Carvajal SA. New York: Fireside Book-Simon & Schuster.

There are three movies I must watch at least once a year from my old video collection, and one of those is *Casablanca* (1942). So it's no surprise that I would choose a book for my library that is illustrated with actual scenes from it and other great films of the '30s, '40s, and '50s. Rick's Bar pops up with Sam at the piano and the other stars seated at the tables. Humphrey Bogart and Ingrid Bergman are about to kiss. Sigh! Each movie featured has a fact flap which includes names of the cast members and quotes a memorable line or two from the film.

TAGS: movie history; movies; Hollywood

King Arthur and the Magic Sword. 1990. Adaptation of the *Story of King Arthur and His Knights* by Howard Pyle; design by Keith Moseley; pictures by John James. New York: Dial Books for Young Readers.

Everyone knows the Arthurian Legends in one form or another. They have been told over and over again through art, books, movies, stage plays, and musicals. The detailed artwork depicting the costumes, the heraldry, the dark interior of a forest inn, and the colorful tents at the tourney makes this pop-up book a favorite rendition of the timeless story set in the age of chivalry, brave knights, and fair maidens.

TAGS: Arthurian legend; King Arthur; knights

Lewis, J. Patrick, and Tom Curry. 2005. *Galileo's Universe*. 1st ed. Poems by J. Patrick Lewis; illustrations by Tom Curry; design by Rita Marshall and Bea Jackson. Mankato, MN: Creative Editions.

This book appeals to my interests in literature, travel, and history. It is a unique combination of poetry and pop-ups that informs the reader about the life and discoveries of the great physicist and astronomer Galileo. The reader's curiosity is peaked with the opening of the cover and sight of a closed door in the end page with the caption "open this door." The setting is defined and a hint of the interest in astronomy is given in the first double-page spread with the child Galileo peering from his window; the Leaning Tower of Pisa is shown in the background against a starry sky. We understand how radical Galileo's ideas were as an angry pope flanked by red-robed churchmen springs from the page, pointing an accusing finger at Galileo.

TAGS: astronomy; discoveries; Galileo; poetry

Meggendorfer, Lothar. 1997. *Lothar Meggendorfer's International Circus: A Reproduction of the Antique Pop-Up Book*. (The original German edition by J.F. Schreiber.) New York: Metropolitan Museum of Art.

It would be impossible for a fan of pop-up books not to love this reproduction of what is considered to be the masterpiece of all the works created by the legendary German illustrator Lothar Meggendorfer. He is considered to be the chief innovator and a master craftsman in the creation of movable books. This title was first published in 1887, but the universal theme of a circus lends it contemporary appeal. As with all masterpieces, its execution is as appealing today as it was in the 19th century.

TAGS: circus; history of pop-up books; *International Circus*; Lothar Meggendorfer; paper engineers

Milne, A.A. 1994. *The Poems and Hums of Winnie-the-Pooh. The Songs of Winnie-the-Pooh*. Hand-coloring of Enest H. Shepard's decorations by Robert Cremins; design by Marcy Heller. New York: Dutton Children's Books.

Each of this pair of miniatures is described as "A Pooh Window Book." Each poem or song in the respective volumes is placed opposite a triple-layered pop-up. There is the watercolor painted background, a pop-up middle ground featuring Pooh and friends that adds dimension, and finally, a transparent foreground with painted tree limbs, bushes, or snow to complete the illusion of depth of landscape. Each tiny scene pops up in a box-like enclosure—the window. I find this unusual format to be charming but not often seen. These are the only two books in my collection to make use of it.

Milne, A.A. 1993. *Winnie-the-Pooh's Pop-Up Theater Book*. Paper engineering by Helen Balmer and Jose R. Seminario; adaptation of illustration by E.H. Shepard by Mark Burgess; design by Jim Deesing. New York: Dutton Children's Books.

Stick puppets of the beloved characters from the Hundred Acre Wood can be inserted into a pop-up theater stage and are ready for reenacting one of five familiar stories written by A.A. Milne. Christopher Robin and friends have been popular since the first stories were written in the 1920s thanks to decades of book reprints, television specials, and cuddly stuffed animals. This very unusual format is an interesting and refreshing departure from the usual fare of versions of Winnie.

TAGS: classic children's literature; dioramas; narrative nonfiction writing; plays; puppets; theater

Moerbeek, Kees. 2000. *Goldilocks Roly Poly*. Swindon Auburn, ME; Sydney: Child's Play (International).

An ageless fairy tale is given a fresh look when it is presented in a most unusual format: a cube. The cube literally unfolds to reveal 3-D scenes of the Goldilocks story, and each small scene has a pop-up, with the story provided on the back of each scene. This title is part of a series of Roly Poly Books: *Goldilocks*; *Three Little Pigs*; *Cinderella*.

TAGS: Cinderella; cubes; dioramas; math; children's literature; fairy tales; *Goldilocks and the Three Bears*; *The Three Little Pigs*

Moerbeek, Kees, and Carla Dijs. 1987. *Hot Pursuit: A Forward-and-Backward Pop-Up Book*. Los Angeles: Intervisual Communications.

    Hot Pursuit was one of the first pop-ups I acquired for my collection, and it remains one of my favorites. Everyone who looks at it is enchanted by it—as you should be with a fairy tale. It is a never-ending story. Open the book flat and keep rotating it. It is a tale of pursuit, with classic fairy tale icons such as dragons, trolls, and knights endlessly chasing each other.

TAGS: fairy tales; pursuit

Nister, Ernest. 1982. *Merry Magic-Go-Round*. New York: Philomel Books.

    Nister is an early master of movable books, and reproductions are readily available. This book of changing pictures intrigues me today much as it must have thrilled readers when it was first published in 1897. Images appear on the right hand side of a picture that were not on the left-hand side before the wheel is turned. It's magic! The poems describing the scenes are delightfully complemented by Nister's illustrations of children at play. They are done in that English Victorian style that radiates with sweet innocence.

TAGS: history of pop-up books; paper engineers; poetry; children's play activities; art; Victorian era

Osborne, Richard N. ca. 1940s–1950. *A Child's Book of the Nativity*. New York: Triad Binding Corporation.

Moore, Clement Clarke. 1988. *The Night before Christmas: A Revolving Picture and Lift-the-Flap book*. 1st U.S. edition. Illustrated by Penny Ives, design and paper engineering by Claire Littlejohn; creation and production by Sadie Fields Productions. New York: G.P. Putnam's Sons.

    It was a tradition on Christmas Eve to read aloud as a family *The Night Before Christmas* and also the story of the birth of Jesus. It continued on, even when some others might have considered the children too grown up for picture books, because it was such an integral part of our celebration. The two books we read are still lovingly displayed each Christmas season and bring forth a flood of memories.

    It was imperative to me that I include movable versions of those wonderful stories in my dream library. Penny Ives's book of revolving pictures positioned across the pages from Moore's narrative poem is one of my favorite renderings of that classic. The circular transformations, especially the snowy scenes, effectively evoke the era and the winter season. The story of the birth of Jesus that I wanted to include in my dream library required some research on my part. A gift from my brother, *A Child's Book of the Nativity* is a wonderful metal spiral-bound book of progressive scenes. The first page opens as an easel showing the manger and some animals. As each succeeding page is raised, it adds a layer to the nativity scene: Mary and Joseph, angels, shepherds, and wise men, along with a simplified text of the Biblical story. It ends with the words to the song "Silent Night." The book gives no publication information and credits only the illustrator, Richard N. Osborne. I finally discovered through Alibris.com that it was published by Triad Binding Corp., ca 1940s–1950.

TAGS: Christmas; the Nativity story; *The Night before Christmas*; Santa Claus

Pelham, David. 2007. *Trail*. Production by White Heat. New York: Little Simon.

> This is a visually stunning book because of the incredible, intricately detailed white and silver pop-ups and the clear attachments that make butterflies flit above the pages as if without support. It may be the most beautiful pop-up book that I have seen! The verse that blends unobtrusively into the background is read by turning a wheel on each page, taking you on a nature walk to the trail's end at a pond. Here, on the underside of the last pop-up is the only color in the book: a touch of green leaves and a brown snail reflected in a shimmering pond. The cover, also done in white and silver, says "paper poetry" and it is indeed sheer poetry in both word and art.

TAGS: art; nature; nature walk; poetry

Pieńkowski, Jan. 1996. *Botticelli's Bed & Breakfast*. Paper engineering by Rodger Smith and Helen Blamer, with special thanks to Hilary Sanders. New York: Simon & Schuster.

> This is my very favorite popup book! I love the carousel format of an old world mansion, with famous works of art hidden in unexpected places, from where they pop-up and slide out. I also really appreciate the use of humor, such as Whistler's mother rocking in front of the fireplace and Michaelangelo's David brushing his teeth in front of the bathroom mirror. A miniature guidebook is included to help identify the master works if needed.

TAGS: art; art appreciation; art masterpieces

Priceman, Marjorie. 2001. *Little Red Riding Hood: A Classic Collectible Pop-Up*. Paper engineering by Bruce Foster. New York: Simon & Schuster.

> There are many versions of *Little Red Riding Hood*, but I am always drawn to the illustrations and use of color in this pop-up. The dominant use of red flows throughout the book, playing on the name of the title character. This variation follows the original storyline of the classic fairytale, but its revised happy ending makes it less scary than some retellings are for small children.

TAGS: children's literature; classic children's literature; fairytales; *Little Red Riding Hood*

Prokofiev, Sergei. 1986. *Peter and the Wolf*. Scenes by Barbara Cooney; paper engineering by John Strejan and David A. Carter. New York: Viking Kestrel.

> Prokofiev's symphony for children, written to introduce them to the instruments of the orchestra and with the story spoken by a narrator, is illustrated beautifully by Caldecott Award–winner Barbara Cooney. I was awestruck by the dense woods and historic structures in parts of rural Russia when I visited there. I did imagine Peter and the wolf in those forests. Cooney has captured the flavor of the setting perfectly. The pages of the book fold down so readers can easily visualize themselves in a concert hall, with the pop-up scenes depicting what they might be seeing with their mind's eye as the music is played. Just pop in a CD, open this book, and savor the whole experience.

TAGS: music; *Peter and the Wolf*; Sergei Prokofiev

Provensen, Alice and Provensen, Martin. 1984. *Leonardo Da Vinci*. 1st edition. Paper engineering by John Strejan. New York: Viking Press.

> The activities of Leonardo da Vinci as artist, astronomer, inventor, and scientist in 15th century Florence are highlighted in this movable book. Pop-ups, wheels, tabs,

and pull-down stages by one of my most admired paper engineers, John Strejan, and pictures by Caldecott Medal–winners Alice and Martin Provensen, combine to produce a book that encompasses many of my favorite things: a great artist, a beautiful city, history, and the creative use of paper as a medium making it a work of art.

TAGS: art; art history; inventions; Leonardo da Vinci; Florence, Italy

Reinhart, Matthew. 2005. *The Ark: A Pop-Up by Matthew Reinhart.* 1st ed. New York: Little Simon.

This is my favorite Reinhart production. The technique of outlining everything in white—contrary to the more common practice of outlining in black—the stylized figures, and the use of brilliant color makes this book an eye-catching work of art. Even when the rains come, the only darkness is in the clouds and sky. The frightened villagers are still depicted in vivid color. The motion of the waves, the Ark being tossed about, and the yellow flashes of lightening show the fierceness of the storm. I love the animals, the color, and the movement! It is a visual treat.

TAGS: animals; the Ark; Bible; floods; math; measurement; nature; natural disasters; Noah

Sabuda, Robert. *Alice's Adventures in Wonderland: A Pop-Up Adaptation of Lewis Carroll's Original Tale.* 1st ed. New York: Little Simon.

Almost everything Robert Sabuda has done would be in my dream library—and is! As much as I admire all of his work, I do have a favorite, *Alice's Adventures in Wonderland*. The artwork is done in the style of Sir John Tenniel, who illustrated the first edition of Alice. But, anyone who might balk at reading that classic won't have a moment's hesitation once they open the cover of Sabuda's adaptation and a giant tree pop-ups, complete with the Cheshire cat, the Hatter, and the Queen camouflaged in its leafy branches. Lift a wonderful tunnel from the page, peer through its little peephole, and down the rabbit hole you go! The most amazing pop-ups occur throughout the book. The croquet game extends outside the pages, a deck of cards flutters in an archway over Alice, even teacups pop-up. Alice's Wonderland is nothing compared to the wonder of Sabuda's creations in this fabulous book.

TAGS: classic children's literature; *Alice's Adventures in Wonderland*; John Tenniel; Lewis Carroll; math

Sabuda, Robert, and Matthew Reinhart. 2001. *Young Naturalist's Pop-Up Handbook: Beetles.* 1st edition. New York: Hyperion Books for Children.

Pop-ups enhanced with shiny paper and a detailed text often written with a touch of humor (a tiny book of *Beetle Memories* can be read as pages turn when a tab is pulled) make this book both visually appealing and informative. What makes it truly unique is that fact that it is packaged together with a colorful three-dimensional beetle in a paper frame ready to hang on the wall.

TAGS: beetles; insects; nature

Scarfone, Jay, and William Stillman. 2000. *The Wizard of Oz.* Design by Jim Deesing; photo retouching by B. Scott Hanna and Metafor Imaging; paper engineering by Rodger Smith. Santa Monica, CA: Intervisual Books.

Watching the now classic movie version of *The Wizard of Oz*, starring Judy Garland, every time it was shown on television was a special event in my family. The pop-ups in this book are photos taken from that film. The beloved characters are given dimension, movement, and placed against the memorable scenes we saw on the screen. The book comes with a music CD of favorite songs from the soundtrack. There are other movable book adaptations of *The Wizard of Oz*, but the approach taken in this one is most unusual and definitely makes it my favorite. Where's my popcorn?

TAGS: classic movies; Judy Garland; L. Frank Baum; movie soundtracks; music; popular songs; *The Wizard of Oz*

Schulz, Charles M. 2004. *Peanuts ®: A Pop-Up Celebration*. Based on the comic strips of Charles M. Schulz; art adaptation by Paige Braddock; paper engineering by Bruce Foster. New York: Little Simon.

Who can resist Charlie Brown, Snoopy, Lucy, Schroeder, and the rest of the Peanuts gang!? Black-and-white reproductions of the original comic strips are featured on the end pages. Inside the book, colorful pop-ups give action to some of those so-familiar scenes such as Lucy moving the football just as Charlie Brown runs up to kick it. Smaller pop-ups on a double-page spread expound each character's philosophy on happiness, which, according to Snoopy is "defeating the Red Baron!" If you read the comics and watch the TV specials, then this book is for you just as it is for me.

TAGS: comics; Charles M. Schulz; Charlie Brown; humor; *Peanuts*; Snoopy

Smyth, Iain. 1994. *The Mystery of the Russian Ruby: A Pop-Up Whodunit*. 1st U.S. ed. Assistant illustration by Jacqueline Crawford; assistant writing by Alison Cook; typography by Adrian Leichter. New York: Dutton Children's Books.

As an inveterate mystery reader, I cannot resist this pop-up that has a plotline and characters reminiscent of the board game Clue. Readers will enjoy analyzing the hidden clues to deduce which of the six suspects stole the ruby. Read the story, turn a dial, read again, and the clues will change to offer three different endings to the mystery. Sharpen your critical thinking skills while enjoying a whodunit written in classic mystery style.

TAGS: critical thinking; detectives; literature; mysteries

Spiegelman, Art. 1997. *Open Me . . . I'm a Dog!* [New York]: Joanna Cotler Books.

Even though it has only one pop-up (the dog's tail), I love this clever book. It has a dog's leash handle, velvety end papers, and a wonderful story of a dog turned book by a wizard's curse, trying to convince the reader that it really is a dog. Makes me wonder: What would my book be if it weren't a book? Fans of the Pulitzer Prize–winning *Maus* will recognize the name of graphic artist Art Spiegelman because of that work, but this book is very appropriate for anyone of any age who enjoys a good fairy tale told with a twist and a sense of humor.

TAGS: Art Spiegelman; books; dogs; fantasy; humor; magic; writing

Stevenson, Robert Louis. 1991. *A Child's Garden of Verses: A Pop-Up Book Illustrated by Jannat Messenger*. 1st U.S. ed. Illustration by Jannat Messenger; design by Doug Bergstreser; paper engineering by Dennis K. Meyer and Rodger Smith. New York: Dutton's Children's Books.

The style of Messenger's illustrations, nostalgic without being syrupy, and the artistry of the paper engineers bring this selection of poetry from the works of Robert Louis Stevenson to life for those just being introduced to it and to those who haven't read it since their own elementary school days. The poems and accompanying movable art invoke thoughts of childhood experiences, those experienced and those we wish had been. For example, the soaring kites that accompany the poem "The Wind" fly off the top of the page, and the wings of the rooster in the poem "The Hayloft" flap enthusiastically as the book is opened. A personal favorite has always been "The Land of Counterpane." Who can't recall the confinement in bed, imposed by colds, measles, or other illnesses of youth, made more bearable by a vivid imagination?

TAGS: children's poetry; poetry; Robert Louis Stevenson; *A Child's Garden of Verses*

Tieman, Robert. 2005. *Quintessential Disney: A Pop-Up Gallery of Classic Disney Moments.* Paper engineering by David A. Carter; illustration by Toby Bluth; design by Katie LeClereq Hackworth; editing by Adrienne Wiley; production coordination by Sheila Hacker. New York: Disney Editions.

As a mother and grandmother, these classic Disney movies have been part of my life and the childhoods of my children and granddaughters since the first born was old enough to be a moviegoer. From the sepia-tone illustrations of the beloved characters on the cover to the interior pop-ups, which fold out like movie sets, this book is classic nostalgia that captures those Disney movie moments that linger in everyone's heart. Accompanying each "set" is a small fold down fact sheet that gives the release date of the movie and a little inside info on the making of the movie. It is notable that Tieman has the experience of being manager of the Walt Disney Archives.

TAGS: adaptations of children's literature; animation; children's literature; movies; Walt Disney

Van Der Meer, Ron, and Frank Whitford. 1997. *The Kids' Art Pack.* [New York]: DK Publishing.
Combine a movable book with a clear and easily understood resource that introduces kids to art techniques, art history, and art appreciation, and you have a winner! A booklet nicely tucked into a pocket in the back cover is full of step-by-step activities that young artists can do themselves.

TAGS: art; art appreciation; art history; art instruction; children's art

Wildsmith, Brian. 1996. *The Creation: A Pop-Up Book.* Written and illustration by Brian Wildsmith; design by Jim Deesing; paper engineering by Bruce Reifel and Jose R. Seminario; production by Intervisual Books. Brookfield, CT: Millbrook Press.
Internationally acclaimed illustrator Brian Wildsmith's interpretation of the story of Creation according to the book of Genesis captures the joy and brilliance as darkness is transformed into light. A variety of paper engineering techniques is used: pop-ups, pull tabs, and wheels. Text is so well hidden under flaps in the artwork that I first thought this was a wordless book. The use of color is stunning: Bright patterned geometric designs in the planets and in the robes of heavenly figures are set against a dark sky, depicting the creation of the universe on the first day. It continues throughout the book until a lush green landscape bordered with flora and fauna ends the telling as God creates the Garden of Eden on the sixth day. The last end pages offer a brief biography of Wildsmith and his comments on each of the double-page spreads in the book. Of note: Wildsmith is the winner of the 1962 Kate Greenaway Medal for the picture book *Brian Wildsmith's ABC.*

TAGS: Bible; children's illustrators; Creation story; geometry; math

Wood, Audrey. 1994. *The Napping House Wakes Up.* 1st ed. Illustration by Don Wood; design and paper engineering by White Heat. San Diego, CA: Harcourt Brace & Company.

    This cumulative tale is the perfect example of an award-winning picture book with a storyline that lends itself so well to the addition of movement that in doing so it makes a great book even better. As granny slumbers comfortably in her bed, she is joined by a small child and several animals. As each one climbs unto the bed, it sinks lower, and the pile of sleeping companions gets higher until at last, through a predictable chain of events, the bed collapses. Thankfully, Don Wood's original illustrations were retained for this movable adaptation. From the snoring granny, to the composition of the figures in the bed, to the color palette of blues and yellows that capture the quiet of the night and the bursting forth of the dawn, they are priceless.

TAGS: Audrey Wood; children's literature; *The Napping House Wakes Up*; prediction; sleeping

Zelinsky, Paul O. 1990. *The Wheels on the Bus.* New York: Dutton Children's Books-Penguin Books.

    I purchased this book because Paul O. Zelinsky mentioned it as a forthcoming publication when I heard him speak at a public library many years ago. As I turned the pages and pulled the tabs, I saw how precisely the motion in the illustrations fit the words of the familiar children's song and enhanced the visual appeal of the book. As a librarian who was always promoting reading, I considered how the use of movement could be a powerful tool to hook readers of all ages. As an art enthusiast, I was struck by the realization that the complex process of creating movement with paper is an art. This book reached me on so many levels that I have been passionate about movable books ever since. It definitely has a place of honor in my dream library.

TAGS: music; songs; "The Wheels on the Bus"

REFERENCES

The Leprechaun. 2001. 2002. Illustration by Peter Rutherford; design by Tony Potter; poem by Robert Dwyer Joyce. Dublin, Ireland: RiRa, an imprint of Gill & Macmillan.

Si j'étais . . . Boucle d'Or: Un livre anime des Editions Ouest-France [If I were . . . Goldilocks: A Book of Anime Editions Ouest-France]. 1990. Pour l'edition originale publiee sous le titre *When Sue Pretends.* Illustre par Linda Hill Griffith; concu et realise par Dick Dudley. Long Beach, CA: Compass Productions; pour l'edition Francaise: Rennes France Editions Ouest-France.

Glossary

Here we provide our explanations of some basic terms related to pop-up books. Following the definitions, we have listed resources that offer their own glossaries of this specialized vocabulary. We should note that there are often several words or phrases that can mean approximately the same thing when talking about these wonderful creations. In these definitions, we have strived for a short and easily understood explanation that reflects a common understanding of the terms.

Carousel book   The book is opened and its covers are fastened back, and thus the illustrations inside the book become three-dimensional. Sometimes this is called a **star book**, because the shape of the opened book resembles a star.

Lift-the-flap   A flap attached to a page, and as it is raised, another illustration is revealed underneath it.

Paper engineer   Individuals who devise the motion in pop-up books.

Pop-up book   A book that provides the reader the possibility of interacting with the book to create movement.

Pull-tab   The tab is connected to a figure or illustration that will move when the reader pulls the end of the tab.

Rotating wheels   *see* Transformation

Scroll   Much like the scrolls from the Middle Ages, pop-up books can use two handles at either end of the "scroll" to move a very long strip of paper and create the action.

Slide   Part of the page slides, creating a different view.

Transformation   The reader manipulates the page, often by rotating a wheel or disc, and the original illustration is transformed into a different one. Montanaro (1993, xii) says that the transformations can be circular, vertical, or horizontal. Sometimes the transformation is called a **metamorphosis** or **dissolving wheel**.

Tunnel books   Similar to peepshows of other eras, the tunnel book uses mechanisms such as folds to create a tunnel, with visual access through peep holes. Sometimes this is called a **peephole book**.

Wheel   *see* Transformation

SOURCES WITH GLOSSARIES OF POP-UP BOOK TERMS

The following resources provide glossaries of terms related to pop-up books and to their production. We have also used them as background for composing our definitions in this glossary. We should note that there is variation in the wording of terms from resource to resource. For instance, we have seen "lift-the-flap" expressed as "lift flap."

Carter, David A., and James Diaz. 1999. *The Elements of Pop-up: A Pop-up Book for Aspiring Paper Engineers.* Design assistance and illustration by Leisa Bentley; photography by Keith Sutter; digital production art by Rick Morrison, White Heat; production by Intervisual Books; development by White Heat. New York: Little Simon.

 This must-have book for those interested in creating their own pop-ups not only provides 3-D models of the mechanisms for creating pop-ups, but it also has a glossary of 50 terms.

Hutchins, Edward H. Exploring Tunnel Books. Artistbooks.com. http://www.artistbooks.com/abr/index.htm.

 Two-and-a-half web pages explain the tunnel book format, including the history, and are illustrated with several color photographs of examples.

Montanaro, Ann R. 1993. *Pop-up and Movable Books: A Bibliography.* Metuchen, NJ.: Scarecrow Press.

 The preface to Montanaro's book defines eight terms used to describe the movement in the books included in her extensive bibliography.

Rubin, Ellen. Glossary of Pop-up Terms. The PopUpLady: Specializing in Movable Paper. http://www.popuplady.com/about03-glossary.shtml.

 This glossary on the website of a pop-up book collector/author explains approximately 20 terms applicable to pop-up books; some are illustrated with color photographs.

Index

About the Contributors

GAYLE BAAR holds both MS and MLIS degrees and has experience as a school librarian, including opening new schools, but she also has experience in the public library sector. She has worked as an elementary teacher and as the children's programming coordinator at Cleveland Heights/University Heights Public Library in Ohio. She uses pop-up books with pre-kindergarten, kindergarten, and first grade. The pop-books that she's used belong to all areas of the curriculum: science, math, language arts, and social studies.

She finds that children absolutely love pop-ups. There are any number of toy or moveable books that can be used to teach various concepts. She finds it wonderful to hear the oohs and ahhhs as the pages are turned. When budgets sometimes limit purchases, she always has a few of her own pop-ups to supplement lessons.

She agrees somewhat with concerns about the fragility of pop-ups. While educators try to prepare children for the use of pop-ups, they cannot go home with the children. Sometimes in their excitement and exuberance, pages get destroyed. Because they are library books, the child doesn't have the pride of ownership that comes with actually receiving the books as gifts or purchasing them. When she buys pop-up books, she tends to buy less paper construction and more fold-out and hidden surprise types of books, such as the "Spot" books and Ed Emberley's *Go Away Big Green Monster*.

MERRY GRAVES has experiences of being a teacher-librarian in the Grapevine-Colleyville (Texas) Independent School District and being a teacher of secondary English and Latin. She uses pop-up books for K–5 grades and for reading interest and research activities. She is a proponent of the Big Six method of research and uses it extensively with her students at all grade levels. She frequently conducts workshops and staff development programs on the topic for teachers and librarians in her region.

Her advice to other teachers and librarians is that for the library, it's best to think of pop-ups as something that will be weeded after several years, since they do wear. Her practice has been to try to buy two copies: one to circulate and one as a library copy to use in the library only. When Robert Sabuda's book was on the Texas Bluebonnet Book list, she bought two copies to keep in the library and let the children read them in the room. This worked very well.

STACEY IRISH-KEFFER has been a youth services librarian with the Denton Public Library for over 14 years.

She has been active in the Texas Library Association's Children's Round Table and was chair of the Family Literacy Committee from 2006 to 2007. Through a quirk of fate, not to mention some really cool puppets, Stacey found her calling as a children's librarian shortly after she graduated with her MLS and has not looked back since.

Her advice to public librarians is to not be afraid to use pop-up books in story-time programs or other programs with young children. Children find pop-up books amazing and should get opportunities to interact with them whenever possible.

LORA KRANTZ is chair of the math department, Drane Intermediate School, Corsicana, Texas. Before teaching, she was a technology aide/instructional aide and worked in the lab and took care of campus equipment. Then she moved into a math class and worked one-on-one with students. She also spent some time teaching math in the special education department. She has been a workshop presenter in summer teacher development institutes.

She works with sixth graders. She loves using pop-up books because they offer a cross-curricular medium. She is able to teach angles, cause/effect, and simple machines through them. During the school year, she shares pop-up books with students at the end of class meetings, often from her own collection. Students really enjoy this activity and always want to try to construct something they see in the books.

Her advice to teachers and librarians who want to use pop-ups is first to start simple. There are many sources about pop-up books and how to make them. Many sources are free, so it's not necessary to spend a lot of money to do this. For instance, Robert Sabuda's website (http://robertsabuda.com) is a great source with lots of printable cards and is good for getting started. When shopping for pop-up books, she suggests checking out eBay and Amazon.com. Their prices are better than chain bookstore prices.

As for fragility of pop-up books, she notes that there is going to be some wear and tear with all books. Explain to students that the books are fragile and will not work if they are torn. Students don't want the books to "not work," so her experience has been that they tend to take better care of them than their text books! The light in their eyes testifies about how they enjoy reading and making pop-up books!